A POLITICAL HISTORY OF CHILD PROTECTION

Lessons for Reform from Aotearoa New Zealand

Ian Kelvin Hyslop

P

First published in Great Britain in 2022 by

Policy Press, an imprint of
Bristol University Press
University of Bristol
1–9 Old Park Hill
Bristol
BS2 8BB
UK
t: +44 (0)117 954 5940
e: bup-info@bristol.ac.uk

Details of international sales and distribution partners are available at:
policy.bristoluniversitypress.co.uk

British Library Cataloguing in Publication Data
A catalogue record for this book is available from the British Library

ISBN 978-1-4473-5317-1 hardcover
ISBN 978-1-4473-5318-8 paperback
ISBN 978-1-4473-5320-1 ePub
ISBN 978-1-4473-5319-5 ePdf

Cover design by Nicky Borowiec
Image credit: Adobe Stock 58060571 Lookinout

To Peg and Fred, who came to the antipodes on a wing and some sort of a prayer. I have you both to thank for my good fortune.

And to Ted Pōmare, Mātua Whāngai mōkai – good of you to visit e hoa – although I know you have your reasons.

The good fight must be fought on all fronts and in all forms
Advancing and outflanking
Retreating and retrenching
Restocking and replenishing
Reimagining and reinventing
For the guises of oppression are many
And the road to Damascus has many donkeys

Ian Kelvin Hyslop

Contents

Glossary of Māori words

It is important to recognise that these translations are brief and proximal/simplistic.

Hapori	public/wider community
Hapū	kinship group/sub-tribe
Hui ā-whānau	a meeting/family gathering subject to appropriate Māori protocols
Iwi	extended kinship group/tribe of common descent
Kaimahi	worker
Karakia	prayer/ritual blessing
Kaumatua	an elder/person of status
Kaupapa Māori	Māori approach/doctrine/agenda
Kia ora	hello!/best wishes!
Mana	Prestige/standing/power
Mātua	parents
Moemoeā	dream/vision
Mōkai	servant
Mokopuna	grandchild
Motu	country/area/island
Ngāi Tūhoe	tribal group of the Kutarere-Ruātoki-Waimana-Waikaremoana area
Pākehā	Exotic/foreign – name given to settler 'newcomers'
Pēpi	baby
Rangatahi	youth/young person
Rangatiratanga	chieftainship/right to authority
Rohe	area/territory
Rōpū	organised group
Tamariki	children
Te tino rangatiratanga	ultimate/maximum authority
Tikanga	Correct procedure/customary lore
Waiata	song
Whakapapa	genealogy/lineage
Whānau	family/extended family group
Whāngai	rear/feed/customary foster-child

About the author

Ian Kelvin Hyslop is Senior Lecturer in Social Work in the School of Counselling, Human Services and Social Work, Faculty of Education and Social Work (Te Kura Akoranga me Te Tauwhiro Tangata), at the University of Auckland, Aotearoa New Zealand. He worked in statutory child protection social work for 20 years prior to becoming an academic. Ian is passionate about child protection social work and the development of socially just policy and practice, both in Aotearoa and globally.

Acknowledgements

Many people have supported me in the writing of this book. Nobody travels alone. My partner, Jan Patricia Rimmer, has been a magical oasis of patience and humour. I would also like to acknowledge my beautiful children, Rory, Jade and Bianca, for being who they are, and their mother Donna for helping to make them that way. And Jan's children as well – you have all tolerated the guy in the back room. Thank you too brother Stuart for caring for our mum when it looked like this book had no chance.

My comrades in the Reimagining Social Work collective have provided much-needed solidarity and support. My ancient blues brother friends and my casual supervisor David Kenkel have helped to ground me in the possible. Thanks to my colleagues in the faculty who supported my research leave and carried the weight left behind. It is only fair to mention Imogen Moyne, who helped me out significantly with the archival material. Isobel Bainton, Commissioning Editor, somehow seemed to quietly believe this would all happen. I appreciated that greatly.

Finally, to all the whānau whose lifeways I crossed as a social worker: you were my real university and I have written this book for you. All gifts demand a return.

Power structures and problem definition

Introduction: Orientation and focus of this text

This book examines the politics of child protection in Aotearoa New Zealand (hereafter, Aotearoa).[1] The intent is to contribute to growing debate about the trajectory of the modern child protection project – to trouble the deceptive common sense of these neoliberal times and to envisage another future. The text aims to weave a nuanced historical account of child protection policy and practice within the unique context of Aotearoa. As such, the argument is not purely linear or descriptive. It is, however, informed by exploration of the conditions of possibility inherent to a particular liberal capitalist society. This introductory chapter outlines the conceptual building blocks that underpin the analysis developed and presented here. The intent is to provide a framework that will assist the reader to engage creatively with the unfolding narrative.

The concept of a specific 'child protection project' refers to the development, over time, of the role of the state in identifying risk of harm and responding to the care needs of children when caregivers are deemed to be a threat to their safety or well-being. It will be argued that this project has consistently turned a blind eye to the way in which such caregivers are drawn from a section of the population that poses a threat to the perceived safety and security of the liberal capitalist state. As a result of this conflation, the historical and contemporary practice of child protection social work has persistently generated raced and classed outcomes in Aotearoa and in comparable societies. To understand and address this systemic bias, it is necessary to examine the generative influence of economic and political structures.

Such an approach is largely counter-intuitive to the way in which child protection theory and practice is currently understood. The aim of this book, in this sense, is to invite the reader to critically interrogate the mainstream discourse of child protection social work. This reconsideration can be usefully informed by an understanding of child protection as a historical project of social care and control that has developed within the context of liberal capitalist economic and social relations. It is proposed that a critical analysis of the political economy of child protection can contribute to a deeper understanding of this emotive subject and help to inform the development of more effective and enduring responses.

Although the implications are seldom explored in depth, the socio-political location of the child protection project is, as Tawney (1978: 103) suggests, self-evident: 'It is merely to recall the commonplace that the tension between human wants and the limited resources available for satisfying them takes place, not in a vacuum, but in a specific cultural environment, by which the character both of the wants and of the resources, is determined.' Drawing on the work of Parton (2014a), child maltreatment is conceptualised in this text as a problem that is defined and responded to within a contested and conflicted political framework. As with all social problems, child protection policy is influenced by economic structures, the social relations that serve these structures and the political arrangements that govern these relationships. Liberal societies are configured by relations of power, but they are also inherently unstable; change happens, and we are currently at something of a crossroads in Aotearoa and internationally.

For many years now, academic commentators have questioned whether current anglophone child protection systems are part of the problem, rather than an effective solution (Gupta, 2017). The following is an excerpt from Dorothy Scott's (2006: 1) address to the tenth Australasian Child Abuse and Neglect Conference:

> Most child protection services in countries such as Australia and New Zealand have become demoralised, investigation-driven bureaucracies which trawl through escalating numbers of low-income families to find a small minority of cases in which statutory intervention is necessary and justifiable, leaving enormous damage in their wake. The point has been reached in many places where we are exceeding the use of the State's coercive powers to protect children without causing further harm.

More recently, Featherstone, White and Morris (2014: 3) have advocated for a re-engagement with the moral complexity of child protection, asking: 'Is it ethically desirable to focus on rescuing children and leaving their parents behind in a society riven by inequalities?' Although the primary focus is on Aotearoa, particularly developments since the 1970s, some reference is made to policy history in England and wider anglophone jurisdictions. It will be argued that recognition of the systemic social and economic inequalities in liberal capitalist societies is crucial to understanding the political bones of the child protection project and for constructing a fresh vision (Hyslop, 2012).

The initial chapters of this text have a historical focus that allows for the identification of deep patterns and for connections to be made with the challenges that currently beset this field. Abiding legacies associated with the 19th-century roots of child protection are considered in relation to capitalist economics, liberal politics and the emerging role of social science. The 20th-century transition to statutory practice within a unified welfare state apparatus is also critically interrogated. The later chapters explore the development of child protection in Aotearoa since the 1980s: the way in which a vision of bicultural practice was inevitably derailed by the managerial austerity of neoliberal politics and the continuing moral construction of child abuse in a class society. The book concludes with an examination of the contemporary crisis of child protection policy and practice, and the implications for radical reform. Reference is made to the outcomes of a series of inquiries into the discriminatory relationship between the state and Māori, with a particular focus on the 2021 findings of the Waitangi Tribunal.[2] The challenges of practice reform are considered in the cold light of the conclusions reached through this process.

Personal dimensions

Some brief disclosure of my own influences and biases (at least the ones that I recognise) is a necessary part of the narrative process. I am an Aotearoa-born **Pākehā** – the third child of an English mother and a Scottish father. My family emigrated to Australia after the Second World War and eventually settled in Auckland. My parents looked for work, opportunity, stability and education for their children, as migrants have always done.

This text is an account developed from an academic distance, but a distance informed by a prolonged and intimate encounter with its subject. I was employed in statutory social work in Auckland, in direct child protection practice, as a team supervisor and later as a practice manager for approximately 20 years of my working life (Hyslop, 2007). As Ferguson (2004: 1) identifies, statutory child protection work is often experienced as a consuming world of its own. Children are vulnerable; humans can be very dangerous. I went into social work with a distrust of the control functions of the state and concerns about the classed, gendered and raced biases of child protection practice. I left direct practice with those suspicions confirmed by experience.

I put my heart into this work. At times, I encountered harrowing abuse, including the deaths of children, both at the hands of their parents and in foster care. I learnt from the vicarious pain of these events, and I realise how difficult it is to consistently practise well in this demanding context. In hindsight, I also appreciate that the energy expended in this vocation was not without cost to those around me. I have subsequently made use of the reflective space that academic work allows to endeavour to articulate this experience of engaged and embodied practice – and what might be required to do it well:

I recall the experience of all those tension-filled allocation meetings when the white noise of practice anxiety filled the air; of workers breaking down at the threat of 'one more case' – and subsequently talking them in to taking it anyway. This vignette stays with me as much as the gut-wrenching memory of child deaths. (Hyslop, 2007: 8; see also Hyslop, 2009, 2013b)

Increasingly, I have moved from an interest in the mechanisms that enable 'best' practice in statutory bureaucracies to a focus on the way in which the child protection project has been politically constructed over time (Garrett, 2013; Hyslop, 2017; Hyslop and Keddell, 2018). The unfolding text illustrates the way in which child protection social work is connected with relations of power, that is, 'whatever its ethical principles and philosophical commitments, social work is prone to take on the features of the political culture in which it is practised' (Jordan, 2012: 12). However, liberal capitalist societies also contain generative tensions, producing conflict and change. The analysis developed and presented in this book sets out to contribute to a gathering agenda for progressive reform, both in Aotearoa and internationally.

Political economy

Analysis of context is critical, both in social work generally and for understanding the constraints and possibilities that apply to child protection specifically. As O'Brien (2014: 6) has observed: 'Social work practice and social work literature regularly emphasise the significance of "context" in shaping both the lives of the individuals, families and communities that practitioners work with and the nature and scope (in the widest senses of those two words) of practice itself.'

Referencing a generic social work text widely used in Australasia, *Social Work: Contexts and Practice* (Connolly and Harms, 2013), O'Brien (2014: 8) highlights the following assertion: 'In the third edition of this text, Williams (2013, v) comments in the Foreword, "if there is one truism of social work it is that it is context bound, situated and shaped by the socio-economic, political and cultural milieu in which it operates".' This milieu is the bone to be picked. The concept of 'political economy' refers to the way in which economic structures are not simply neutral arrangements that regulate the conduct of commercial life. Rather, economic systems are entwined with social interests that exist within material relations of power and privilege. Accordingly, since child protection is enmeshed with the liberal state, it is necessary to critically consider the structure and function of this form of social organisation and governance.

Three abiding and related elements are woven throughout the history of policy and practice in Aotearoa. First, child protection work is situated within the capitalist model of development. Capitalism is a system of ownership, production and exchange that shapes social life in a manner consistent with market-driven processes. It is an extractive system that facilitates the accumulation of private profit and generates inequality (Heilbroner, 1985). The children and families on the receiving end of child protection services are drawn disproportionately from the edges of the capitalist social fabric: the relatively impoverished margins of the working class (Dominelli, 2004: Pelton, 2015).

This phenomenon is as evident in modern anglophone states as it was in the late Victorian liberal capitalist societies where the first wave of the child protection project arose. The original targets of the child rescue movement were the children of the disreputable and dependent poor (Ferguson, 2004). This pattern has been modified over time, but it has not changed fundamentally. In important ways, contemporary forms of social distress are reminiscent of the dislocation generated by industrial capitalism in the 19th century. Individual and communal identities that were linked with secure working-class occupations up until the 1970s have become frayed and tenuous in recent decades (Bauman, 2000; Bourdieu, 2005; Cummins, 2018). Poverty and visible social suffering have been re-naturalised.

Second, Anglophone jurisdictions operate within the dominant rubric of liberal politics, which delimits the way in which the causes of child maltreatment (and the range of possible responses) are configured. Liberal individualism, with its associated overlay of personal responsibility for poor social outcomes, is the primary ideological vehicle that legitimates the capitalist mode of economic and social life (Žižek, 2014). Historical analysis reveals other persistent patterns within the liberal tradition: the ideological construction of threatening social groups; moral notions of deservingness; and social exclusion. Along with growing inequality, populist political rhetoric directed at the spectre of a feral underclass has been revived in the neoliberal era (Welshman, 2013; Beddoe, 2014; Jensen and Tyler, 2015). The relevance of this phenomenon for modern child protection is developed in Chapter 6.

In Aotearoa, and in comparable societies, child protection systems are fundamentally shaped by liberal capitalism. As referenced here, 'liberal capitalism' is understood as an amalgam of liberalism and capitalism. The state is immersed in this context: it is not a neutral arbiter of social relations. Finally, in Aotearoa, child protection is also framed by a living legacy of colonial oppression (Hyslop, 2020; Stanley and de Froideville, 2020). The child protection system has consistently delivered blatantly racist outcomes since the mid-20th century.

In the chapters that follow, the current challenges facing child protection social work in Aotearoa are explored through the lens of this economically, politically and culturally calibrated history. It is argued that the dominant model of policy and practice is not an adequate framework for responding ethically and equitably to child maltreatment in liberal capitalist societies characterised by social disparities across dimensions of class, gender and ethnicity. Both the moral imagination of the late 19th century and the assimilationist goals of the colonial state have an enduring reach into modern child protection. The intent is to identify lessons that may be applied to the design of socially just responses to child protection in the here and now.

In common with Indigenous populations in comparable postcolonial societies, Māori are over-represented on the social margins, and this disparity bleeds into the child protection system (Cram et al, 2015; Choate, 2019; Keddell, 2019). Child protection intervention is disproportionately directed at **whānau** Māori ('extended Māori families')[3] but generally not middle-class Māori. Pasefika[4] peoples are also over-represented. In my experience, and in academic research findings, the parents engaged by the statutory social work system are often young brown women living in relative poverty (Roberts, 2002; Hyslop, 2007).

This assertion is unlikely to surprise informed readers. The challenge is to recognise the implications for the way in which we understand and conduct this work. It is argued that some serious rethinking and recalibration is required. More importantly, in a capitalist settler society structured by racial inequality, there is an underlying issue of power and control. Bluntly, who has the authority to answer such questions, how is power configured and who decides?

There is significant historical (and contemporary) friction between the liberal politics of child protection and the communal identity of Indigenous Māori (Harris, 2007; Provan, 2012). Modern child protection cannot be divided from this history. Accordingly, it is contended that an agenda for child protection reform cannot be separated from the need to redress inequalities in the distribution of power and control at the intersection of class and race in the settler colonial state of Aotearoa (Poata-Smith, 2002).

Re-politicising child protection

It is more convenient to blame the poor than confront the systemic relationships between poverty, racism and child protection in liberal societies. In relation to toleration of the extensive collateral damage caused by overloaded child protection systems, Scott (2006: 9) makes a further observation:

> Is this because, like our predecessors in the history of child protection, we cannot allow ourselves to acknowledge that we cause such suffering when our intent is so well-meaning? Is it because we prefer to engage in self-protective 'defensive practice' regardless of the cost to children and their families? Is it because we do not readily identify with the

anguish of parents because they are mostly 'other'? If this happened to middle-class families on the scale it is happening to indigenous and non-indigenous working-class families, the pain would not be inaudible.

Technocratic, science-centric practice assumptions, pervasive managerial strictures of audit and efficiency, and denial of the complex intersections between child maltreatment and structural inequality are all part of the historical house training of child protection social workers.

Warner (2015) has explored the way in which an almost primal discursive landscape influences responses to child maltreatment. Child protection is saturated with emotive drivers that 'are embedded in the entire child protection system and in the wider context for its development' (Warner, 2015: 1). Who, after all, is in favour of child abuse? Warner's 'emotional politics' functions as a kaleidoscope, fracturing and distorting more objective understandings of child abuse and neglect. Shifting political imperatives to blame abusive individuals and inadequately protective systems for child death tragedies, or destructive over-intervention, deflect attention from the wider social and economic context within which child abuse is generated, understood and responded to (Parton, 2014a). As discussed in later chapters, all of this has played out in the contemporary history of child protection in Aotearoa.

Within the operational context of statutory bureaucracies, the conflicted injunction to safeguard the innocent and vulnerable, while protecting family integrity, lends its own sense of centrifugal intensity and an associated incapacity to think laterally – an inertia of urgency and motion. It is as if the care and control functions of statutory child protection are imagined within an imperative vacuum – a sealed bubble of professional and managerial expertise. This bubble has been on the brink of rupture in Aotearoa for some time. Indigenous voices are not prepared to be co-opted and silenced any longer. There is a lineage of resistance here, which this book examines.

To be even-handed, child protection is also often regarded as an ambiguous and morally complex subject, at least by those who have any significant experience of practice. How this complexity is unpacked and analysed is critically important to our understandings of what has happened in the past and what is possible in the future. Stan Houston (2014: 61) asserts that one 'of the significant gaps in modern social work is the lack of an embedded "sociological imagination": one that irrefutably draws the connection between private ills and public issues; one that debunks political rhetoric and deconstructs ideology'. Accordingly, this text endeavours to get under the skin of the Aotearoa child protection project, unsettle underlying assumptions and signal a better way forward.

Tensions and intersections

As suggested, liberalism generally provides the primary narrative for economic and social history in Aotearoa. As a body of theory and practice, it also encompasses a range of tensions and contradictions (Duncan, 2004). Capitalism is a continually moving mode of development, driven by economic expansion, commodification and accumulation (Hewlett, 2007). It is a system prone to crisis (Callinicos, 2010). The liberal state accommodates and, to some degree, manages the negative social consequences that capitalism inevitably generates. In this analysis, liberal capitalism is not necessarily a fixed or stable form of political organisation; rather, there are always fracture lines (Žižek, 2014).

Although the state ultimately functions in the service of capitalist social relations, it is a site of contestation between antagonistic class interests (Ginsberg, 1979; Bourdieu, 2005). Similarly, the historical and contemporary accommodation between the Crown and Māori in Aotearoa is characterised by shifting dynamics of resistance, conflict and compromise (Walker, 2004). There is, however, a fundamental, persistent and generative disconnect between the liberal foundations of postcolonial politics in Aotearoa and the communal social fabric of the Māori world. This tension tracks directly and profoundly into the politics of child protection.

It is important to grasp the complexity of this relationship. Colonisation was not simply about cultural imperialism. It entailed the imposition of liberal capitalism: the systematic separation of Māori from communal land ownership and collective subsistence to provide the capitalist economy with wage labour (Poata–Smith, 2002: 11). Colonial dispossession is common to Indigenous people in comparable settler societies, particularly in relation to the racist configuration of child protection systems (Stewart-Harawera, 2005; Gray et al, 2013). This book will consider the implications of this experience for the past, present and future orientation of child protection social work in Aotearoa.

Correlation and causation

As Featherstone, White and Morris (2014) assert, to conflate social work with child protection and to essentialise child protection as a process of child-centred rescue in a grossly unequal society is a very problematic undertaking. This narrow ideological construction has distorted our collective understandings of child welfare practice – in the imaginations of neoliberal policymakers, in the moral panics induced by media-driven scandals and in the minds of the urban poor, who fear that their children may be taken by the state (Whānau Ora Commissioning Agency, 2020).

In his influential exposition of the micropolitics of child protection practice, Ferguson (2004) noted the centrality of social work to the child protection mandate, as well as the pressure that unreasonable expectations have placed on the credibility of the profession. He proposed that the rehabilitation of child protection (and perhaps social work itself) requires a deep appreciation of the historic and contemporary nuances of applied practice: 'It is no exaggeration to say that the very future of social work itself rests on reaching a deeper understanding of child protection' (Ferguson, 2004: 7).

Ferguson advocated for a comprehensive interrogation of the liminal space that social workers occupy, encompassing the emotive sights, sounds and smells that infuse this practice setting. There is a focus on late Victorian encounters with the squalor of poverty and comparable experiences of filth, disgust and fear of contamination that, he argues, continue to haunt modern child welfare. Significantly, given the storm of creative destruction that is the hallmark of capitalist development, Ferguson's Irish practice study revealed a common perception that families encountered in child protection work were somehow 'left behind', having failed to keep up with the times:

> My point here is not to argue that such children are not really at risk, but to lay bare the embodied practices and the psycho symbolic as well as scientific knowing which makes risk what it is. The notion, expressed by different workers, that working with the family was like being in a 'time warp' reflects how such families are viewed as being stuck in a different age ('sixty years ago'). In such a future-oriented practice as modern child protection, their failure to keep developing means moral decay, with potentially deleterious implications for the children and the community. (Ferguson, 2004: 182)

As many others have done (Pelton, 2015; Saar-Heiman, 2020), Ferguson (2004: 165) identifies the inconvenient truth that it is generally the children of the poor who repeatedly come to notice:

> In an important sense, child protection systems have been chronically enmeshed with certain kinds of high-risk children and families for as long as there has been a child protection movement. There is a discernible intergenerational transmission of child protection work where generation after generation of the same family (or types of families) and welfare systems are caught up in intense relationships. This is reflected in a core pattern of long-term, multi-problem, multi-referred child protection cases which keep coming (back) to professional attention and which are at the heart of high-risk work.

This analysis is consistent with my own experience of practice in Aotearoa and with the findings of recent research (Hyslop, 2007; Keddell, 2019).

Nevertheless, it is important to critically deconstruct the preceding excerpt because identification of the relationship between poverty and child protection can pave the way for some pernicious assumptions about fault and remedy. Simplistic suppositions that conflate correlation with causation are politically convenient and potentially dangerous.

As suggested, the clients of child protection social work are drawn today, as they were in the 19th century, from the outskirts of the working class, that is, from the 'underclass' so often demonised in populist rhetoric (Welshman, 2013; Parton, 2014a; Beddoe and Joy, 2017). Social disadvantage can be reproduced in poor families, particularly in contemporary neoliberal societies, where intergenerational social mobility is both lauded and increasingly constrained. High-needs families are often multiply re-referred. However, locating the genesis of social ills in the behaviour of a deficient substratum of the poor has a notorious pedigree (Hyslop, 2016b; Cummins, 2018).

There is a resilient history of racist and pseudo-biological explanations for poverty, disadvantage and criminality (Gillies et al, 2017). This lingering social Darwinist thread within the liberal tradition is often clothed with a persuasive chimera of scientific credibility (Flanagan, 2018). The associated application of ostensibly neutral science to child protection – technical fixes for socially generated problems – can serve to disguise and mystify the socio-political context of this field. This book sets out to unhorse this fallacy.

The inference that a limited group of dysfunctional families can be identified, isolated and treated as a means of addressing the social ills of late capitalism is a distorted, politically naive (or, more often, ingenuous) and oppressive representation, with its roots firmly planted in 19th-century eugenics (Flanagan, 2018). It is also important to recognise that the families who become clients of the child protection system are not passive objects to be identified, assessed and treated. Rather, the children and adults who are constructed as 'clients' are active agents in processes of engagement and decision-making (Smith, 2001). The intensions of policymakers and social work practitioners are not always met with enthusiasm by those on the receiving end of state-sponsored intervention. According to Jones (1983: 6), there is a 'long tradition of suspicion towards social work as a predominantly middle-class moralistic welfare activity which hinders rather than assists solutions to working-class problems of poverty'.

Modernisation and child protection

The spectre of a threatening underclass has continuously stalked public policy in societies that are structured by economically generated inequalities of class, wealth and power. Ferguson (2004: 28) prosaically invokes an image linked with processes of urban expansion and renewal, specifically, the disorder of the Parisian slums of the late 1800s, exposing middle-class sensibilities to the gaze of the working-class poor:

> Faced with such stares, as well as the threat of being literally touched by the 'dangerous' classes, a major social, moral and political dilemma opened up concerning how to deal with the poor. The decisive Bourgeois response was to contract out – mainly to social work – the dirty work of dealing with the 'refuse' of modernity in order to try and sanitize these new spaces and seal up these wounds that modernization was creating.

I first read Ferguson's classic text in 2005. It was refreshing to engage with an academic account sympathetic to the centrality of the 'smell of practice' in the context of relative poverty because this interactive relational experience is endemic to child protection social work. As an experienced child protection practitioner, I was well aware of the way in which differences of class and culture can distort communication, and of the way that historically conditioned fears, gendered expectations and racist stereotypes can skew practice judgements (Hyslop, 2007).

Nevertheless, as instructive as such insights can be, a preoccupation with the way in which socially conditioned class differences, prejudices and insecurities impact upon child protection decision-making can also obscure the material dimensions of social inequality. Featherstone, White and Morris (2014: 12) express the risk of overdeterminism in relation to danger and dirt as follows:

> Relationship based approaches have been promoted which are absolutely vital and there has been some acknowledgement of extending the ethic of recognition to parents. ... But the focus generally remains on the child, on entering the home to see the child, on inspecting the home to see the child is safe and has enough to eat. Danger is emphasised – danger of dogs, violence, of being lied to, of entering liminal spaces, no-go areas, places different and dirty. We are not dismissing danger and dirt, but we do want to argue for the importance of understanding how 'othering' and distancing processes operate in unequal societies.

Poverty and inequality impact upon the lived experience – the life chances – of children and parents, and these dynamics clearly influence relationships with state social workers (Hyslop and Keddell, 2018). However, an introspective preoccupation with the microphysics of class politics in child protection – the sensual and emotional subtleties of communicative engagement – deflects attention from the way in which inequality is systemically rather than individually generated. If poverty is the elephant in the child protection room (Gupta, 2017; Hyslop and Keddell, 2018), the rest of the herd is lurking behind the cloak of liberal politics and capitalist socio-economic relations (Garrett, 2018).

Class analysis revisited

Although the late Victorian genesis of child protection is enmeshed with bourgeois concern about the threat posed by the urban poor, the relevance of social deprivation has generally been downplayed in the modern child protection project (Krumer-Nevo, 2016). Reasons for this oversight are complex. Morris et al (2018) have stressed that pervasive poverty among those on the receiving end of services has, ironically, diverted attention from this structuring reality – poverty has become the 'wallpaper' of practice.

The urgent mandate to respond to the suffering of individual children at risk of harm from dangerous caregivers tends to invalidate concern with the identification of wider patterns in favour of a focus on individual pathology. Further, an analysis that links harm to children with the shortcomings of the capitalist economic system is not likely to find favour within the rubric of contemporary neoliberal governance. Specifically, and no less ironically, the lack of a simple and constant correlation between poverty, social distress and child maltreatment is often used to diminish the importance of the association (Featherstone et al, 2014).

Nevertheless, comprehensive research has recently established a glaring association between relative poverty and the involvement of child protection systems with children and families (Bywaters et al, 2018; Bywaters and CWIP Team, 2020; Keddell, 2020). Although, as Ferguson (2004) has so eloquently illustrated, the origins of social work were clearly about middle-class people delving into the 'disorder' of working-class lives, the enduring implications for contemporary policy are seldom examined. It is as though the classed nature of child protection intervention has been rendered invisible, in the same way that the class configuration of advanced capitalist societies is masked by contemporary neoliberal discourse (Sugarman, 2015).

A socialist perspective

The analysis developed in this book is ideologically situated. I am interested in exploring the relationship between child protection and the systemic (economic and political) reproduction of inequality, arguing that contrary to liberal constructions of personal responsibility for social failure, unequal social outcomes are an inevitable product of capitalist social relations. This process has accelerated and intensified globally over the last 40 years as the rate of exploitation has risen and the social support functions of the state have been reduced in response to the neoliberal political turn (Harvey, 2005). The implications of this analysis for current and future child protection policy development will be explored and exemplified.

It is not being suggested that a global critique of the failings of capitalism provides a complete answer to the challenges facing contemporary child protection. However, it is contended that this lens of analysis is pivotal to understanding the evolution of modern child protection regimes: although the relationships are complex rather than linear, child protection is as much a classed and gendered undertaking now as it was in the late 19th century. Moreover, in Aotearoa, the relationship between the colonial liberal capitalist system and Māori has generated a specific set of contradictions and struggles that are both connected with and distinct from a class-centred analysis of child protection (Poata-Smith, 2002). Unpicking this knot can illuminate a progressive pathway for future policy and practice development.

When looking to escape from contemporary neoliberal hegemony, it is instructive to consider a time when a social-democratic/embedded liberal doxa held sway (Garrett, 2018). A collection of critical texts produced in the early 1980s as the neoliberal political project began to gather momentum offers useful source material. The advantage of a Marxist analysis is that it moves beyond the identification of inequality and poverty per se to an appreciation of how relative deprivation is linked to wider class relations. Although this critical tradition is alive in the scholarship of a small minority of social work academics (Gray and Webb, 2013a), it is seldom applied to an analysis of contemporary child protection.

Critical Texts in Social Work and the Welfare State – a series of books edited by Peter Leonard – is inevitably time-bound. However, the broad Marxist-inspired critique of the British welfare state that these volumes develop provides some very helpful conceptual foundations for the analysis of child protection policy as it has evolved in Aotearoa. As Ginsberg (1979: 10) asserts:

> While the working class has exerted little 'real' control over welfare policy and administration, it is equally true that the welfare state is a response to the presence of the working class, and the continuing plight of either some or all of its members in inadequate or insecure living conditions.

Ginsberg (1979: 11) maintains that public policy in capitalist states has always paid attention to groups who are perceived as outside of the mainstream of acceptable social relations, that is, groups identified by difference, being involved with agitation, resistance or protest, or simply marked by visible and disproportionate social inequality:

> While none of these phenomena have represented an organised threat to the state, they forcibly bring home to the bourgeoisie the existence of

a class or fragments of it which either rejects or is rejected by bourgeois values and whose needs must to some extent be accommodated or repressed to ensure the survival of capitalist social relations.

In summary, the analysis developed throughout this book proceeds from the position that child protection policy is historically situated within the political economy of liberal capitalism. Further, it perceives the social structure of Aotearoa and comparable societies to be constituted by active, productive contradictions. In this vein, the apparatus of the state is embedded with conflict, rather than serving the interests of capital in a simplistic or monolithic sense (Bolger et al, 1981).

Class, race, gender and history

Contemporary historians often question the hegemony of grand narrative templates, focusing instead on the submerged stories of those without power. In the North American context, Jacobs (2018: 263) has argued that Indigenous narratives tend to be rendered invisible within orthodox progressive histories, effectively replicating the cultural imperialism of settler colonial societies:

> The problem, I believe, rests with the particular nature of the sweeping twentieth-century epic historians have created. We often cast twentieth-century U.S. history as a showdown between liberal and conservative forces over the development of a welfare state and the increasing power of the federal government through two world wars, the New Deal, and the Great Society. The history of race, which historians have framed primarily around African American experience, has played a prominent role in explaining this showdown. One common and still powerful narrative portrays the early 1960s as an era when liberal white legislators, under pressure from but in concert with African American civil rights leaders, ended legal segregation and advanced African American voting rights. That moment ended, the story goes, as a separatist Black Power movement, urban race riots, and intractable poverty exposed the limits of the liberal agenda and as a conservative backlash regained the political upper hand. Twentieth-century Indigenous histories do not fit neatly into this epic narrative, although ... they have much to contribute to the subjects around which it revolves.

I will illustrate how statutory child protection in Aotearoa is enmeshed with the Māori history of struggle in and against the institutions of the settler colonial state.

Textured histories such as Harris's (2007) doctoral study, 'Dancing with the state: Māori creative energy and the policies of integration, 1945–1967', also look to give appropriate weight to the agentive role of social actors engaged in the creative negotiation and resolution of outcomes, rather than seeing people as mere pawns of place, time and powerful socio-economic forces. Harris (2007: 66) argues that excessively structural 'critiques can be problematic in that it can appear that the actors within the structure concerned are passive, behaving in ways that the structure dictates as opposed to responding to, engaging with and influencing the structure'.

This book does not aspire to be a mediated work of history in this sense. To draw on Marx's aphorism: people make their own history but not in circumstances of their choosing. The unabashed intent is to make explicit connections between a broad left-wing political analysis of capitalist social relations and the development of child protection social work. Accordingly, the narrative of this book is painted with a broad brush that aims to highlight how the intersections between capitalism and colonisation have coloured the child protection project in Aotearoa.

The connections between capitalism, liberalism, colonisation and child protection are not simple and linear. Accordingly, the relationships between working people, the interests of capital, the state and the role of social work are complex and nuanced. Nevertheless, it is argued that these relationships are generally configured by the conditions of possibility inherent to liberal capitalism. Capitalist society is confronted with a perennial problem in terms of how to deal with the impoverished population of surplus and residual labour it inevitably produces (Jones, 1983: 55). Since Victorian times, the liberal state has sought to divide and differentiate the residual or dependent poor from the respectable working class.

Governments provide various justifications for this endeavour, and as illustrated in subsequent chapters, it is a practice that is alive and well in the present political landscape. Foucault asserts that this division is an ideological and material necessity:

So that instead of saying, 'There is the working class and the marginal,' we would say, 'Within the overall lower class, there is a divide between those who work and those groups who are not part of the system of production.' The institution of police, the legal system, and the penal system are one of the means to deepen this partition, which is needed by capitalism. (Foucault, in Chambon, 1999: 94–5)[5]

The poor and recalcitrant are constituted as a practical and moral danger to the wider body politic. This categorisation deflects attention from the systemic causes of poverty (and the associated social suffering of children) while also serving a disciplinary function in relation to the wider working class. Broadly speaking, social work and the modern social sciences that inform and justify policy and practice have played (and continue to play) a significant role in 'othering' those on the margins of the capitalist social form. Statutory child protection does not sit in a room apart from these dynamics; rather, the families engaged by the system have always been drawn from the marginalised working class – a disproportionately 'brown' and feminised sub-proletariat in the Aotearoa context.

Conflict and change

Tension between the liberal humanist values espoused by the social work profession and the constraining political and managerial environment within which practice is enacted is also not a new phenomenon. The following passage was written by Peter Leonard in 1982 in an editor's introduction to Chris Jones's (1983) book, *State Social Work and the Working Class*. After suggesting that the focus in the 1950s–60s on psychotherapeutic understandings of the relationship between workers and clients obscured the essentially class-centred nature of that relationship, Leonard goes on to make the following statement:

> Later, from the early 1970s, as social service agencies grew in size and complexity and as the managerial component became more confident, social workers experienced mounting problems in their organisational roles. At the same time, increasing emphasis was given to the monitoring and control of individuals and families deemed 'at risk', culminating in various moral panics, most notably in the area of non-accidental injury to children. (Leonard, in Jones, 1983: xi)

Here, 50 years ago, we have many of the elements associated with the contemporary functioning of anglophone child protection systems: excessive control and direction within large managerial bureaucracies; a focus on the identification and surveillance of those classified as high-risk; and moral outrage as a driver of (or justification for) politically motivated reform.

The interaction between state social workers and those who are constructed as clients continues to occur in an ambiguous intermediary space situated at the nexus of care and control (Dominelli, 2004). As well as being instruments of state policy, social workers mediate and negotiate outcomes, and, at times, advocate vigorously for the children and families they engage with. In this sense, social workers can be notoriously 'difficult' employees: reluctant or resistant agents in the administration of social discipline (Hyslop, 2016b).

In his introduction to Jones's (1983) text, Leonard makes the further observation that 'social workers have continued to be *contaminated* by this contact with the working-class poor – a material experience deeply challenging to dominant ideologies' (Leonard, in Jones, 1983: xiv). This conscientisation process has also influenced the course of policy and practice development in Aotearoa, particularly in the watershed decade of the 1980s, when opposition to structural racism first came to dominate both practice innovation and the wider political reform agenda.

Although this positioning is a historical constant, the role of social work also changes with the times, or, more accurately, with the shifting imperatives of capitalist economics. The relationship between state social workers and service recipients is influenced by the changing needs of the labour market, preferred family forms and desired social norms. Practices perceived as necessary and desirable in the post-war welfare state era differ considerably from the desired function of social work within contemporary neoliberal 'modernisation' regimes (Parton, 2014a).

As the economic ground and the political balance has shifted to the right internationally, the ideological underpinnings of child protection social work have altered accordingly. Wallace and Pease (2011: 133) point to the inevitability of this accommodation given the place of social work within the apparatus of the state: ' "social work" is a continuous activity, conditioned by and dependent upon, the context from which it emerges and with which it engages (Harris, 2008: 662), changes in welfare regimes will shape the way in which social work is constituted and practiced'. As suggested, however, this transformation is not a straightforward or mechanical process; rather, the state is a site of struggle (Ginsberg, 1979). Ballantyne's (2019) discussion of the recent rejection of predictive risk modelling in relation to pre-emptive child protection intervention in Aotearoa highlights Rose and Miller's (2010) distinction between 'political rationalities', which look to normalise particular ideological perceptions of social problems, and 'technologies of governance', which aim to give effect to political projects. Both categories of governance engender resistance: 'In the words of Miller and Rose (1990), "Whilst 'governmentality' is eternally optimistic, 'government' is a congenitally failing operation. ... The 'will to govern' needs to be understood less in terms of its success than in terms of the difficulties of operationalizing it" (pp. 10–11)' (Ballantyne, 2019: 17).

Parton (2014a) has long maintained that the level of autonomy assigned to family life in the liberal mode of governance creates tensions in relation to expansive state 'interference' in the realm of the family, though a much lower bar is often applied to reordering the lives of the children of the para-proletariat. In Aotearoa, the experience of Māori will be considered through this lens of analysis.

The liberal inheritance

It is contended that the principles underpinning the liberal political tradition shape child protection policy and practice by setting the discursive 'common-sense' boundaries around how the problem of child maltreatment is understood and responded to by the state. It is further suggested that Māori conceptions of collective well-being present another, oppositional, claim to the 'common-sensing' of child protection work.

Accordingly, it is necessary to devote some attention to the philosophy and history of the liberal political tradition in Aotearoa. Grant Duncan (2004: 43) classifies the entrepreneurial activities of Edward Gibbon Wakefield and his flawed project of systematic colonisation as representative of 'the importation of capitalist economics and class structures in New Zealand'.[6] The concept of individuated, commodifiable private property rights is fundamental to liberalism and to capitalism; it was alien to Māori.

The modern origins of capitalism are normally associated with the period of rapid economic development in 19th-century Europe and Great Britain in particular (Polanyi, 2001). The exponential growth of bourgeois economic power is entwined with the unprecedented profit-driven rise in industrial production, urbanisation, the global development of commodity markets and associated processes of imperialism and colonisation.

Duncan (2004) sketches the broader horizon of societal change that prefigured this economic and social upheaval. In late feudal times, a small class of merchants and free craftsmen, as distinct from the land-owning aristocracy and rural peasantry, began to emerge. Over time, these shifts in the class configuration of power led to changes in the distribution of political authority, specifically, the expansion of limited-franchise parliaments. In England, the capacity of the rural poor to sustain themselves was undermined by the 1760–1840 Enclosure Acts, which restricted the use of common land for grazing and the traditional 'gleaning' of crops post-harvest. In Scotland, people were driven from the land during the highland clearances to facilitate the efficient, large-run farming of sheep (Duncan, 2004: 45–6). These processes dovetailed with the subsequent demand for mass factory labour and the urban migration that fuelled the growth of British capitalism.

Polanyi (2001: 174) has argued that the 1834 Poor Law, with its workhouse test for the provision of relief for the destitute, was effectively the birthday of the working class: 'Politically the British working class was defined by the Parliamentary Reform Act of 1832, which refused them the vote; economically by the Poor Law Reform Act of 1834, which excluded them from relief and distinguished them from the pauper.' This radical process of industrial change and the associated shift in economic, social and political power was underwritten by the philosophy and politics of liberalism. This was, in turn, the dominant political philosophy applied by the colonial authorities in Aotearoa. In modified form, it remains the primary lingua franca of contemporary political discourse.

The modern age of Enlightenment is intimately connected with understanding the nature of humankind and our relationship with the material and moral world through processes of scientific rationality and the motif of continuous progressive development (Ife, 2016). According to Descartes, reason separates man from nature and legitimates human dominion over all things (Hyslop, 2012). This duality is also what differentiates the 'Western' world view from cosmologies common to the Indigenous peoples of the colonised anglophone world – 'organic' societies where humans are viewed as an integral part of nature rather than its natural masters (Gray et al, 2013).

John Locke (1632–1704), the so-called 'father' of liberalism, was an English philosopher whose ideas influenced the broad corpus of intellectual work developed by subsequent French and Scottish Enlightenment thinkers, particularly the political economy espoused by Adam Smith (2010).[7] Locke's philosophy of private property proceeded from the building block of individuated freedom, that is, that individuals exercise autonomy over their own person. This 'original' property right is then extended to parts of the earth that individual labour is expended upon, such as the cultivation of land, effectively separating it from the claims of others by enclosing it from the commons.

It is a short and convenient step from this presumption to argue that uncultivated land, such as that occupied by Indigenous communities, is no more than 'wasteland' and therefore ripe for appropriation. The conflation of moral and economic good with individual entrepreneurial effort and the productive use of private property is the backbone of the liberal value system. Liberty is equated with unfettered business activity, so that it becomes possible to classify all potential impediments to commercial profit as barriers to 'freedom'.

It follows that government activities that interfere with the sanctity of the market or undermine private ownership and enterprise, such as worker protections, trade barriers or special interest subsidies, work against the interests of human liberty. State assistance damages the poor, discouraging the work ethic and robbing them of their agency. This has proven to be a potent and enduring justification for exploitative capitalism. For our purposes here, questions of child abuse and maltreatment can be disconnected from structural inequality and vested entirely in notions of individual morality and responsibility.

In common with most political ideologies, liberalism is an internally contested doctrine, though this contestation occurs within confined theoretical parameters. Duncan illustrates this by comparing the liberal doctrines of Adam Smith with the writings of the influential theorist and social activist Tom Paine (1737–1809). Whereas Smith saw state activity (beyond the protection of private property rights) as undermining liberty, Payne advocated for liberal freedom as a universal right. In this iteration of liberalism, the state has a role in ensuring that individuals are afforded some degree of capacity to exercise choices. This argument opens the door for a claim to social entitlements, as the state has a duty to enable citizens to exercise their freedoms.

At the risk of oversimplification, these contrasting interpretations loosely align with the right- and left-wing orientations of modern liberal politics, leaning as they do to a lesser or greater role for the state in regulating the functions of the market economy and enabling belonging and participation in society. According to Duncan (2004: 57): 'these two versions of liberalism – one that emphasises equality of rights and the other favouring freedom of choice – have become fundamental to many of the policy debates that we hear today'. He goes on to underline the symbiotic connection between liberalism and capitalism: 'It is no coincidence that the political ideas introduced earlier (private property, economic liberty, civil rights) were highly appropriate to the advance of capitalism and the forms of political and social organisation that accompany it' (Duncan, 2004: 57).

Despite the opposing poles of the liberal continuum, there is broad agreement on the sanctity of private property, the private ownership of productive resources and the role of government in encouraging and policing these fundamental foundations of the capitalist social form. In this analysis, mainstream liberal politics is essentially a family feud. The classical liberal political theory refined by the likes of John Stuart Mill (1806–73) and Herbert Spencer (1820–1903) resonates with the popular mythology, if often not the experiential reality, of settler society. Colonial Aotearoa was imagined as a vigorous, 'new' country that could avoid the ills of the old world. Individual and wider civic reward was associated with the productive use of land and natural resources, that is, hard work and astute investment. Liberalism provided the ideological backcloth to the colonial settlement narrative. It was also essentially oppositional to the collective social world of whānau, **hapū** and **iwi** Māori.

Belgrave (2012: 4) argues that the canvas provided by the liberal theoretical spectrum, in combination with variable economic influences, set the scene for emerging approaches to the provision of social security and wider welfare programmes:

> Nineteenth century liberalism was exported from Europe worldwide and its role in the expansion of a globalised economy based on capitalism cannot be understated. At the same time, major economic events with their international implications, such as periods of depression or sustained economic growth, had a major impact on New Zealand's systems of charity and welfare, providing greater or lesser opportunities for government to sustain existing programmes or develop new ones.

I have emphasised the centrality of liberalism to the political (and economic) history of Aotearoa because of the way that this ideology has played out historically in child welfare and protection, particularly in distinctions between the deserving and the morally threatening poor, and in conflict with the values and practices of Māori. As explored in later chapters, there has been a complex renaissance of liberal fundamentalism and resistance in the recent past, which is reflected in an ongoing process of contested reform. The formative history of the liberal colonial child welfare project in Aotearoa is canvased in Chapter 2.

Origins of child protection in Aotearoa

Sanitation

The positioning of social work as a profession that targets the working-class poor in the provision of services and interventions inevitably gives rise to productive tensions in a class society such as Aotearoa. Critical writers have long pointed to the associated 'sanitation' of state-sponsored social work:

> The de-politicisation of clients' problems, by which is meant the manner in which they are presented and understood in ways which deny or obscure their connections with the capitalist process, for example emphasising personal inadequacy, has been a central feature in the development and practice of social work. While this process is also evident within every state agency that has dealings with the working-class poor, it is particularly significant within the personal social services given that this part of the state apparatus deals almost exclusively with the residual and problem poor. Within the history of social work there exists a tradition which not only attempts to redefine the nature and causes of poverty and human brutalisation, but also to promote a view of clients not as casualties of a barbarous social system but more as a special and unique sub-species of the human race. (Jones, 1983: 59–60)

Arguably, the concept of depoliticisation is a misnomer. Social work that concentrates on addressing deficits in individual and family conduct, rather than targeting structural inequalities, can be said to perform an explicitly political function in terms of reinforcing mainstream liberal orthodoxy.

This orientation is professionally unsettling, particularly given the difficulty of reconciling statutory child protection with national and international social work definitions and practice codes, which aspire to the universal pursuit of human rights and social justice (Cree, 2013: 154–5). The argument developed here is that effective reform of contemporary child protection must take explicit account of the social and economic location of policy and practice – placing sociological and political understandings firmly back on the table.

Patterns and connections

In Chapter 1, it was proposed that perceptions of child maltreatment and responses to it are best understood within the context of wider society, not a society structured as a fixed totality, but nevertheless a society based on a given set of socio-economic arrangements: liberal capitalism. It is equally important to realise that societal forms are influenced by struggle and contestation – by conflicting class interests.

Socialist ideology (both revolutionary doctrine and the softer Fabian concept of evolutionary reform) has also contributed to the historical development of anglophone society, including the shape of social work in child welfare (Bolger et al, 1981). Further, the role of science and its relationship to modern political economy is important as something of a third pillar to support a critical, historically informed understanding of child protection theory and practice (Hyslop, 2012).

The modern construction of child protection is littered with connections to earlier liberal responses to child and family welfare. Awareness of this is important because, in contrast to the ahistorical understandings generally promoted in neoliberal discourse, it is argued that the present cannot be well understood without some reference to historical processes (Hyslop, 2016b, 2017). As Parton (2014a: 14) has asserted, past patterns are complex and textured, though not indecipherable, given that:

> what we now call 'child protection' has a history and line of development that has been influenced by a range of social, economic, cultural and political changes over a century and a quarter, and that a knowledge of this history is crucial to explaining and understanding the current form and function of this area of policy and practice. This is not to suggest that the developments have been straightforward or linear, or that what is referred to as child protection is in any way solid, as a whole range of complexities, tensions and contingencies have led to its emergence.

Approaches to the welfare of children are embroiled with the changing role of the state in the development of social policy and the delivery of social work services to systemically disadvantaged sections of the population. Historical accounts are also inevitably ideologically contested.

The orthodox periodisation of welfare history normally begins with the rudimentary 19th-century origins of charitable and state intervention with individuals and families in need. Such responses were motivated by concern with the maintenance of social order and morality, that is, with disciplining the poor and unproductive, as much as with addressing the impact of social suffering (McClure, 1998; Bauman, 1999). The associated focus on the 'deservingness' of those in receipt of assistance from the state or community was drastically modified, though never completely eradicated, by the construction of Western welfare states in response to the shared experience of insecurity occasioned by the Great Depression and Second World War. In Aotearoa, this history is also shaped by the development of a unique settler colonial society, specifically, the conflicted relationship with Māori.

The liberal bones of welfare

This chapter will signpost historical tensions and identify patterns in the relationship between the state and those who are positioned as welfare service recipients – tensions and patterns that reverberate in the present. With reference to comparative research into child protection system design, Parton draws attention to the conclusions reached by Hetherington (2006), which emphasise the crucial role that 'culture' plays in differentiating national orientations: 'By culture, she meant the nexus of views, understandings, habits of mind, patterns of living and use of language that are built up in a community, nation or state by the shared history, experiences and social circumstances in which people live' (Parton, 2014a: 7). The colonial settlement project was animated by the values and myths of liberal 'culture', which centred on the sanctity of private property, paid employment and self-reliance. The evolution of child protection policy and practice needs to be understood within this wider rubric and in the context of accompanying attitudes to problems of poverty, social distress and the distribution of rights. In this sense, Victorian ghosts still wander at large in the contemporary social work imagination (Hyslop, 2016b).

Belgrave (2012) connects the history of the modern welfare state back to the Liberal governments of the 1890s, specifically, the precedent set by the introduction of old-age pensions in 1898. He also locates the wider evolution of responses to social need in Aotearoa squarely under the umbrella of the liberal economic and political tradition:

> Liberalism provided the intellectual and policy underpinnings for the expansion of British capitalism and British constitutional institutions to settled colonies such as New Zealand. Liberalism assumed the autonomy of the individual and provided a justification for laissez-faire capitalism. Earlier writers (and to some extent popular mythology today) assumed that New Zealand had from its creation a more progressive approach to providing welfare, in creating a 'workingman's paradise'. (Belgrave, 2012: 2)

Tennant (2007) suggests that the early iterations of state welfare in Aotearoa were, if anything, more confined, both morally and fiscally, than the modest and punitive services provided in the 'old country'. The colonial project presupposed an even more dismissive orientation to poor relief, particularly state-sanctioned assistance, than in the English setting:

> At the time when organised European settlement of New Zealand began, antagonism towards a poor law was stronger than it had been in the previous century, and a sense of the colony as a 'new world' free from the taint of the old was to give this an even sharper edge. (Tennant, 2007: 26)

The English Poor Law of 1834 standardised the variable pattern of parish relief that dated from Elizabethan times, replacing it with a 'spur of poverty' ethos designed to ensure the supply of disciplined labour required to fuel the engine of industrial capitalism:

> This measure heralded the era of the New Poor Law, in which the principle of 'less eligibility' – that aid given to the needy should be less 'eligible' or attractive than the living achieved by those on the lowest wages – underwrote publicly funded assistance. 'Outdoor' assistance to people in their own homes contracted, and entry to the workhouse was made a condition of help for the able-bodied. (Tennant, 2007: 23)

The 19th-century policy settings reflected a synergy between the requirements of the capitalist labour market and moral condemnation of economically marginalised people. This formula has proved to be resilient over time and continues to influence contemporary responses to impoverished families. The wider aim of work enforcement and the ideological link between state dependence and moral degeneration is plainly evident in the workfare and benefit-sanctioning initiatives associated with the modern neoliberal political turn.[1] The National Party 'mother of all budgets' benefit cuts of 1991 have never been adequately readjusted and have effectively consigned two generations of children to relative poverty in a land of plenty (Boston and Chapple, 2014).

In Aotearoa, poverty and inequality are demarcated by class, gender and race: Māori and Pasefika women are over-represented (Bell et al, 2017). Although the children who come to the attention of state child protection services are disproportionately drawn from the working poor or families in receipt of state-mandated income support, concern with the structural causes of social suffering is largely absent from mainstream child protection discourse. Contemporary child protection social work is primarily directed to the identification of risk to individual children and the resolution of the perceived parental deficits that impact on their safety and well-being. Moral judgements are better concealed but no less influential than in the

19th-century beginnings of state welfare. Arguably, such judgements are masked by ongoing efforts to frame assessment and intervention in terms of objective evidential science.

Recent research has highlighted this problematic misalignment between the socio-political realties of family life in grossly unequal societies such as Aotearoa and the current model of centralised investigation and intervention-driven child protection bureaucracy. Analysis undertaken by Keddell (2020) documents stark statistical divergences, begging imperative questions about the processes and outcomes of child welfare practice. There is an uncomfortable disjunction between the narrow causative rationale embraced by detect and 'fix or rescue' child protection systems and the poverty and inequality that underpins care and well-being disparities for children in Aotearoa:

> In 2014, children living in the most deprived 10% of neighbourhoods in Aotearoa New Zealand had 21 times the chance of having a substantiated finding of child abuse than children living in the least deprived 10%, were 35 times more likely to have a family group conference held about them, and over nine times more likely to enter foster care (Keddell, Davie and Barson, 2019). Each step-increase in deprivation resulted in a sequentially higher chance of child protection system contact, clearly illustrating the systematic relationship between living in high deprivation areas and contact with the child protection system. (Keddell, 2020: 36)

The implications will be discussed in depth in the concluding chapters of this book, where the current revisioning of child protection is canvassed in some detail.

Middle-class benevolence

The genesis of modern child protection social work can be traced from Victorian responses to social 'misfortune', as best exemplified in the work of the English Charity Organisation Society (COS), established in 1869: 'The pivot of this new guise of benevolent activity is the "visitor of the poor", the true forerunner of social work, the instrument at once of the capillary distribution of "household relief", and of the "study of character" which was beginning to be considered indispensable for good social administration' (Procacci, 1991: 165). Since the origins of social need were perceived to reside largely in personal failing, eligibility for assistance required an assessment of moral deservedness and capacity for reform. This orientation casts a long shadow down to the contemporary assessment of caregivers' ability and willingness to learn and apply new behaviours to meet the care or protection needs of their children. When I began as a state social worker in 1984, my office manager passed on the following piece of advice: "Look son, there's three kinds of people in this world: winners, losers and swingers. Forget about the winners, they can look after themselves and forget about the no-hopers too – see if you can do something for the swingers." Old constructions die hard.

Jones (1983: 83) suggests that an idealist personal redemption ethos was embedded in the education and training systems that the COS developed to support 'good casework'. The drive to professionalise philanthropy involved integrating the morality-enhancing attributes of the 'friendly visitor' (the archetype deliverer of personal social services) with technical tools selectively appropriated from the emerging social sciences. The legacy of this notion of social workers as good and upright citizens bringing individuated change through instruction and example is evidenced in the contemporary regulation of the social work profession.[2]

Science and contamination

The relationship between social work and social science is saturated with questions of professional methodology and legitimacy. In turn, social science tends to experience a fraught relationship with the physical sciences (Cnaan and Dichter, 2008). Over time, the push to invest social work with empirical clarity has become inseparable from questions about the desired function of social work, how it might best be done and the knowledge that is required (Barretta-Herman, 1994). According to Jones (1983: 89), scientific trappings have historically served to disguise 'social work's class-based morality'.

Faith in the political neutrality and predictive certainty of social and behavioural science has continued to inform the design and development of professional social work to the present day, particularly as a means of neutralising the emotive and ambiguous context of statutory child protection. As in the 19th century, ostensibly objective scientific methodology is often employed in the service of morally and politically constructed policy objectives (Pease, 2013). Elements of social Darwinist thinking persistently recur in rational 'evidence-based' interventions designed to identify and target a morally reprehensible underclass (for discussion of problem families and population groups, see Chapters 6 and 7).

Charles Booth's meticulous study of poverty and inequality in late 19th-century London is significant for several reasons. The ideological foundations reflect both the moral prejudices of the day and a faith in the utility of empirical evidence as the basis for solutions to social problems such as urban poverty. The search for objective facts as a prerequisite to rational intervention was informed by the notion that studies in social science should be made as exact as those in natural science, as propounded in the philosophy of Auguste Comte (1798–1857).[3]

Booth's rigorous collection and analysis of detailed information has continued to be influential in terms of social research methodology, particularly statistical approaches to studies of poverty (Orford et al, 2002). His weighty *Life and Labour and the People in London* (1904) divides the population of London into eight distinct groups (classes A–H), based on a mix of assigned social status and material circumstances. This germinal work is inevitably saturated with the classical liberal morality of the times (Spicker, 1990). Those occupying the bottom rung of Booth's classification (class H) are variously described as semi-criminals, loafers or the 'vicious' poor. The denizens in this category are implicitly regarded as lacking the moral capacity to exercise rational liberal autonomy. This toxic status is seen as a form of degenerative quicksand into which the honest poor may fall, or be dragged, through association with the feckless and indolent.

Booth proposed the concept of 'state industrial homes' as a means of separating the upright poor from the moral danger posed by this contaminating influence. This thinking has been repackaged in recent decades in support of neoliberal/neoconservative approaches to the political economy of welfare and child protection. In Aotearoa, the contemporary reach of these ideas is evidenced in recent policy documents, specifically, the implicitly biologised socio-economic categories of poverty and social service client status set out in the New Zealand Productivity Commission's 'More effective social services' (NZPC, 2015) report, as well as in the work of the Modernising Child, Youth and Family Expert Panel (canvassed in Chapter 6).

Biopolitics

Booth pioneered the demographic identification and detailed statistical delineation of population groupings with the intent of enhancing the well-being of the wider 'population'. This project is consistent with Michel Foucault's (2003) theorisations of an emerging 'biopolitics' of the social. Essentially, this concept addresses the increasingly sophisticated way in which mechanisms of control have come to operate in advanced liberal societies.

Foucault examines the lineage of state concern with the future development of the life of the 'species' and the associated significance of biological understandings of human development.[4] He argues that the focus of liberal governance has expanded in various complex ways from the 18th-century preoccupation with the punishment of deviance to a more productive, 'freedom-enhancing' focus on population health. Foucault is interested in the complex relationship between dominant knowledge forms, political power and human subjectivity. From this perspective, the nascent role of biological science and medicine from the late 19th century (and the pastoral care that Foucault associates with social work) provided technologies to promote social health and hygiene, as well as to shape and serve economic and political order (Tudor, 2019: 74).

The eugenics movement that flourished in the early 20th century is perhaps the starkest example of this orientation. Tudor (2019: 17) draws attention to a spectrum of policy approaches influenced by this kind of population-centred view of social development, stressing a distinction between supressing weakness and developing strength:

> In New Zealand, Wanhalla (2001) notes that the eugenic history fits more with the positive variant of population management. Positive eugenics was 'designed through state intervention, to encourage the reproduction of the best, or "fittest", stock while negative eugenics devised strategies to identify the "unfit" and to prevent their reproduction' (Wanhalla, 2001). The objectives of New Zealand's eugenic welfarist approach were centred on ensuring a healthy, functioning society, which involved ensuring all facets of society were able to contribute to the common good (Belgrave, 2012: 6).

However, the distinction between positive and negative orientations is not necessarily clear, as in more (or less) subtle ways, one approach implies the other. The notion of enhancing well-being at the level of the population – 'race improvement' – continues to be evident in the development of public policy in Aotearoa. Social work has a long association with biological forms of knowledge, importing concepts from human developmental and behavioural science into work with individuals and groups in the social world (Gillies et al, 2017).

In Foucault's original formulation, 'biopower' was conceived as an amalgam of internalised disciplinary authority and forms of regulatory governance that required social division, that is, the designation of population groupings as exterior to the norm, hence the central role for demographic and statistical differentiation. His later work developed the link between biopolitics and the concept of governmentality. Regulatory power was reworked as 'the technology of security' – techniques for the management of the population at the level of internalised individual sovereignty (Tudor, 2019: 28).

Such theorisations are consistent with both the naturalisation of liberal values at the level of individual consciousness and the identification of deviant social groups as targets of remedial intervention: 'Foucault ... observes how the division of the population occurs according to a range of norms including mental illness, degeneracy, and social class divisions, enacting a kind of cultural racism' (Tudor, 2019: 29). It is a short step from perceiving child abuse as undesirable deviance to the delineation of an external class who pose a biological threat to the collective health and 'security' of the wider population. Advanced contemporary demographic data collection and processing technologies potentially provide mechanisms for the identification and tracking of sub-populations associated with social risk (Ballantyne, 2019). The relevance of this analysis to contemporary child protection will be developed in Chapter 6.

Going native

The 'scientisation' imperative can also be instructively linked to a range of complex tensions associated with the positioning of social workers and the conduct of practice. Social work is something of a conflicted occupation historically, and child protection practice is certainly no exception. At the risk of oversimplification, the impetus to work alongside, or in some degree of partnership, with groups or individuals experiencing social and economic hardship can be contrasted with a focus on diagnosing and remedying the failings of individuals perceived as inadequate and in need of social repair.

In this sense, social work can be understood as a broad church, ranging from community development to coercive statutory intervention. Even at the authoritative end of this continuum, practitioners tend to take some account of the way in which individual lives are influenced by wider social systems. To this extent, social work is always a contentious field, not least because of its 'location' at the point where the role of the state interfaces with individuals, families and communities who are marginalised in capitalist processes of production and distribution:

> Since its beginnings in the late nineteenth century, social work has had the particular societal mandate of going amongst the poor, and working with the poor, but with the clear injunction 'not to go native' (the analogy with Christian missionary work in the remotest parts of the Empire is, of course exact and early social work was often seen explicitly in these terms ...). Jones refers to the ever-present danger of social workers becoming 'over-involved' with their clients as the problem of contamination and sees the development of social work education as being part of a strategy to arm budding social workers against this danger (Jones, 1983). The dilemma this involved was evident from the earliest days of the Charity Organisation Society (COS). (Ferguson, 2008: 20)

In various forms over time, the danger of 'going native' has been an abiding concern in relation to practice 'safety' in child protection. State regulation of problem populations (in the Foucauldian sense described earlier) by means of personalised engagement perennially entails the risk of social workers getting too close to the 'contaminating' material and narrative realities of their clients. This intimate work potentially generates insight into the link between social problems and private troubles, as well as a desire to embrace political rather than personal solutions to social difficulties embedded in economic inequality. This is evident in Chapter 4, which discusses the quasi-political agitation and practice innovation embraced by state social workers in the 1980s. Given that this was motivated by anti-racist sentiment, the label 'going native' is particularly ironic and resonant.

Jones (1983: 86) identifies the historical emphasis, both in social work education and in organisational practice, on maintaining a safe distance: 'It is little wonder, therefore, that so much of the social work literature focuses on the manipulative qualities of clients, highlighting the manner in which clients can exploit the sympathies of the unguarded social worker.' Although the accepted technical orthodoxy of child protection practice has changed dramatically since the late 1800s, or, indeed, since the early 1980s, the importance vested in dispassionate practice informed by the science of the day persists. This is illustrated, for example, in the modern practices of tabulating cumulative risk factors, assessing attachment deficits or eliciting evidence of intergenerational trauma for the purpose of individual or familial diagnosis and treatment.

The spirit of colonial welfare

The formative influences canvassed earlier carried over, and were adjusted, to the settler state society of Aotearoa. Echoes continue to reverberate in contemporary child protection. Emerging welfare services were primarily directed to the needs of Pākehā. In this sense, the evolution of a recognisable welfare system and the postcolonial Māori experience reflect separate histories, though they are, of course, intertwined. The complex interplay of conflict, resistance and accommodation that characterised the colonial relationship was played out on a much broader canvas concerned with the procurement of land for settlement and the commodification of Indigenous labour (Poata-Smith, 2002). When touching on the minutiae of development, it is important to hold this bigger picture in mind.

State welfare provision in Aotearoa is also connected with the growth of parallel services and institutions, so that the provision of material support and social assistance cannot be neatly divorced from, for example, the development of health and education services. In fact, these areas of state activity and professional expertise have had significant implications for the shape and form of social welfare bureaucracy, and for child welfare services more specifically. The early hospital system was initially significant for Māori, and the programme of native schools under the auspices of the Native Department from 1867 was central to the assimilationist colonial agenda.

The often destructive later 20th-century history of residential care and schooling for Māori can be linked back to this early faith in the 'civilising' role of educational institutions.

The 1846 Destitute Persons Ordinance created a legal right for the penniless to pursue family members for support. Although its practical effect should not be overstated, this regulation exemplifies a commitment to the classical liberal expectation of self-help and family responsibility (Tennant, 2007: 28–9). Legal frameworks for state assistance, institutions and administrative infrastructure only began to develop significantly from the late 1870s as the ideal of a liberal 'new world' utopia began to pale before the harsh realities of colonial life. This process was hastened by the poverty that arose from economic recession in the 1880s. Related concerns about worker exploitation and damaging industrial conflict influenced the reform agenda of the Liberal government (1891–1912): 'As social divisions appeared increasingly entrenched – divisions between town and country, between landholders and landless, between capitalist and worker, between the haves and the have nots – a number of public figures began to lament the appearance of the old world in the new' (Tennant, 1989: 23).

The Liberals represented a divergent alliance of interests. As in comparable societies, the state was compelled to broker compromises with the increasingly militant demands of the trade union movement (Weir, 2002). They responded to the needs of workers and the protection of trade unions through the Industrial Conciliation and Arbitration Act 1894 (IC&A Act), which provided a template for industrial regulation in Aotearoa up until the 1970s. This legislation forced employers to the bargaining table, but it also constrained the power of radical organised labour by curtailing the right to strike.

There was a limited policy focus on enabling rural settlement/small farm ownership and development. Conflict between small (or aspiring) landowners and the vested interests of large-run holders was a central friction in the process of Pākehā settlement – an ideological and material tension that touches squarely on the liberal 'dream' of social mobility through sharp investment, enterprise and hard work. The link between family wealth and the opportunity to 'get ahead' by investing in private property and/or small business enterprise continues to underpin liberal conservative 'Kiwi' ideology in Aotearoa (Hyslop, 2007: Provan, 2012). It can also be transposed to the 'working man's paradise' mythology associated with the post-war welfare state. The tenuous and conditional place for Māori in this national identity narrative, and the powerful relevance of this for child protection, are developed in subsequent chapters.

Political debate in the late 19th century was informed, as it often is today, by the various, sometimes inconsistent, strands of thought associated with liberal political economy. As indicated, liberalism comprises a diverse body of ideas that can combine and interact in unforeseen ways in terms of policy agendas and outcomes. For example, the groundbreaking old-age pension legislation of 1898 was promoted as a guarantee of dignity and security, but it was increasingly administered through strict and miserly criteria: tests of need and fitness of character, and the exclusion of individuals and groups construed as undeserving. In his commentary on the legacy of Liberal government, Roper (2008: 11) concludes that 'the provision of pensions and benefits was blatantly discriminatory towards women, Māori, Asians and those who were referred to as the "undeserving poor", while public provision of health and housing remained far from extensive'.

In addition to oppositions and contradictions, public policy can also be influenced by unexpected convergences. The ideology of evolutionary social progress espoused in the Fabian socialism of William Pember Reeves, the architect of the IC&A Act (Moloney, 2002), contrasted, and at times overlapped, with the cautious and morally saturated approaches to state assistance associated with social Darwinism. Belgrave (2012) identifies synergies between the Fabian concept of incremental social improvement and the population-strengthening ideology evidenced in public health initiatives developed from the early 20th century. The zealotry of the Plunket Society carried the mark of positive eugenics as consistent with the biopolitics later theorised by Foucault. As suggested, this thinking also continues to resonate in the field of contemporary child protection.

Charitable inheritance

To a degree, the overtly gendered 19th-century 'golden age' of voluntary welfare in Britain was mirrored in Aotearoa, though the scope and financial security of benevolent organisations was not of a comparable scale (Tennant, 1989: 20). However, the moral frame that coloured Victorian charitable responses to recipients of aid or institutional shelter was replicated. Formative responses to poverty and social need also reflected an uneasy relationship between state responsibility and benevolent or faith-based service provision that continues to the present day.

The Hospital and Charitable Institutions Act 1985 (H&CIT Act), which Tennant (1989: 30) describes as 'effectively a colonial version of the Poor Law, minus the right to relief', provided 'a mean and limited form of public assistance'. Administration involved a blend of voluntary and state services. A network of hospital and charitable aid boards were funded by local rates, private donations and central government. The commitment to material provision was parsimonious and conditional, but it did signal the beginnings of state responsibility for social assistance.

No discussion of this period would be complete without reference to the self-important and imposing figure of Dr Duncan MacGregor, Inspector-General of Hospitals and Charitable Institutions (1886–1906).

McGregor regarded poverty and dependence on state relief (pauperism) as a self-perpetuating social disease and was apt to dispense these sentiments in excoriating reports and blustering prose:

> MacGregor believed that the 'hopelessly lazy, the diseased, and the vicious', who would once have been weeded out by natural selection were 'eating like a cancer into the vitals of society.' Regretting that society would no longer leave these 'waste products to struggle and die unaided', he concluded by advocating the lifetime incarceration of hopeless drunkards, criminals and paupers. (Tennant, 1993: 285)

The harshness of McGregor's invective was not necessarily matched by his political influence. It is, however, powerfully symbolic of a thread of moral condemnation within the liberal heritage: a blaming and casting out of those who have failed to display the necessary self-reliance. Receipt of state or private benevolence is associated with a further degeneration of character.

In 1889, a proposed amendment to the H&CIT Act looked to segregate the most socially infectious by confining 'idlers, drunkards and tramps and those whose families were likely to become a burden on the state' to prison-like state refuges (Tennant, 1989: 32). This proposal did not become law, despite the support of politicians actively involved in the eugenics movement. Tennant (1989: 33) notes the influence of Charles Booth, the early English researcher, who ' recommended labour colonies for the very poor in 1887 and 1888'.

As discussed briefly, Booth's work was driven by mixed motivations and yielded mixed outcomes. Forensic attention to the life of the poor revealed that poverty was associated with erratic work and low wages, and was not solely the province of the immoral and itinerant. However, the classification of the poor as an isolated object of scientific study with identifiable gradations of risk and moral failing has left a lasting inheritance.

The process of segregating the recalcitrant and irredeemable as a separate class of client requiring a different approach to intervention is clearly illustrated by Tennant (1989: 116) in the practice of an early refuge for 'fallen' women:

> Before 1891 the Canterbury Refuge was divided into two sections – Class A for 'first falls', and Class B for older, more intractable cases. Conditions in Class B frequently verged on the riotous, inmates reported as 'behaving infamously', cursing and assaulting staff, refusing to work, having tantrums on the back lawn and absconding.

The larger legacy is evident in the persistent discourse of 'feral' underclass families reproducing social disadvantage and in contemporary efforts to harness big data to identify sub-populations who are more likely to abuse their children (Ballantyne, 2019). In my experience, it is also bound up in the attitudes of statutory social workers when confronted with children and families who present as uncooperative and irredeemable. A profession motivated by the concept of redemption and inclusion must find a means of justifying exclusionary practices:

> In my twenty years of experience in child protection social work in Auckland, New Zealand, I often observed groups of social workers in social or out-of-hours gatherings engaged in the exaggerated mockery of individual parents and/or children who were perceived as inadequate and often as somehow grotesque. It was as if repetition in the form of tribal incantation would exorcise doubt. (Hyslop, 2016b: 11)

Although the charitable aid ethos was discredited by the shared experience of insecurity generated by the Great Depression of the 1930s, punitive and moralistic approaches to poverty and the poor have proved to be a resilient theme in the governance (and conservative common sense) of liberal capitalist societies. From the vantage point of the late 1980s, Tennant (1989: 8) notes the persistence of this form of stigmatisation:

> The 1970s preoccupation with 'dole bludgers' and 'solo mums' smacked more of charitable aid in the 1890s than of the supposed altruism of social security in the 1930s; the 1980s rhetoric of efficiency, targeting, and incentives would have appealed immensely to the most austere of New Zealand's nineteenth century 'poor law' inspectors.

As the initial neoliberal wave of doctrinaire market fundamentalism cascaded across the social fabric of Aotearoa from the 1990s, policies predicated on these sentiments were further legitimised and reinvigorated.

Child welfare and social work: tracing lines of descent

Children are something of a special case in terms of liberal conceptions of morality and rights. As emergent citizens tied to the programme of family life, children and young people occupy a liminal space, attracting ambivalent and sometimes contradictory responses from the state (Parton, 2014a). According to Tennant (1989: 46), even the austere gaze of Duncan McGregor discerned 'total support for children, whom he considered educable and still worthy of investment'. The notion of children as worthy of future investment has become a central, and ideologically loaded, 21st-century policy discourse.

Responsibility for the well-being of children is also spread historically across intersecting and disputed territories, between the state and civil society, and between the various arms of central government: health, education and social welfare bureaucracies. This is unsurprising given the broad nature of children's developmental needs and the overlapping disciplinary and administrative perspectives that inform these policy and service systems: 'Historically, responsibility for children has been contested between government and the voluntary sector, between state sector agencies (most especially Child Welfare, Health and Justice) and amongst professional groups (social workers, educationalists, and the medical profession)' (Tennant, 2007: 108).

It was not until 1972 – when the Child Welfare Division of the Department of Education was amalgamated with the Department of Social Security to form the Department of Social Welfare (DSW) – that child welfare became explicitly aligned with the wider delivery of personal social work services within the welfare state. Significantly, the professional designation 'social worker' replaced the title of 'child welfare officer' when the Child Welfare Act 1925 was superseded by the Children and Young Persons Act 1974. Tensions around the roles and responsibilities of social workers in relation to children, particularly in the area of child protection, have continued to generate debate and policy swings, as reflected in the multiple reorientations and restructurings that have taken place over the last 40 years.

This contested terrain is evident in the early history. The establishment of state institutions for the reform and containment of recalcitrant children dates from the Neglected and Criminal Children Act 1867, 20 years earlier than rudimentary state regulation of provision for destitute adults. Child welfare initially came under the auspices of the Justice Department. Transfer to the Education Department in 1880 signalled a shift to a more reformative orientation. Debates about the relative merits of 'justice'- or 'welfare'-centred approaches to juvenile offending are enduring, as evidenced in the return to a justice orientation in the Children, Young Persons, and their Families Act 1989 (CYP&tF Act).

Synergies, intersections and tensions between state and 'voluntary/ charitable' welfare services have also been an ongoing feature of child welfare policy and practice in Aotearoa. Varying formative elements of child protection social work as we know it today can be identified in the early iterations of both voluntary and state-sponsored practices, not least in the notion of the disciplined 'inspection' of individual and family circumstances against preset criteria for assessment and intervention. The present-day maintenance of focused case-note records corresponds to the 'painstaking casework and classification of the poor' undertaken by the English COS and much admired by Duncan McGregor (Tennant, 1989: 46).

These practices were replicated to a degree in the conduct of charitable aid relieving officers. The assembly of written client records in the shape of narrative accounts of conduct and character, hierarchical reporting systems and, to some extent, the mediating, pragmatic interactions with those seeking relief are all reminiscent of modern social work. Although eligibility for assistance was determined by meetings of board members, 'case reports became the basis on which most relief decisions were made in the largest centres' (Tennant, 1989: 69).

Tennant (2007) also suggests echoes with other challenges commonly associated with contemporary practice: a need to be wise to the risk of manipulation by people in need; occasions of physical risk; and the temptation to abuse the power imbalance inherent in the helping relationship. Some late 19th-century charity workers performed wider functions more directly comparable to the professional practice and identity of modern social workers, assessing and intervening broadly – in terms of the dominant causal perceptions and available resources – into the 'problems of others' (Tennant, 2007: 58). As with the COS template, the exemplary moral/reformatory function of the worker–client 'relationship' was considered a key component of this role.

Care services

Technically, the charitable aid boards were responsible for destitute children while those in care due to criminal behaviour or parental neglect were the financial responsibility of the state through the Education Department. In practice, the blend of Church, voluntary and state provision of a limited pool of resources resulted in a more flexible and pragmatic system: 'Indigent parents might be relieved of one or two children so that they could more easily support themselves, and it was not unknown for "unfit" parents to have their children forcibly taken from them. Poverty and family dispersal were closely associated' (Tennant, 1989: 127). The scale and zealotry of the 19th-century English rescue movement (as exemplified in the work of Thomas Barnardo) was not replicated in Aotearoa, though it was influential. Institutions for the containment of various categories of destitute or socially censured people were established, principally by Christian organisations, from the 1880s, including the provision of charitable orphans' homes. For orphanage children, accounts indicate a dull and disciplined existence, with elements of the neglectful and abusive practices that have continuously blighted the institutional care of children and young people.

Historical accounts of care systems that focus exclusively on the coerced removal of children can risk assigning an unduly passive role to the working-class targets of such services. Recent scholarship has questioned this excessively passive positioning of families on the receiving end of evangelical care services (Murdoch, 2006). This is not to suggest a benign relationship. In retrospect, it is abundantly clear that state and charitable services have often resulted in destructive outcomes for children and their families. This is particularly the case for Māori from the latter half of the 20th century.

However, Murdoch's work is a useful reminder of the interactive, albeit often stilted, nature of contemporary state social work. There are inevitably points of resistance, that is, ways in which service users actively look to meet their own interests or, at least, modify system responses in ways that better match perceived needs. As is the case with colonised peoples, the relationship between the state and the marginalised poor can be a complex dance of hostility, suspicion and accommodation.

Tennant (2007) suggests that the early orphanage system in Aotearoa, which peaked in the early 20th century, may have effectively 'complemented' the more rigid court-mandated care regime of state industrial homes. Significantly, it appears that children in care were seldom 'true' orphans. There was a 'high incidence of temporary admission, with children being reclaimed by family members weeks, months or years later' (Tennant, 2007: 48). This suggests elements of agency, with families seeking to access care for children in times of dire need rather than callously seeking to relinquish responsibility as per the popular construction of the time.

Complex 'negotiated' relationships often inform the practice of modern statutory social work, though this element of practice is seldom clearly visible in systems driven by concern with efficiency, risk management and procedural compliance (Hyslop, 2009). The efforts of statutory social workers to engage, 'treat' or otherwise intervene with 'client' families are, unsurprisingly, met with varying degrees of mistrust and resistance. In this context, parental behaviour that is perceived as oppositional, non-compliant or manipulative is often more about families' attempts to exercise some degree of agency, that is, to meet needs on their own terms rather than as defined by the state or contracted service providers (O'Leary et al, 2013).

In the 1890s and early 1900s, charitable aid boards were motivated by the question of cost to ratepayers (and the related incentive to avoid liability) as much as by the suffering of children, whereas the Education Department was more likely to take (or be pushed into) a more interventionist/reformatory position. Education came to assume the dominant role in child welfare provision and became increasingly associated with the 'boarding out' of children in private foster-care arrangements, while smaller 'children's home' institutions became the province of the churches.

Foster care was legitimated, in part, by much earlier successful practice in Australia. As is the case today, the adequate care and safety of children was not necessarily assured by boarding-out arrangements given the financial needs of caregivers, the disciplinary practices of the time and the stresses perennially associated with caregiving. Concern with 'baby farmers' and the potential for abusive practices generated the Infant Life Protection Acts of 1893 and 1896, which set down some minimum standards for approval and inspection, though the practical effect was likely limited (Tennant, 1989: 138).

Fostering of 'state wards' was the entrenched policy preference of the Child Welfare Branch of the Education Department, established in 1925. The 'division' was staffed by workers accustomed to practices of home visiting and assessment, setting in place the framework for a developing professional child welfare identity:

> By 1918 the Department employed juvenile probation officers, attendance officers, district agents under the Infants Acts, visiting nurses, and the personnel of the special and industrial school branches. Many of these men and women had some mandate to investigate private homes and worked closely with schools and voluntary workers. From 1925 the appointment of Child Welfare Officers provided a core of professional social workers with a well-defined career structure to oversee the welfare of children. (Tennant, 1989: 143)

Somewhat paradoxically, it was not uncommon for women supported by charitable aid to take on foster-care responsibilities as a way of generating income. Foster care is significantly cheaper than institutional care as a rule. At times of deinstitutionalisation, although the political rhetoric is often focused on the shortcomings of managed-care facilities, cost reduction is often an unspoken driver.

Although the larger charitable aid system and its morally engrained mandate of minimal necessary assistance was overwhelmed and significantly discredited by the Great Depression and unemployment of the 1930s, Tennant (1989: 201) concludes that notions of 'discipline, less eligibility and deservedness, and the fear of pauperisation and of inbred degeneracy, are part of the heritage of our welfare state'. I would argue that these influences are alive and well in statutory child protection practice and in the critical contemporary debate about the future of this work.

Echoes of class and gendered discipline

The eugenics movement, with its quasi-medical focus on the reproduction of a deficient social residuum, became increasingly influential in the early decades of the 20th century. Tennant (1989: 123) identifies a 'growing range of state and voluntary agencies anxious to guide "problem" families after the First World War. Always subject to censure from the relieving officer, poor women were obvious targets for the new social workers, although many remained staunchly resistant to interventions.' Gendered ideals and class-based judgements coloured practice:

> Such women carried the burden not only of poverty, frequently of brutal or broken marriages, of chronic ill-health and overcrowded

homes, but they were held collectively responsibility for racial decline and social disorder. Their experience was a far cry from the almost spiritual picture of radiant–motherhood and cosy family life promulgated by women's organisations and in popular magazines of the time. (Tennant, 1989: 124)

Writing, as I am here, in the winter of 2020, it is instructive to consider the abiding parallels between contemporary child protection and the emerging social work practices of 1920 in order to reflect on what has changed and what has remained 'essentially' the same. As was the case a century ago, poor women living on the frayed edges of the mainstream social fabric are the targets of child and family social workers. Chapter 3 will discuss the way in which this classed and gendered inequality developed a racialised dimension as the 20th century unfolded in Aotearoa.

3

Post-war child welfare

Ideological boundaries

I have argued that child protection is politically constructed in a broad sense – that deep, often opposing currents reflect tensions within the liberal capitalist project. These economic and political parameters have set the boundaries of child protection reform, even when apparently radical departures from past models have taken place. In an important sense, this space became no less contested after the neoliberal turn that has informed state policy in Aotearoa from the mid-1980s.

However, room for manoeuvre has narrowed as successive centre-left/centre-right administrations have attempted to grapple:

> with the legacy of state sector reform ushered in by the State Sector Act 1988 and the Public Finance Act 1989. Beyond formal structures, these reforms have had a pervasive impact on the public service, changing its culture and performance and redefining the relationship between politicians, officials and the public. (Garlick, 2012: 10)

The final chapters of this book focus on this volatile period of change and the current trajectory of child protection reform. To background this discussion, it is necessary to devote some attention to the development of child and family practice during the welfare state era. Many of the issues that currently assail child protection are rooted in this history.

Despite significant local variations, the development of post-war state services followed a comparable path across anglophone jurisdictions, being a period of relative political consensus that Garrett (2018), following David Harvey, refers to as 'embedded liberalism' – as distinct from the neoliberalism of recent decades (Spolander et al, 2015). I have also suggested that these 'new' liberal reforms can be instructively compared with the political backdrop to the 19th-century wave of capitalist fundamentalism, that is, that political ideology generally serves economic interests and development imperatives: 'The ideas of the ruling class are in every epoch the ruling ideas, i.e. the class which is the ruling material force of society, is at the same time its ruling intellectual force' (Engels et al, 1970: 64). This chapter broadly highlights developments in state-sponsored social work between the end of the Second World War and the early 1980s, exploring the ways in which practice developed in response to wider economic and societal influences.

The welfare state era

The progressive welfare state period in Aotearoa is generally charted from the election of the 1935 Labour government and the Social Security Act 1938. The underlying shift towards left-liberal/social-democratic reform is mirrored in the policy platforms adopted in comparable societies in response to the experiences of the Great Depression. McClure (1998: 6) stresses the way in which the shared experience of economic vulnerability discredited notions of moral failure and personal responsibility: 'Poverty became more public and state and charitable provision proved chaotic, inadequate and humiliating.'

A broad appetite for a reliable system of social protections was profoundly influenced by the insecurity of the Great Depression and reinforced by the hardships of wartime life. However, the partial realisation of working-class demands for protection against the fickle winds of capitalism also needs to be understood in terms of historical struggle and the Labour Party's mandate as the mainstream political voice of the working class. As Roper (2008: 11) suggests, the radical political shift seen in the mid-1930s did not fall from the sky; rather, it was 'the culmination of fifty years of working-class, trade union and political activism'.

The scope of reform was not as expansive as sometimes portrayed, but it did largely replace the notion of aid for the morally deserving with the concept of universal entitlement. The associated principles of relative equality and opportunity were based around a protected full-employment economy and a well-unionised workforce.

Tensions and contradictions

Although the aim was never fully realised, the ideological horizon of the welfare state envisaged inclusive entitlement to social support. However, as McClure (1998) suggests, the dominant trope of social cohesion reflected a monocultural vision of political community. Harris (2007: 49) argues that the 'good citizen' inhabited an assimilated liberal capitalist community:

> The good citizen – male, female, Maori, Pakeha, short, tall – was a product of the good family, and it was the solemn duty of all families to be good families: to be well-behaved, law-abiding, healthy, educated, employed and economically independent. These are not particularly enlightening desires, surely they are fundamental to what most families want for themselves. However, for Maori citizens this kind of talk was

code for integration, Maori citizenry could only occur in a mainstream (Pakeha) frame. Thus, good citizens owned their land individually and not communally as Maori did; and good citizens ensured all the land they did own was productive, and therefore contributing to and not burdening the national economy.

The middle decades of the 20th century are often portrayed as a time of remarkable stability in Aotearoa. This was undone by the collapse of the long boom: macro-economic developments associated with changes in the configuration of global trade, commodity and investment markets (Callinicos, 2010). However, submerged internal divisions and contradictions also fermented from the 1950s.

Historians such as Belgrave (2012) and McClure (1998) contend that the protection of full employment became the central plank of the post-war political consensus. In this sense, the model developed in Aotearoa amounted to a white working man's welfare state, rather than a universal settlement. This distinction was obscured by the dominant patriarchal discourse. The tenure of this supposed egalitarian identity, in combination with the earlier ideology of good fortune naturally accruing to worthy, hard-working individuals, has had a long reach into the national psyche, despite the fact that much of the scaffolding for state-sponsored material security has been systematically dismantled since the early 1980s (Kelsey, 1995).

After 1945, the welfare state ethos was increasingly adapted to the needs of a conservative agenda, being bent to the interests of what today's politicians refer to as 'middle New Zealand'. The welfare state consensus was significantly captured by conservative (albeit interventionist) political interests: property ownership, protected private industry and a guaranteed supply of labour. If equality was the professed aspiration, it was the notion of espoused, if counterfactual, 'sameness' that came to characterise Aotearoa from the 1950s. Assumptions of shared identity masked differences of class, race, sexuality, gendered opportunities and widespread disparities in wealth. Dissenting discourse was silenced.

This suppression of plurality fuelled the protest movements of the 1960s and 1970s. Diverse demands for social freedoms clashed with the state apparatus, establishing a legacy of left-wing agitation and conservative containment. Paradoxically, the social security that this monocultural and family-centric 'consensus' delivered stimulated demand for expanded visions of equality, opportunity and social freedom. In this sense, the welfare state fell victim to the prosperity that it enabled, particularly the new-found educational and vocational opportunities for working-class people.

In common with social movements in similar societies, a mixed chorus of voices demanded social progress that went beyond the vision of a protectionist, male-dominated, heterosexual and monocultural society.

Demands for the inclusion of silenced or marginalised social groups found a degree of synergy with calls for economic liberalisation in the 1980s. Social opportunity came to be associated with economic privatisation and consumer choice as the driver of development – policy prescriptions that ultimately privileged corporate interests and delivered greater material inequality.

This political and sociological process is reflected in struggles to define and control the operation of the child protection system in the 1980s, 1990s and beyond. Finally, the conformist ideology that underpinned the welfare state consensus has maintained a stubborn place in the script of national identity. The concept of a middle New Zealand comprised of 'good Kiwis' is lucratively milked by conservative political parties, effectively disguising the glaring social inequities within contemporary Aotearoa. This fragile identity claim also inevitably leads to the demonisation of outsiders. Provan (2012) argues that the vehement 'othering' of Māori women became central to recent processes of child protection reform. This analysis is explored in Chapter 5.

Professional identity

Social work gradually began to develop a broad professional identity after the Second World War. A social work training course was established at Victoria University in 1949, and the first conference for social workers took place in 1950 (Nash, 1998). The professional association, the Aotearoa New Zealand Association of Social Workers, dates from 1964. As in similar jurisdictions, however, the process of professionalisation has not been a straight road.

Social work is subject to intra-professional tensions. Personal social services are delivered in a range of settings. This leads to identification with a variety of specialist skills and organisational loyalties. The profession has also struggled to assert credibility among the more established disciplines with clear claims to expertise in areas such as medicine, jurisprudence or the hard sciences. This explains, at least in part, the attraction of the notion of social treatment or intervention supported by theories and practice tools that have a basis in objective, evidential science.

There is also a lengthy history of social workers aiming to work alongside, as opposed to 'on', those who are constructed as their clients. This is arguably a product of the location of social work within the interstices of care and control (Parton and Kirk, 2010). Community-oriented social workers have actively resisted the development and regulation of an expert professional identity, arguing that this elite positioning disrupts bonds of solidarity with people in need of services. These debates are intrinsic to social work education and have also influenced statutory practice. Chapter 4 illustrates that state social workers have not always been passive vehicles for government policy.

State social work and child welfare

Although statutory social work was shaped by the welfare state, the foundations of bureaucratic administration were prefigured in earlier decades. Similarly, the 19th-century inheritance of class-based moral reform has continued to resonate in policy and practice. Garlick (2012: 12) credits the Public Service Act 1912 with initiating 'the "unified, non-political, permanent career service" which was to characterise public management in New Zealand for the next 75 years'. The place of child welfare in this schema was cemented by the Child Welfare Act 1925:

> The Child Welfare Act 1925 set the basic contours of the state's approach to the welfare of children and young people for most of the rest of the century, consolidating a range of earlier developments into a broad system. This encompassed Children's Courts to dispense justice, Child Welfare Officers to investigate and assess family situations, and an expanded supervisory role through the extension of probation and greater use of 'boarding out'. (Garlick, 2012: 13)

The early work of the Child Welfare Branch was marked by the progressive intent of its first Superintendent John Beck (1926–38) and his successor Jim McClune (1938–45), who both sought to reduce reliance on institutional remedies and extend the provision of social assistance to families. Dalley (1998: 191) links this family-centred orientation with the progressive mood of the times:

> By the 1920s, family-based, community work was the mainstay of child welfare services. The growing emphasis placed on the social value of child life in Western nations, especially after the First World War, turned the tide against the confinement of children in industrial schools and reformatories for lengthy periods.

These expansive aims helped to position fieldwork 'officers' as the forerunners of modern caseworkers, so that 'by the time the Branch was renamed the "Child Welfare Division" in 1948, preventive supervision made up a quarter of all child welfare cases' (Garlick, 2012: 14).

For much of the remainder of the 20th century, child welfare policy was aligned with the functions of broader state bureaucracy under the umbrella of a liberal/democratic welfare consensus. It is important to understand something of the tensions that simmered beneath this ostensibly even-handed bureaucracy because they reflect the contradictions inherent to welfare systems in liberal capitalist societies. These tensions have vividly played out in the history of child protection policy and practice, and they continue to fuel contemporary debate.

The fifth social service

Consumer demand and the protectionist policies of the Keynesian settlement delivered relative growth and security after 1945, but prosperity was far from universal. As Jones (1983: 15) notes, in the English context, a section of the community remained excluded:

> The evacuation programme after the war, followed by the growing involvement of social work agencies such as Family Service Units, among the slum populations of inner cities ... heightened awareness about the ways in which a substantial cluster of the population seemed to be locked in poverty and destitution. Popularly known as the 'problem families', writer after writer ... drew attention to the manner in which these families not only constituted a huge drain on the newly expanded range of state welfare resources, but also produced more than the average number of children, many of whom never made it to the labour market in an employable state.

Social work developed a central place within the welfare state from the mid-20th century. The idealised notion of communicative redemption was sustained and sheltered within this ethos (Parton, 2014b). Although practice has always balanced the twin mandate of care and control, social workers aspired to an inclusive function:

> In his recent ruminations concerning the relationship between social work, child protection and politics, Parton (2014[a]) reminds us of the central place historically afforded to social work within the Western welfare state. Focusing on the English setting, Parton revisits the designation of social work as the fifth social service, alongside health, education, social security and public housing. These state services were directed at taming the five giant evils that William Beveridge famously associated with poverty: disease, want, ignorance, squalor, and idleness. (Hyslop, 2016a: 21)

Social work became a key part of what Bourdieu has termed the enabling 'left hand' of the state, arguably blunting the worst excesses of capitalism (Lorenz, 2017). As the 'fifth social service', social work set out to 'provide the personalised, humanistic dimension of the welfare state, the primary tool being the social worker's personality and use of relationships' (Parton, 2014b: 2047).

This mission has come adrift as contemporary policy orientations have taken a punitive turn (Featherstone et al, 2014). It has become increasingly difficult to reconcile progressive aspirations with the neoliberal economic and political template, particularly in the field of child protection. As I have argued, there is an inglorious tradition in social science and conservative liberal politics of blaming a recalcitrant underclass for the reproduction of social ills. The connection between social work, the poor and the welfare system has left the profession vulnerable to a critique of guilt by association: the populist notion that supportive practices have increased inequality by enabling anti-social behaviour, encouraging poor parenting and generating dependency (Jensen and Tyler, 2015; Cummins, 2018).

Child and family bureaucracy

The aspirations of the early Child Welfare Division to broaden supportive intervention in the lives of children and families came to fruition through the 1950s and 1960s. Social work was perceived as a harmonising force, enabling the integration of those who had failed to partake in post-war prosperity. High-needs individuals and families became the target of corrective interventions informed by the behavioural and psychological ideas of the times, as they are today: 'From its somewhat amateurish origins in the 1930s and 1940s, "field work" became an increasingly professional and specialised field in the post-war period; "field officers" became "social workers" and increasingly adopted a psychological approach in their casework' (Garlick, 2012: 14).

An uneasy mix of moral reform, enablement and empowerment has always been present in state social work. Practices of careful recording and assessment against predetermined criteria for entitlement and remedy can be tenuously traced to the lineage of 19th-century Poor Law visitors. There are other important continuities. The trust-based communicative engagement that was regarded as pivotal in the charitable beginnings of social work was central to practice in the 1960s and remains so to this day. It also says something about the power relationships that accompany child welfare work to consider that suspicion, or at least what Munro (2010: 55) has termed 'respectful scepticism' (of 'client' honesty and motivation), is also tied with this legacy of inspection.

A sense of practice confidence and competence was imparted by the clear procedural structure of child welfare work within a unified public service. Interventions were subject to supervisory approval and sign-off within strict financial delegations. Differing assigned 'statuses' allowed for corresponding levels of authoritative intervention. Something of the regulated structure of mid-20th-century child welfare practice is captured in the following reflection from Vaughan Milner (2004: 60).

As a beginning social worker in southern New Zealand in the mid 1970's I was told the story of a Boys Welfare Officer employed by the

Child Welfare Division of the Department of Education in the Otago/ Southland area in the 1960s. The worker put up a case to the Head Office in Wellington for the installation of a heater in his car. The argument advanced was that working in Tapanui in the winter meant a lot of time in sub-zero temperatures and snow. Traveling in a car without a heater was depicted by the worker as injurious to health and above and beyond the call of duty. The proposal was supported by local management and duly forwarded to the superintendent. The reply was brief. It read 'If Mr x proceeds about his duties with the briskness and efficiency expected of a Boys Welfare Officer, he will have no need of a heater. Request declined'. (Comer, circa 1976)

This passage suggests a halfway house between 19th-century sensibilities and the modern demand for efficient practice. The notion of disciplined 'casework' with individuals and families has had an enduring influence. Procedures were prescribed in a service manual, and records were painstakingly accumulated in voluminous paper files. Paradoxically, although the rule-bound hierarchies of the 20th-century public service are often portrayed as a rigid maze of inertia, a detailed process of manual references and approvals potentially enabled significant practice creativity and the timely provision of practical assistance. However, from the 1970s, serious cracks began to appear in this system. Unprecedented economic and demographic pressures coalesced with demands for effective intervention in relation to 'delinquency' and child abuse. The casework home-visiting approach of state social work was increasingly overmatched.

Welfare visions and realities

The growth in service demand throughout the 1960s stimulated government interest in the coordination of welfare provision. This culminated in the establishment of the DSW in 1972, amalgamating the Child Welfare Division with the Department of Social Security. Some of the contradictions that were beginning to trouble the 'late' welfare state are evident in the New Zealand Association of Social Workers' submission on the bill that introduced this reform. This paper argued for expanded state responsibility under a larger Ministry of Social Development, directly alleviating social distress while also promoting community-led service development (Garlick, 2012: 89).

While the structure of the new Social Work Division remained unchanged, an expanded vision looked to 'implement a broader range of social services to cover the whole field of personal and family welfare' (Garlick, 2012: 92). Significantly, the 1972 Royal Commission on Social Security reaffirmed the welfare state commitment to ensuring that everyone should be 'able to feel a sense of participation and belonging to the community' (Garlick,

2012: 15). The public policy implication – as in the left–liberal ideology of Tom Paine – is that the state is obliged to enable this right to participate and belong (Duncan, 2004). Benefit payment levels were raised and a statutory domestic purposes benefit to support lone parents was introduced in 1973.

The Children and Young Persons Act 1974 further embedded the professional structure of state social work and supported an expansion in residential care. Not for the last time, as we shall see in subsequent chapters, policy aspirations and resource-constrained practice realities were like ships that passed in the night:

> Increasingly preoccupied with urgent matters relating to children and young people, the Social Work Division had little ability to provide a preventive service based on the family environment. An early report on social welfare services noted that preventive work continued to be limited to the homes of children who had come to the notice of the authorities; statutory responsibilities and heavy caseloads meant that the 'impetus which might have been given to the development of State social welfare service' had 'not been sufficiently realised'. (Garlick, 2012: 92)

The desire of the welfare state administration to keep up with the demands of a changing society was not adequately supported by its resource base, and the rising level of economically generated social distress was not about to be resolved through its personal social service methodology.

Changing times

When I began my career in statutory social work in the mid-1980s, I was allocated, among other 'cases', a range of high-needs families under the informal umbrella of preventive supervision or 'supportive service' (Hyslop, 2007). This 'status' was reviewed at 12 monthly intervals and commonly extended if underlying family troubles had not been remedied.

To borrow loosely from Antonio Gramsci, this was a troubled time of interregnum when the old was dying but the new could not yet be born. Many social work practices remained embedded in bureaucratic routine. As well as enabling professional discretion, state bureaucracy can also be a refuge for fools. This sense of a system running on its own logic but stretched beyond capacity and no longer fit for purpose is captured in the following reflection:

> Social workers within the intact, yet crumbling, welfare state bureaucracy of the mid 1980s balanced child protection cases alongside youth offending services, some community funding functions,

foster care/institutional placements, housing needs, even services to 'individual adults with personal problems'(!). Paradoxically, material resources for child-centred intervention were probably easier to access than in the more focused and accountable child protection ethos of the new millennium. Practice quality was variable; many social workers laboured tirelessly, and many became emotionally spent, as is the case today, while others concentrated on their personal survival. Many families received intermittent attention while others were under closer, if variably productive, surveillance in the guise of 'supportive service' or 'preventative supervision'. Such client families experienced stresses associated with factors like alcohol and drug abuse, violence, physical and mental ill-health, child neglect and developmental impoverishment, sexual and/or physical exploitation. Long-term client families were variously labelled in the state social work culture as multi-problem, severely dysfunctional, or, if applicable, as 'white trash' (in the covert lexicon of practice). This 'truth', and mistrust of 'the welfare' born of experience, can be woven into the historical wisdom of some client families. Ironically it is such resource-scarce, impoverished and excluded families, with an associated unwillingness or inability to accept their alleged failings or to adjust their parenting practices, who are the most likely to be confronted with the power of the State in the form of adversarial care proceedings. (Hyslop, 2007: 5–6)

Among this alchemist's mix of order, chaos and contradiction, the notion of 'lofty calling' continued to animate statutory practice. A sense of 'making a difference' within a challenging context, in combination with the wider public welfare/service orientation, tended to obscure the more controlling and punitive dimensions of practice. This is equally true in contemporary contexts, where the overriding demand to protect vulnerable children can be used to shield practitioners from the ambiguous and oppressive dimensions of child protection.

Benign authoritarianism

Statutory social workers in the welfare state era tended to see themselves as agents of a largely benign social service system, albeit an increasingly overworked and under-resourced one. This sense of identity was reinforced by the wide range of service activities and entitlements available from the Department of Social Welfare and within the associated bureaucracies of Health, Education, Housing and Māori Affairs. In my own experience, information was routinely shared across these networks, often with little thought to issues of privacy or confidentiality.

Given the assumptions and trappings of state authority, social workers often conflated their professional identity with the scope of practice undertaken by 'the Department'. There was more than a hint of moralistic 19th-century benevolence embedded in the variable mid–20th-century child welfare practices. A culture of paternalism was reinforced and disguised by the apparently neutral operation of detailed procedures: visiting books, submissions, notification slips to authorise care payments and paper file records of sometimes gothic proportions.

Recourse to institutional remedies for the perceived threat posed by undisciplined children and youths found favour as urban stress and struggle surfaced in the expanding cities and suburbs of post-war Aotearoa: 'The Child Welfare Division's workload exploded in the 1950s and 1960s, as anxieties about juvenile delinquency and youth offending rose along with Children's Court appearances and follow-up work. To cope with the influx, the Child Welfare Division boosted its staff and expanded residential institutions' (Garlick, 2012: 15). Children were placed in temporary/short-term care during times of financial and/or emotional crisis. Children and young people entering long-term care as 'state wards' were disproportionately Māori and generally inducted through a youth-offending pathway. Essentially, an escalating tariff system eventually culminated in a court-mandated state guardianship order.

Parents were also encouraged to enter into voluntary extended care agreements when children were deemed to be 'out of control'. Social workers were secure in their authority and largely confident that 'they' knew best and that 'the Department' could provide the best-available solutions. This confidence was severely shaken in the 1980s when this veneer was torn away by the rising voice of Māori protest.

A building crisis of faith

From the mid-1970s, a complex combination of factors produced a more questioning workforce and a bureaucracy less confident in its capacity to produce positive outcomes. This crisis was, in part, produced by the nature of the close encounter between social workers and the social circumstances of those who are designated as their 'clients'. Direct experience of the raced, classed and gendered social differentials that inevitably go with the territory of social work practice in structurally unequal societies makes for a troubled and troubling profession. Practitioner disaffection with the old order and wider concerns over racism and inequality in Aotearoa were part of the drive for systemic change that emerged in the 1980s.

In the longer run, the unravelling of the welfare state vision has produced something of an existential crisis for social work (Rogowski, 2010). Although the critique of bureaucratic modernity that emerged from the economic strains and conflicts of the late 1970s was politically stilted, it was not without colour of truth. Welfare work was, and is, filled with tensions: an espoused commitment to empowerment and respectful humanist values jars with the performance of regulatory functions. Professional discretion within strictly defined bureaucratic boundaries was exposed as a contestable and power-saturated endeavour, rather than a purely benign force for social good. The postmodern critique of state structures has also served as justification for retrenchment and privatisation, disguising the crisis of capitalism that precipitated a neoliberal political resurgence (Hyslop, 2012; Gray and Webb, 2013b: 218–19).

Changing lenses: Indigenous narratives

Globally, social work has been reluctant to recognise oppressive aspects of its history (Ferguson et al, 2018). Social work in Aotearoa was, and is, enmeshed with colonisation. As O'Malley (1998: 11) reminds us, the process has been disputed and interactive, as Māori have engaged in a complex process of adaptation and resistance to the imposition of a foreign political and cultural order:

> the fact that Maori attempts to engage with the new colonial order on terms beneficial to both Maori and Pakeha were ultimately thwarted by settler self-interest does not mean that Maori were somehow passive victims of this process of disempowerment. Indeed, attempts by Maori to assert the autonomy they believed the Treaty had guaranteed them generally intensified as the process of marginalisation and disempowerment gathered force.

Official accounts of the development of settler colonial states such as Aotearoa have seldom reflected Indigenous realities. Writing from a North American perspective, Jacobs (2018: 262) argues that, until recently, Indigenous histories have been absent from the record: 'This selective and minimal incorporation of twentieth-century Indigenous histories not only perpetuates the long-held notion of Indians as amodern and thus outside modern history, but it also inadvertently fulfils the settler colonial logic of elimination that has driven American engagement with Indigenous peoples since the founding of the nation.' As economic and demographic stresses escalated from the 1960s and the numbers of institutional and foster-care placements escalated, the 'welfare system' experiences of whānau Māori were often marked by separation, loss and abuse or insecurity in care.

Māori and the post-war state

There are fundamental tensions in the relationship between Māori and Pākehā that stem from the process of colonisation. The much-disputed Treaty of Waitangi (Te Tiriti o Waitangi) covenant has been central to understanding and mediating this relationship, particularly over the last 50 or so years.[1] Te Tiriti o Waitangi has been a vehicle for the assertion of Indigenous rights and, more recently, a mechanism for the resolution of colonial injustice. Apart from related issues concerning the legality and morality of specific Crown actions over time and the difficulty of reconciling conflicting world views in relation to land, liberty and 'ownership' (including differing cultural institutions and governance processes), the nub of the problem has always been the degree to which Māori have a right to sovereignty in postcolonial society.

This desire for social, political and economic self-determination has played out in complex and varied ways over time, but it has never disappeared. As asserted in Walker's (2004) path-breaking exposition postcolonial struggle for Māori, efforts to retain control over collective well-being and development have produced a continuous process of contestation, both in and against the settler state government. Naturally, the area of child welfare and protection is no exception.

Harris (2007) examines the complex interactions between Māori interests and the state (through the Department of Māori Affairs) in the immediate post-war decades. She describes the framework created by the Māori Social and Economic Advancement Act 1945 as follows:

> Central to the operation of that framework was the Welfare Division of the department. The team of Māori welfare officers who staffed the division worked in particular with the community-based leadership that expressed itself through newly formed units of social organisation, that is, branches of the Māori Women's Welfare League and tribal committees. The ultimate goal was to instil, in Māori, confidence in the department's policies of integration. It was an old approach made new: the idea that the leadership and energies of iwi Māori, appropriately organised and guided, could be influenced to support a government policy (equally as old) of 'whitening' Māori. (Harris, 2007: 1)

The following excerpt is infused with the smell of liberal capitalist ideology, specifically, the touchstone of individuated private property. There are echoes of John Locke's doctrine of wasteland ripe for appropriation:

> Matters of Māori land development and Māori land title provided some clear examples of the systematic erasure of difference: the government could not tolerate Māori owning their land differently than other New Zealanders. In the post-war years, the government regarded it the duty of every good citizen to make full use of the soil, the foundation of prosperity. However, Māori farming was impeded by the multiple

ownership of Māori land which in turn obstructed the overall cultural adjustment of Māori people to the modern world and indulged their so-called sentimental attachments to the land. (Harris, 2007: 43)

While recognising the overarching intent of assimilation, Harris (2007: 1) develops a layered account, depicting the process as organic and creative, with Māori leadership structures endeavouring to make their own peace with modernity:

Māori relations with the state, or more accurately the Department of Māori Affairs, were intersected and underpinned by the state's unrelenting pursuit of assimilation and its various mutant forms – integration, amalgamation, and even mainstreaming. Simultaneously, those relations were both tempered and challenged by the Māori world's ongoing policy-defying act of balancing the old and the new, the traditional and the modern, the rural and the urban.

In the post-war decades, the state was dealing with a Māori world in a complex process of change, but it was interacting with a distinct people rather than a passive object. According to Harris, diverse tribal bodies, and Māori organisations with varying degrees of distance from the apparatus of government, engaged with the state in an elaborate dance.

State education in the mid-20th century portrayed Māori as a people of the past rather than 'of the now'. Māori were, in fact, very much a people of the present, and a present very much animated by a narrative of the past. This is captured poignantly is the following quotation, written in 1892, by the great-grandfather of activist and thinker Moana Jackson:

Those who came after are the ones who believed in new stories and turning new pages hoping in that way to change the way that we tell our stories to ourselves. But I will struggle on with the old stories about our **tikanga** [customary procedure], about our history, about our Treaty, about what has happened to our people since then. And I will struggle on in the hope that before those stories are finished, they will have made it worth all the trouble for us now and for our **mokopuna** [grandchildren] tomorrow. (Jackson, 1995: 248)

Harris (2007) challenges one-dimensional understandings of the urbanisation process, stressing the means through which traditional practices were translated into city life. She emphasises cultural resilience, arguing that the rich diversity within hapū and iwi identities – urbanisation and responses to it – are all part of a distinct, interconnected history. This message of the ongoing existence of a diverse Māori world as a coherent cultural entity is important in the sense that this continuity is often buried in analyses of relative deprivation and cultural loss.

She portrays Māori affairs policy in the 1950s – and the role played by Māori welfare officers – as an intermediary activity. It was a dance of tensions, simultaneously recognising and developing distinct tribally based Māori cultural authority, while promoting a unified national identity. However, it is recognised that the negative consequences of urban assimilation are consistent with late colonial experience of Indigenous peoples internationally:

> In brief, the literature tells us that, for Māori, the net result of the post-war experience was an increasingly detribalised and bereft population, living at the margins and ghettoes of society, lacking in leadership and social control, emerging in the 70s as an angry under-class. This is demonstrably true, especially demographically, and the situation was far more complex than this picture usually depicts. (Harris, 2007: 8)

A policy shift to a more overtly integrationist policy in the 1960s led to greater, or at least more overt, resistance. There was, for example, direct opposition 'to the department's power to intervene in their proprietary rights. In some districts, conversion came to be regarded as a kind of confiscation, a view which would gather momentum and feature amongst the catalysts for the initiation of modern Māori protest movements in the late 1960s' (Harris, 2007: 44).

As Poata-Smith (2002: 174) illustrates, ongoing resistance to land confiscation led to the radicalisation of Māori protest in the 1970s:

> The public release of the Pritchard–Waetford Report on the Maori Land Courts in February 1966 and the subsequent embodiment of its crucial recommendations in the Maori Affairs Amendment Act of 1967 precipitated an immediate upsurge in Maori protest activity. Under the Act, the Crown could purchase compulsorily 'unproductive' Maori land and sell it to business interests that would make it productive and profitable. Widely perceived by Maori as the 'last big land grab', the opposition that crystallised around the report and the proposed legislation united Maori organisations with radically different temperaments, political philosophies and strategies.

In a categorical formula reminiscent of Charles Booth's methodology, the integrationist Hunn Report (Hunn, 1961), classified Māori into three groupings along the journey to 'modernisation':

> group A was comprised of assimilated Māori, a 'completely detribalised minority' retaining mere traces of Maoritanga; group B comprised the

integrated majority of Māori comfortable in both Māori and Pakeha societies and able to participate in both; and group C, the unassimilated and unintegrated, 'another minority complacently living a backward life in primitive conditions'. Hunn advocated that Māori policy should aim to eliminate the complacent and backward minority and raise it up to join the comfortable majority. (Harris, 2007: 44)

In Harris's (2007: 45) judgement, it was, ironically, 'Hunn's group C and its "backward" lifeways that gave group B the cultural wherewithal to maintain its Māoriness'. As will be discussed in later chapters, this persistent and inventive 'Māori world' (and the leaders it produces) has continued to dispute and shape the future of child protection.

Class, colonisation and racial inequality

Poata-Smith (2002) presents a Marxist materialist analysis of the post-war Māori experience. Urbanisation was generated by demand for wage labour, the larger story of land alienation and the associated destruction of an economic base outside of capitalist social relations. He stresses the social positioning of working-class Māori, while also emphasising the function of assimilation:

The assimilative ideology of 'one people' functioned to conceal the reality for the majority of Maori. Although drawn into the working class, Maori workers found themselves in the worst jobs, crammed into inadequate housing, and with inferior technical education that limited their opportunities for economic advancement. Moreover, finding employment was not a forgone conclusion. (Poata-Smith, 2002: 149)

The blunt and uncomfortable reality is that racist beliefs and practices intersected with the structural location of Māori. This confluence propelled Māori into disproportionate contact with the child welfare system. The consequences generated a history of violence and harm. This is graphically illustrated in the following sections of this chapter, which focus, first, on the insights provided by Cook's (2020) statistical examination of the demographic basis of care disparities for Māori and, second, on Dr Oliver Sutherland's account of the work undertaken by the Auckland Committee on Racial Discrimination (ACORD) in the 1970s and early 1980s.

Demography, inequality and state care

In the late 1990s, Dalley (1998: 194) noted that calls for autonomous child protection services 'by Māori with Māori' were echoes of similar demands articulated by Māori groups shortly after the passage of the Child Welfare

Act 1925. This position was expressed more stridently as the 'welfare' needs of Māori children came to wider public attention from the 1940s: 'Maori offending and over-representation in children's courts also became of major concern in Maori communities from the 1940s. A number of Maori groups, including the Maori Women's Welfare League, argued that Maori themselves were best suited to solving their own problems' (Dalley, 1998: 196). Dalley (1998) also argues that counter to popular assumptions, early child welfare policy and practice intent was averse to state care for Māori. This is supported by the documentary and case-record evidence that is drawn on. It is also recognised that efforts to maintain a whānau and/or community-centric approach to child welfare practice were not necessarily driven by respect for Māori independence:

> The policy of trying to keep Maori children in Maori communities fitted the broader enunciation of a family-based care for all children, but it also reflected a reluctance to have Maori welfare issues 'intrude' on Pakeha society. Resolving Maori welfare problems in Maori communities may have been presented as being in the interests of Maori, but it also served the interests of a Pakeha society and state chary of engaging thoroughly with Maori social and economic conditions. (Dalley, 1998: 197)

Child welfare officers attempted to work alongside Māori communities, with varying degrees of energy and understanding. However, the post-war process of urbanisation and the state policy of integration meant that the social and economic struggles of whānau Māori presented an increasingly apparent and unsettling problem.

Cook (2020) examines the historically disproportionate rates of Māori children in state care and of adult incarceration in terms of the experience of specific population cohorts. The statistical evidence illustrates grossly biased outcomes for Māori within the child welfare and justice systems, suggesting time-specific relationships between care entry and subsequent imprisonment. The assembled data also beg questions about the negative flow-on impact of state care and imprisonment for Māori, that is, the destructive intergenerational consequences for the well-being of whānau.

Cook's (2020) analysis raises an issue that goes to the heart of liberal capitalist institutions, namely, the illusion that procedural impartiality is an adequate proxy for justice. This convention disguises the effects of structural inequality: 'that different outcomes for Māori have resulted from the purportedly universal application of laws and institutional practices' (Cook, 2020: 5). Māori are often subject to biased responses in the welfare and justice systems, and even when equality of treatment is applied, it does not result in equitable outcomes in unequal societies.

He outlines something of a demographic tsunami for the Māori population after the Second World War. A high birth rate and falling infant mortality saw the number of Māori children double between 1951 and 1966. By 1966, at the apex of this trend, 50 per cent of the Māori population was aged 14 and under. This phenomenon occurred in the context of unprecedented urbanisation: 'The intensity of Māori migration to cities remains one of the most significant experiences of rapid urbanisation seen by a people anywhere in the world. Individuals, whānau, hapū and iwi were affected by the speed at which whānau structures, cultural ties, economic underpinnings, and community were eroded' (Cook, 2020: 7–8).

Two particularly significant periods when child welfare policies and practices had negative consequences that resonate in the present are identified: the post-war spike in forced adoptions up until 1980; and the rapid rise in the institutional placement of Māori from the 1960s through to the early 1980s. The socially and culturally damaging legacies of these practices of intensive state intervention correspond to the oppressive policy prescriptions applied to Indigenous populations in Canada, Australia and the US:

> As noted with the earlier forced removal of babies from unmarried teenage mothers, both Canada and Australia had parallel experiences, in their case with an intense focus on placing indigenous children with European parents. In Canada this is referred to as the 'Sixties Scoop', and in Australia 'the Stolen Generation'. (Cook, 2020: 29)

Disproportionate state care for Māori children escalated radically from the 1970s. The visibility of relatively poor urban Māori children, often distanced from traditional social support structures, led to scrutiny from loosely integrated education, welfare and justice systems. Placement processes and outcomes for children taken into state care were complex and variable. Younger children entering care in relation to perceptions of neglect, abuse or unmet needs were placed in a variety of settings, including Pākehā or non-kin foster placements, private children's homes, and residential settings. Older children generally became 'state wards' as an outcome of cumulative juvenile offending, and were placed in state-run institutions that often served as gateways to adult imprisonment:

> In 1966, Māori children aged under 15 had become half of the Māori population. Their number almost doubled from 1951 to 1966. ... Within five years there was a rapid rise in the rate of detention of Māori boys and girls by the State through the Children's Court. By then, some 7 percent of Māori boys and 1 percent of Pākehā boys ... born between 1955 and 1974 had been placed in a youth custodial institution. (Cook, 2020: 29)

Prison disproportionality

Cook's analysis tells us that between 1860 and 1920, the relative share of Māori imprisonment per head of population was generally lower than that of Pākehā. This trend began to reverse from the mid-1920s as Māori were drawn into closer relationships with state systems. By 1935, the Māori imprisonment rate was twice that for Pākehā, rising significantly to four times the non-Māori rate by 1945, where it remained until 1990. The rate of Indigenous incarceration was six times that of Pākehā for a lengthy period between 1970 and 1985 (Cook, 2020: 12).

The reasons for increases in adult imprisonment are not linear. Social stressors for Māori were exacerbated by economic restructuring, which impacted disproportionately on workers in unskilled and semi-skilled occupations. However, the rising rate of incarceration in the 1980s was 'dominated by the coming of age of those cohorts which had been placed in the custody of the State as children' (Cook, 2020: 31). Cook (2020: 34) illustrates how the disproportionate care intake of Māori children and youth has continued to ripple through to the subsequent age and ethnicity structure of the prison population:

> After experiencing the extreme rates of State custody of children during the 1970s and up to 1984, in general, this particular cohort of children grew into the 20–29 year olds of the 1980s, and then the 30–39 year olds of the 1990s. The ageing of this birth cohort has been the most significant trigger for rises in the age-specific incidence of imprisonment of Māori men and women, for three decades now.

Researchers and academic commentators are only now beginning to come to terms with the enormous scale of racist and abusive outcomes resulting from the care policies and practices applied in the 1970s and beyond (Stanley, 2016; Royal Commission of Inquiry into Historical Abuse in State Care and in the Care of Faith-Based Institutions, 2020).

Racism and institutional abuse

The current Royal Commission of Inquiry into Historical Abuse in State Care and in the Care of Faith-Based Institutions is arguably part of a process of healing and atonement for damage inflicted in the name of child welfare. In the following discussion, I have included some relatively lengthy quotations from evidence recently presented to this commission by anti-racist researcher and children's rights activist Dr Oliver Sutherland (2019) in order to provide a sense of the scale of abusive practice and the reality of personal and family suffering involved.

The work of Dr Sutherland and his associates in ACORD documents a deeply disturbing history of abusive state care in the 1970s and 1980s. ACORD analysed official figures to evidence the operation of racial bias in the child welfare/youth justice system. Dr Sutherland and colleagues also investigated abusive practices (exceptional, customary or, in many cases, officially sanctioned) that were carried out in institutions during this period. ACORD went to great lengths to pursue justice for individuals and system reform from politicians, senior bureaucrats and the human rights watchdog establishment of the time.

Responses to this advocacy were often dismissive, illustrating the blindness and deafness that is often reserved for the suffering of the least powerful and 'least deserving' in the liberal capitalist hierarchy of power. In Dr Sutherland's (2019: para 3) own words:

> From 1970 to 1986, I personally advocated on behalf of scores of children whose cases I drew to the attention of a series of Cabinet Ministers and others. The notes of my interviews and meetings with these children and their care givers are held in the ACORD archives in the Auckland City Library. They are the case histories which I will detail in this submission. ACORD also instigated a number of Ombudsman, Human Rights Commission, Judicial and other official inquiries into the abuses revealed by these cases.

The statistical data that Sutherland refers to echo the glaring disparities in patterns of Māori institutional placement evident in the material collated by Cook (2020). Causation, as Cook suggests, is influenced by socio-economic and demographic variances between the Māori and non-Māori populations. However, within this layered web of structural disadvantage, discriminatory attitudes and practices also clearly contributed to disproportionate incarceration and the associated maltreatment of Māori children and young people:

> There was a marked bias against Māori boys in particular. The results of a study by Ross Hampton of the Justice Department Research Section in 1973 showed that Auckland Police Youth Aid officers, when deciding who to prosecute 'discriminated against Maori boys by sending a disproportionate number of them to court' thus 'inflating their crime rate in comparison with that of non-Maori children'. (Sutherland, 2019: para 6)

Poata-Smith (2002: 150) offers the following excerpt from the Hunn Report (Hunn, 1961) as indicative of the mainstream perception of Māori youth offending as a phenomenon connected with cultural deficit, being entangled with a failure to conform to the liberal Pākehā system of individualised private property rights protected by the rule of law and enforced by the police:

> The report surmised that these property offences were essentially a result of the: '... survival of the communal way of life followed by Maoris [sic] for centuries. Share and share alike was the custom but propriety rights in a modern society make it a crime to take other people's property. Ancient custom dies hard.'

ACORD documented and challenged a long and disturbing list of institutional practices perceived as inhumane and counterproductive: the absence of legal representation in court; the routine use of remand to child welfare custody or police cells for relatively minor offences; remand to adult prisons and psychiatric facilities; the normalisation of harsh physical punishments; the use of pecking-order systems as punishment and control mechanisms; and the customary use of unregulated solitary secure detention in social welfare institutions.

In Foucauldian terms, the excesses of this system were arguably rendered invisible and unspeakable by the disciplinary discourses of the time, particularly in relation to the perception that a particular group of children and young people deserved (and required) resocialisation within a regime of rigid discipline. ACORD also documented routine invasive/forced sexually transmitted disease/s examinations for girls in social welfare custody at Bollard Home in Auckland:

> Tina B, who was in Bollard in 1974 described the admission procedures: 'You were stripped of your clothes and stripped of your privacy when you arrived. You are de-loused − with nit goo and a Dettol bath ... then put in a cell. It was very small, with a bed, rubber mattress and a toilet. You were given four squares of toilet paper for all day. We wore pyjamas all day, even for cleaning out our cells. They often didn't fit too well, which was very demoralising'. Worse was the compulsory venereal disease [VD] check: 'you were moved into another cell and told to take everything off except your top. Then you were put onto a bed and into stirrups like when you have a baby. The old bag shoves your legs around how she likes. She didn't say thank you; she didn't say please: Just "undress!" get up there; spread your legs out, etc'. Tina B noted that some girls who were 'kicking and struggling' were held down by straps. It was a procedure that was described by all the ex-inmates of girls' homes. One, who was aged 13 years at the time, 'wouldn't take the VD test. I was put in secure, but I still wouldn't agree. In the end three or four staff came in and I was taken and strapped down for it.' (Sutherland, 2019: para 53)

ACORD identified the racism within this system, both in a socio-political sense and in terms of the experiences of specific children and whānau. It is enlightening to reflect on how ineffective the liberal human rights system was in addressing the concerns raised:

By mid-1972 we were advocating for the establishment of a national duty solicitor scheme. Our submission strongly supported the case for a duty solicitor to be present at every court in New Zealand whenever that court was in session and urged that two measures should be taken immediately: (1) all children should be accompanied by a lawyer when being questioned by the police; (2) all children on whatever charge should be represented by counsel whenever they appear before a Justice of the Peace or Magistrate.

The Minister's response was: 'Implications that Maoris [sic] appearing before the magistrate's courts in New Zealand are getting less than justice are incorrect ... we have the best of British justice for all'. The response of Ngā Tamatoa's Syd Jackson to the Minister was as quick as it was unequivocal: 'White racism [is] the basis of our law.' (Sutherland, 2019: paras 13–14)

Racially skewed outcomes were denied or minimised, even when they were clearly illustrated by data drawn from the records of relevant government departments. Māori children were far more likely to be detained, locked up and removed from home:

In 1974, of the 269 children remanded to a penal institution, 53% were Māori. In 1975, of the 320 children remanded in custody to a penal institution, 57% were Māori. In 1977, of the 356 children remanded in custody to a penal institution, 63% were Māori. ...

It is very clear that Māori children received heavier sentences than non-Māori children. Any Māori child before the court was more than twice as likely to be sent to a penal institution (detention centre, borstal or prison) as a non-Māori child, while the latter was more likely to be fined or simply admonished and discharged.

The following data is drawn principally from the annual N.Z. Justice Statistics:

Children in Court between 1967–1976:
(a) Total: 116, 595; c.11,000/year – 41% Māori
(b) In one particular year, 1974, there were 10,438 children of which 45% were Māori. (Sutherland, 2019: paras 18, 22–4)

Dr Sutherland's witness statement includes graphic and disturbing accounts of practices at Owairaka Boys Home in Central Auckland: indeterminate secure confinement on admission; use of a rigid 'nodding system' of communication; and humiliating and inappropriate punishments for matters such as bed-wetting, giving cheek, smoking and especially for absconding. This institution was structured along the lines of a military or prison-style regime, and most of the staff were drawn from this background. The nature of punishment at the Wesleydale Home for boys between 10 and 14 years old is described in the following excerpt:

> Absconding led to the heaviest punishments at Wesleydale – strappings by staff and arranged boy-on-boy boxing matches. One ex-staff member told the Human Rights Commission Panel during their Inquiry in 1980 that 'it was common for one staff member to hold a boy down while a senior housemaster strapped him repeatedly on the body ... one 11-year-old boy would not bend over after receiving six strokes on the buttocks ... three staff held him while a fourth administered further strokes until he was severely bruised on the thighs, buttocks and the jaw'. (Sutherland, 2019: para 50)

The 'boxing match' reference relates to a practice known as the 'golden fist', whereby returned absconders were subjected to beatings by another boy selected by staff.

Institutional responses

The United Nations Convention on the Rights of the Child (UNCRC) came into force on 2 September 1989 but was not ratified in Aotearoa until 6 April 1993. ACORD made a creative complaint to the Human Rights Commission in 1979 (established in 1977) on the basis that:

> the state was in breach of the International Covenant on Civil and Political Rights and the International Covenant on Economic, Social and Cultural Rights in relation to treatment of children by the Department of Social Welfare in residential homes. The Human Rights Commission held hearings throughout 1980 and finally issued their report in 1982. (Sutherland, 2019: para 58)

While acknowledging allegations that 'could' constitute breaches of specific articles within these covenants, the report was ultimately timid and loaded towards the powerful vested interests involved:

> In the last section of its Report, the Commission outlined its 'Conclusions and Recommendations'. It was here that the Commission became weak-kneed. Having acknowledged 'the difficulty of the

Department in running residential institutions' the Report stated, presumably on the basis of the evidence of the current managers of the Homes, that 'many, if not all, of the practices and procedures which formed the basis of the representations made by ACORD have been eradicated, and the Department has embarked on a programme of innovative change'. The Commission was, it stated, 'gratified both by the seriousness which the Department accorded the inquiry and by its willingness to reconsider practices and procedures which came to light during these proceedings'. (Sutherland, 2019: para 61)

There is little doubt that the activities of ACORD did ultimately influence some change to care practices. In 1982, the Minister of Social Welfare commissioned Archbishop Johnson and Merimeri Penfold to investigate children's home practices.[2] The subsequent report raised concerns about the use of solitary confinement, leading to the passage of residential care regulations in 1986. ACORD also challenged the morality and legality of the widespread practice of remanding children to adult prisons. According to Sutherland (2019: paras 103–5), encouraging early progress was thwarted by political machinations:

the Ombudsman, Sir Guy Powles, launched a full inquiry into the remanding of children to penal institutions. However, Powles retired having only completed an initial draft report. The draft report included revealing statistics for the years 1974 and 1975. In 1974, 269 juveniles were remanded to adult prisons; of these 53.16% were Māori or other Polynesian. The following year the total had jumped to 320 juveniles and the numbers of Māori or other Polynesian had risen to 57.19%.

Sir Guy Powles' successor George Laking shelved the report after representations by the Department of Justice.

In a press statement dated 8 February we expressed our 'bitter disappointment' at Laking's decision and explained 'Because the investigation was the first ever into this controversial subject and because the report was to provide guidelines for Government action, ACORD has decided to make the factual material of the draft report public'. The Minister of Justice said he deplored the leak of the report and would not take the matter any further. In the meantime, other cases continued to emerge, and ACORD kept the matter in the public eye.

ACORD also continued to highlight the glaring statistical and anecdotal variance in the treatment of Māori and non-Māori within every facet of the juvenile justice system from arrest to relative severity of sentencing:

In 1981, ACORD published its report 'Children in State Custody'. It was a collation of 10 years of date and case histories following our frustration with the lack of positive change by the Department of Justice. We wrote 'ten years which have seen thousands upon thousands of children from the age of eight years or even less, dragged through the police stations, the courts, the welfare homes and the adult prisons. A child, once caught up in this machinery of punishment and retribution, is lucky if he or she escapes without going through the whole progression of a criminal career'. We forwarded our report to the new Minister of Justice, Geoffrey Palmer. ...

Within a week, Geoffrey Palmer had ordered an inquiry and the Secretary for Justice announced that he had requested District Court Judge Augusta Wallace to inquire into and report on the circumstances preceding and surrounding the detention and custody of the teenage boys. (Sutherland, 2019: paras 108, 120)

A judicial inquiry culminated in an unequivocal recommendation for the abolition of this practice, which was accepted by Minister Palmer. At one level, this outcome validates the role of liberal legal human rights institutions in moderating excesses of state power. However, wider questions about social justice in our liberal capitalist settler society also arise from Sutherland's narrative – questions about who is heard and whose well-being is valued.

In hindsight, if the clear and carefully documented message of widespread institutional abuse and dysfunctional programme design (as well as of endemic racism) had been properly heeded, we might be in a very different position today. If time had been taken to digest the wider implications, the current Royal Commission (40 years later) and, more importantly, the underlying suffering of powerless children, young people and whānau that this process signifies may have been avoided.

This chapter has illustrated the way in which social work's accounts of itself tend to foreground benign intensions in a way that sanitises the destructive racist outcomes that it has been associated with historically. In many ways, the institutional abuse of Māori children, and the flow-on effect of whānau suffering, particularly from the 1970s to recent times, is a damning indictment of statutory social work. Equally, it is important to remember that the sins of social work have not been committed in a vacuum. State social work has been a pawn in a much deeper game tied to a wider history of racism and economic marginalisation. These outcomes are embedded in a structural genesis that social work has never been equipped to tackle: the imposition of liberal capitalism upon a communal people.

Rising Māori voices

Māori were subject to the damaging consequences of a discriminatory care system that was sent into overdrive by economic and demographic disparities.

I am not any kind of expert in relation to Māori social life and can only speak to my own subjective experience. I am also wary of presenting an outsider account that overly simplifies, sanctifies or generalises Māori experience. However, it is undeniable that this process left a toxic social legacy.

Māori social structures were severely stressed by urbanisation, but the communal links that sustain Māori identity have also proved resilient, in the sense that social suffering is felt keenly and collectively, and resolutions are pursued steadfastly. As suggested by Harris (2007), it is possible to discern a sustained history of cultural continuity, adaptation and renewal. In this analysis, Māori-led challenges to the policies and practices of the state welfare system that arose from the early 1980s can be understood in terms of persistent opposition to the political and cultural hegemony of the settler state. As will be discussed in Chapter 7, these challenges have boiled to the surface once again at the dawn of the third decade of the 21st century.

A quantum shift in the intensity (and method) of resistance began to emerge in the mid-1970s. Demands for social and economic justice arose, in part, from established Māori voices and the centres of officially recognised tribal or organisational power. However, the more radicalised drivers of protest came from a new generation. According to Poata-Smith (2002: 15), this wave of activism was initially aligned with a groundswell of left-wing militancy that arose in Aotearoa, and internationally, as the economic promise of the 'long boom' began to falter:

> Indeed, Maori protest organisations were very much a product of the progressive social movements of the time. The early Maori protest organisations such as MOOHR [Māori Organisation on Human Rights] and Te Hokioi allied themselves with the Pakeha left and the trade unions.[3] They represented a conscious break from the shared ruling National Party and state sponsored connections that characterised the New Zealand Maori Council.

According to Poata-Smith (2002: 17), this loose alliance between Māori protest and the militant political Left gave way to an increasing focus on cultural recognition rather than material transformation, which 'left the Maori protest movement ill-equipped to resist the anti-working class policies that the fourth Labour government introduced to restore the economic conditions for profitable capital accumulation'. He further maintains that a failure to focus on the significance of class dimensions within Māori society facilitated, at least in part, a politics of appeasement and the settlement of Treaty grievances in favour of elite, corporate Māori interests from the 1990s (Poata-Smith, 2002: 259, 260).

Poata-Smith's exploration of the relationship between the oppression of Māori and exploitative capitalist processes goes some way to explaining the inability of liberal human rights frameworks to consistently prevent biased outcomes in structurally unequal societies such as in Aotearoa. However, as graphically illustrated in Sutherland's research, the fact that there are systemic connections between relative Māori poverty and the capitalist mode of economic and social development does not mean that racism does not operate as a powerful discriminatory force on its own account.

The economic and political dimensions of this argument serve to remind us of the confluence between racism and class-centred exploitation: it is the children on the margins of the capitalist state who are drawn into contact with the statutory child protection system, and these children are disproportionately Māori. I have rehearsed this argument here in some detail because it is a more-than-useful lens for understanding the supposed bicultural settlement that state social work offered Māori from the late 1980s. The genesis and outcome of this manoeuvre are examined in Chapters 4 and 5.

The 1980s: a storm builds and breaks

The child protection imperative

Awareness of child abuse grew internationally from the mid-1960s. Aotearoa was no exception. Initially focused on the deliberate physical injury of children, child protection has developed to include ever-widening categories of concern (Gilbert, 2012). The visibility of intrafamilial abuse reflects a change of consciousness towards children's rights that can be aligned with the wider post-war human rights discourse, particularly the political ascendancy of women's rights, the so-called 'second wave of feminism':

> The broad influence of feminist politics has been important in focusing attention on the rights of children to be free of violence and abuse. Layers of taboo have been peeled back. Societal acknowledgement of physical abuse in the 1960s has grown to embrace awareness of sexual victimization of children, more latterly the abuse of boys as well as girls. (Hyslop, 1997: 61)

The child protection project is also generally traced to the pioneering research work of the American paediatrician Henry Kempe and associates, specifically, their 'discovery' of the battered child syndrome (Scott, 2006). The focus on diagnosis and treatment associated with Kempe's work has arguably set the enduring template for a forensic approach to the investigation and assessment of suspected child abuse:

> The modern child protection system emerged from a concern to stop babies dying or being 'battered' by parents who were considered to be suffering from a lack of empathic mothering in their own lives. Poverty, bad housing and so on were screened out as holding helpful explanatory value (Parton, 1985). ... Despite all the changes, the story honed in the 1960s has proved remarkably resilient in its stress on the actions of individual parents/carer, and its focus on the intra-familial as the locus of cause and consequence. (Featherstone et al, 2017: 191)

Professional interest in the cross-disciplinary management of child abuse came to a head in the late 1970s in Aotearoa (Garlick, 2012: 102). This movement clashed with increasingly politicised concerns about the alienating effect of state care for Māori. The resulting friction precipitated a protracted dispute between the claims of social workers to the 'expert' role in child protection and the claims of other disciplines, particularly the medical profession.

In addition to exemplifying the conflicting currents that continue to influence child protection policy and practice in Aotearoa, the following discussion illustrates internal tensions within the identity of social work itself. If social work is to be the discipline charged with the statutory child protection function, which of its many faces should be to the fore? Is clinical detection, risk assessment and intervention informed by 'scientific' knowledge about the behaviour of abusive families the appropriate practice template?

As Munro (2011a: 16, 17) has argued, the knowledge base of social work deviates from the medico-legal framework. It involves communicative engagement and assessment of social context, being a socio-technical or socio-legal hybrid as opposed to a disengaged diagnostic process. There are related tensions within social work connected with notions of family and community empowerment, as opposed to the measurement of pathology and risk. These antagonisms have been played out graphically in Aotearoa, particularly in the relationship between the settler state and Māori.

The medico-professional wave

The persuasive notion that child abuse is a complex phenomenon requiring multidisciplinary intervention gained serious traction from the late 1970s. This approach was driven by an articulate and relatively high-status medico-legal/professional grouping that promoted child protection as a new frontier requiring specialist expertise. Paediatric and public health professionals assumed a dominant role in this process. The influence of Dr David Geddes, Medical Director of the Plunket Society and chair of the National Advisory Committee on the Prevention of Child Abuse (NACPCA), was significant. In early 1983, the NACPCA recommended the development of multidisciplinary child protection teams for the management and oversight of practice decisions.

At this point, much of the mainstream child welfare establishment appeared to accept that an expert-led multisystemic approach to child protection was the way forward and that an appropriate legislative framework would be required. However, beneath the surface of this apparent consensus, a storm of conflicting interests and perspectives was building. As it transpired, the process of legislative reform was a tortuous undertaking, and the revised legislation that eventually emerged in late 1989 reflected a very different prescription for change.

Following the NACPCA report, initiatives around multi-agency practice planning and oversight were developed in varying forms at the district office level. Local service delivery autonomy was far greater than in the centrally driven contemporary environment. This is clearly illustrated by a DSW national office memorandum requesting information on the nature of the multidisciplinary practice arrangements that had been developed at the site level (Circular Memorandum, 1984: 121).

Local child protection advisory and coordinating teams took various shapes, either connected with public health/hospital board endeavours or in the form of pilot projects endorsed and funded by the DSW but actively driven by paediatricians and allied child health workers. The situation was also muddied by the ad hoc practice of setting up specialist social work teams to work with serious cases of physical abuse or sexual abuse, and to liaise with the police over role boundaries and decision-making at the district level.

New theoretical understandings about the complex dynamics of child maltreatment, particularly intrafamilial sexual abuse, also influenced the promotion of expert clinical practice, as suggested by the following personal reflection:

> When child sexual abuse emerged from the fog of adult blindness in the 1980s any emergent act of genital exploration resulted in a child-centred interview. Some numbing memories of abuse come to mind, none more than the benign clear-eyed smile of a paedophile who systematically manipulated and abused scores of foster children in his care. Subsequently the routine videoing of child sexual abuse disclosures has not removed the need for children to give evidence in Court, albeit with greater privacy, support and sensitivity, and the obstacles to effective prosecution have grown. Anecdotally it seems that the focus on child sexual abuse has waned. Perhaps the sexual victimisation of children has been reduced. Perhaps the consequences of disclosure and the discomfort of adults means that the mist has rolled back in. (Hyslop, 2007: 6–7)

The proposed development of a new legislative framework prompted significant debate about 'case-management' authority. Multidisciplinary initiatives became mired in questions about how teams should be structured, specifically, whether they should provide a parallel advisory service, assume the central child protection decision-making mandate or perform a function somewhere in between these poles.

Slow brewing conflict

The multidisciplinary perspective also brought the relationship between local cultural knowledge and 'expert' clinical perceptions of child protection into question. Justified by claims to such expertise and located in high-needs, low-income areas, these multi-agency bodies were often perceived as elitist and disconnected from community realities. Feedback received from an internal evaluation of the South Auckland Child Protection Coordinating Team (CPC Team) gives a flavour of this community disquiet:

Of the 40% who made comment as to the ways in which the CPC Team was unhelpful, many commented upon the cumbersome size and cultural bias of the team, and the time involved with cases. ... Comments relating to this point: 'There was a lifestyle chasm between the client and the CPC group which had little real appreciation of the client's social make up.' (Todd, 1984: 6)

For social workers on the ground, the process of multidisciplinary accountability and oversight was often experienced as a burden. The following excerpt from the January 1984 meeting of the South Auckland Sexual Abuse Committee is instructive: 'Conferences seem to press harder for constructive action (e.g. removal from home; long term alternative care) than D.S.W. were originally contemplating. This may have consequences for resources. The issue of accountability has not been resolved (e.g. how binding are case conference decisions?)' (Caton, 1984).

The South Auckland/Mangere CPC Team developed a process that was later replicated in the neighbouring suburb of Otara. As a social worker, I was required to attend meetings of this CPC Team. In 2007, my recollection of this experience was as follows:

Otara office was part of a multi-disciplinary Child Protection Coordinating Team pilot initiative in the mid-1980s. This entailed interrupting your hopelessly overloaded work schedule, clutching a 'red-stripe' child protection file and rushing off to explain to a huddle of earnest health-care professionals why it was that you were not doing enough to protect children. It is little wonder that the associated draft legislation which proposed that executive power be vested in such teams was strongly resisted by practitioners. (Hyslop, 2007: 6)

There was a tendency for professional overreach in the multidisciplinary team model, in particular, for decisions to be based on assessments of family capacity without family involvement and for 'concerned' professionals to pressure social workers to exercise their statutory powers. It is easier to objectively support the uplift of children than to confront a distraught mother in the physical and emotional process of child removal.

If the collective pressure applied to social workers in this context was perceived as intrusive, the prospect of executive authority being transferred to the chairpersons of multidisciplinary teams was truly daunting:

The proposals envisage the establishment of one or more Child Protection Teams in each Social Welfare district with each team having its own Team Social Worker attached to it. The latter would work in close consultation with the Child Protection Social Workers. The Child

Protection Teams, which would be multi-disciplinary in nature and have up to five community members appointed to them, would have oversight of all the reported cases of actual or suspected child abuse and would have the authority to take a matter to the Family Court if necessary. (Cabinet Social Equity Committee, 1985)

It is unsurprising that resistance to this proposition took hold. However, the ensuing power struggle was influenced by more than professional rivalry, as powerful socio-political forces were at play. Opposition coalesced around growing awareness of the damaging impact of state care, particularly the culturally destructive consequences for whānau Māori. This, in turn, was symptomatic of deeper social ferment in relation to the racist foundations and outcomes of the post-war political settlement in Aotearoa. An ideological showdown with the medico-professional practice model germinated throughout the 1980s (Hyslop, 2007).

Care planning

As argued, the surety and complacency of the welfare state social work bureaucracy was disrupted by the economic and political changes of the 1970s and 1980s. As critical as it is to understand the way in which broad anti-racist sentiment ultimately dominated the course of reform, it is also important to recognise the subtle interplay of influences at work. As Garlick's (2012) careful reconstruction illustrates, social workers and managers were not simply tossed on a sea of sociocultural upheaval. Rather, they performed significant service planning and 'change advocacy' functions in this watershed period.

The 1980s was a decade of reviews and interest group consultation processes (Barretta-Herman, 1994), though these exercises were not always travelling on ideologically compatible tracks. Growing intra-organisational concern about the cost, quality and effectiveness of foster-care and institutional placements became a bone of contention from the late 1970s, driving changes to policy and practice design:

> Taking the link between foster placement breakdown and child 'maladjustment' as its starting point, a major survey of the Department's foster care between 1976 and 1981 found concerning levels of movement of children between foster homes. Its findings were situated within a broader interrogation of foster care: 'No longer is the fostering system comfortably taken for granted; no longer is it pronounced that fostering transforms children into "decent and useful citizens"; that the system is a source of great satisfaction to the Department, even that it is the best we can do.' (Garlick, 2012: 103)

Abuse in state residences and inadequate resourcing of the significantly cheaper foster-care system have dogged the child welfare system since its inception. In May 1980, there were approximately 7,000 children in state care, and 13 per cent of these were placed in institutional settings. As evidenced in discussion of the work of ACORD in Chapter 3, the care system came under increased external scrutiny. A 1982 Foster Care Federation background paper made the following comment:

> One hundred years after the inception of state care for children, including those neglected and abused, the legal system still leaves the victims and the caregivers in the hands of a social service deficient in social work training. In the context of institutional abuse, the extensive discretion and power awarded to the Director-General and his social workers, could be described as dangerous. (Craig, 1982)

The inability of the state to provide consistent nurturance and support for the children of the poor whom it 'saves' has been a continuous problem for child protection systems. The challenges faced by foster care, as articulated by the Foster Care Federation, included issues with the recruitment and support of foster parents in a highly gendered context, as the domestic role associated with nurturing foster mothers has seldom been well remunerated.

A state-appointed advisory committee raised associated concerns about a lack of effective or consistent planning for children in care. This shortcoming was, in turn, linked with the insecurity occasioned by multiple placement breakdowns. The concept of permanency planning was promoted as the appropriate antidote. These perennial issues and disputed remedies continue to animate contemporary debate. This is evidenced in the recent expert advisory panel review process, which is discussed in Chapter 6.

One of the challenges with reformist reviews of state welfare over time is the tendency to focus on the perceived failings of problematic areas of the system in isolation (Hyslop, 2009). Remedies for the faults of component parts often have unforeseen or unintended outcomes when applied to the system at large (Munro, 2010; Kemp, 2020). As will be illustrated, the 2015 expert panel review was a case in point: recommendations for early permanency within a child-centric system predictably generated the disproportionate removal of Māori infants from whānau care (Hyslop and Keddell, 2019).

The notion of finality in foster-care arrangements to support a secure attachment process appears to be as persuasive as the merits of motherhood and apple pie until the detail of this panacea is examined more closely. The appeal for social workers to make hard decisions in the interest of child welfare is also a familiar refrain. However, questions such as when 'permanency' decisions are made in relation to the age of children, who should be involved in such decisions, what the ongoing relationship with natural parents and/ or extended family should be, and the legal basis for securing permanency are all contentious issues. This has been particularly problematic when it comes to Māori children being cared for outside kinship networks.

For Māori, there are overarching issues of identity and cultural cosmology. In contrast to anglophone jurisdictions such as the UK and US, this notion of deep connection is the reason why stranger adoption is seldom promoted for Indigenous children in Aotearoa. In 1997, I briefly expressed my own outsider understanding of this existential/spiritual dimension as follows:

> A hugely disproportionate percentage of the client group was (and is) Maori. Also, the systems associated with the 'Care' process were chronically monocultural. 'Rescue' mentality foster care does not have a positive track record. For Maori, the foster care system, with notable exceptions, was doubly destructive. Traditionally Maori children are seen as linked to extended family and kinship groups and ultimately to common ancestors. This source of assistance was often ignored and unexplored. Maori children were removed from abusive and/or non-coping urban family environments and placed in foster care on the basis that individual parents were inadequate. (Hyslop, 1997: 62)

This interplay of competing political and cultural perspectives creates an underlying tension in all debate about child protection and state care in Aotearoa. Historically, this dissonance is often not adequately confronted, which tends to fuel pendulum swings in practice development.

A policy of focused planning towards clear practice objectives for children and young people in care was established, at least in name, within the Social Work Division after what, in hindsight, appears to be a lengthy process of internal and external consultation. This consultative orientation was influenced by the decentralised nature of the organisation, a degree of professional commitment to community-centred deliberation and an associated resistance to 'one-size-fits-all' practice design. Significantly, the eventual shape of the CYP&tF Act (now the Oranga Tamariki Act) was very focused on planning and review processes: casework plans were required to support time-limited care orders, and these plans, as opposed to simply the orders themselves, were made the subject of regular judicial review.

Mātua Whāngai

By the early 1980s, the disproportionate number of Māori children entering the care system (in the vicinity of 50 per cent) was being recognised as a significant problem, compounded by a shortage of Māori social workers and foster parents:

The Department of Social Welfare developed a comprehensive network of foster parents, family homes, and social welfare institutions, to accommodate children who were removed from their homes, forming a range of optional settings in which children could be located. However, it failed to identify sufficient foster parents within the Māori community, instead sending Māori children to live with Pākehā parents, who did not know how to connect culturally with them. As a result, Māori children were often dealt with swiftly, by way of supervision, or removal to an institution, rather than through constructive engagement with their whānau. (Workman, 2019: 11)

Archival documents show germinal efforts to develop a Māori foster parenting resource from the early 1980s. Records of these initially small-scale ventures provide glimpses of the 'community versus expert' tensions that continue to colour contemporary practice development, with potential caregivers being 'put off' by stringent approval standards or being disqualified by risk-averse 'Pākehā' vetting processes.

Similarly, there is evidence of cultural blind spots in relation to the generic concept of 'Māori' foster care, as opposed to recognition of **whakapapa** links to hapū or iwi identity. The following understatement attributed to a Mr J. Ngata, a social worker in Gisborne, in the minutes of a working party on the recruitment of Māori foster parents held in Rotorua on 20 August 1981 speaks volumes. Mr Ngata is reported to have mentioned 'the failure to appreciate tribal identity and the need to investigate more fully the possibility of placement with relatives rather than outsiders' (Dean and Pihema, 1981: 2).

It is important to grasp these conceptual misalignments because they have haunted joint Pākehā–Māori policy and practice initiatives over time. There is an extensive history of attempts to forge state–Māori alliances for social service delivery (O'Malley, 1998; Harris, 2007). Ultimate authority is routinely retained by the state in such arrangements, and Māori ways of approaching and understanding care roles, responsibilities and obligations tend to be selectively appropriated and grafted onto existing Pākehā 'professional' systems of knowledge and procedure as and when they are seen as useful. It is unsurprising that the long-run track record of these hybrid models is less than ideal. It is also unsurprising that Māori continue to call for autonomous service development (for a discussion, see Chapter 7).

The Mātua Whāngai programme (1983–92) was born of Māori aspirations (Walker, 2006: 1–2). Initially a joint venture between the Department of Māori Affairs and the DSW, it was concerned with tapping the potential of Māori to 'care for their own'. The Justice Department also made a subsequent and less-wholehearted commitment to the project. According to Workman (2019: 14), Mātua Whāngai arose from two primary drivers: 'First, it was a response to the increasing demand from tribal authorities and Māori communities to control both resources and delivery of services, and to promote Māori empowerment. Second, it was a Māori reaction to the state's racist treatment of young Māori offenders.' The programme encountered many of the problems of cultural dissonance and agenda variance that have marked such ventures. Friction between government attempts to harness the resources inherent to the extended social structure of Māori and Māori efforts to progress a parallel agenda of tribal or, in other ways, 'Māori-centred' development continues to animate debate about the devolution of child and family welfare services.

In this context, it is important to grasp that the root concept of **whāngai** is an Indigenous customary practice that refers to the process of nurturing children within extended family when, for a variety of reasons, birth parents are not in a position to provide care. It is an elastic construct that does not translate at all clearly into Pākehā concepts of foster care, attachment and permanency because it belongs to a very different cultural framework. Walker (2006: 31) refers to the complexities in some depth:

> Mead (1994) discusses this principle in terms of protecting the interests of the child involved in the fostering process: The closer the kinship ties the better, in order to protect interests that could include the social place of the child; its heritage, including physical property such as land; culture and language; and the self-esteem, mana and tapu of the child. Kirby (1994) describes the concept of tamaiti whangai as 'an absolute whanau promise – a spiritual promise' (p.22). As far as Kirby and Mead are concerned the tamaiti whangai is a precious taonga to be protected by the whanau, hapu and iwi. The whanaungatanga (relatedness) principle operated along bloodlines and it was unusual for a whangai to be placed outside the whanau, hapu and iwi, let alone introduced into another culture (Mead 1994, Kirby 1994). In fact, Mead ... says that it was not the prerogative of an individual parent to 'throw a child into another culture' (Mead 1994: 90) and that this type of cultural violence would not happen if whanaungatanga principles were followed.

A Mātua Whāngai position was attached to all DSW offices and integrated to varying degrees with daily operational work. The programme was subject to significant local and regional variations, including the extent of relationship with equivalent dedicated staff within Māori Affairs offices. In Auckland, where I worked, Mātua Whāngai workers were mostly male, and few had orthodox social work backgrounds; expertise was more likely to be grounded in Māori language, wisdom and experience.

Mātua Whāngai workers were influenced by the rising Māori political consciousness of the time, and, simultaneously, they influenced the beliefs and practices of non-Māori staff within the Department. Several of these men were powerful orators with the capacity to build bridges between the state bureaucracy and both traditional and urban Māori life worlds. Initially, the programme was officially described as the facilitation of a Māori foster-care system:

> The aim is to provide an immediate option to foster care for Maori children within whanau Maori by developing a working relationship between the Maori community and the Departments of Maori Affairs and Social welfare. ...
>
> The Maatua whangai programme is primarily an additional placement resource intended to offer a culturally appropriate and community-based form of care in a family setting for Maori children who are coming to notice in some way. (Circular Memorandum, 1983: 1)

Beyond the provision of 'placements', the role was seen to extend to support work with whānau experiencing difficulties and to prevent entry into care or involvement with the court system. However, as Workman (2019) explains, the original vision was far more ambitious than the provision of social support and the procurement of Māori foster parents:

> Tribal networks and work patterns would support whānau, hapū and iwi development, and departmental officials from all three departments would facilitate that process. Involvement in Mātua Whāngai would be on the basis of a mandate from tribal representatives. Whānau, hapū and iwi, would evaluate how well the networking occurred, and how the **rōpū** could meet the needs of Māori. (Workman, 2019: 14)

Cultural tension was sewn into the fabric of the programme. This was only exacerbated with the release of the potentially transformational 1986 report of the Ministerial Advisory Committee on a Māori Perspective for the Department of Social Welfare: 'Puao-te-Ata-Tu (day break)' (hereafter, PtAT) (Ministerial Advisory Committee, 1988).[1]

By late 1987, a new direction was plotted for Mātua Whāngai – one more in line with the broader intent of empowerment and self-determination. An internal memorandum from Doug Hauraki (1987), National Director of Maori and Community Programmes, outlines a specific role as follows:

(a) Prevent the 'flow' of young Maori people in to Government institutions: and

(b) To take young Maori out of the care of institutions and place them in to the care of whanau/hapu/iwi.

This emphasis required that connections be forged and/or strengthened between urban whānau and the hapū/iwi base. Although the practical challenges of achieving the devolution of state care and social work services to iwi Māori were not coherently confronted, there was a generalised intention to reorient the Mātua Whāngai programme as a support system for iwi organisations as they prepared for this function. The memorandum in question goes on to state the following:

(a) In order to meet this objective it is recognised that it is necessary for kin-based support to be developed in partnership with iwi authorities; an equal partnership involving an equal share of resources. (Hauraki, 1987)

Little attention is given to the mechanics of this proposal apart from a directive that the process should be delegated to the local district level:

Accordingly, the Department needs to avoid the development and imposition of a national policy, which ignores the need to consult with Maori and fails to take account of the differing strengths of the 34 tribal authorities.

Each District undertakes responsibility for reviewing with the tangata whenua and other iwi groups, the future direction of Maatua Whangai at the local level and the most effective strategies for implementation and accountability. The review should include the development of general policy guidelines. (Hauraki, 1987)

The idea appears to have been that local initiatives would be developed and piloted in ways that did not interfere with the self-determined needs and aspirations of differing tribal authorities. The momentum for this work unwound rapidly in response to changing political and economic priorities from the early 1990s.

Workman, alongside Doug Hauraki and John Rangihau, the principal architect of PtAT, was personally involved with a review of Mātua Whāngai in the mid-1980s. He passes the following judgement in his witness statement to the current Royal Commission of Inquiry into Historical Abuse in State Care and in the Care of Faith Based Institutions:

Mātua Whāngai became little more than a mechanism for contracting out the delivery of state services and added to prevailing Māori suspicions about the Crown's motivations. The underlying concept never gained acceptance and was derailed by government departments, who turned the programme and the funding that accompanied it, to their own purposes. Māori paradigms were beyond the comprehension of mainstream government agencies, leading to their own interpretation of responsiveness to Māori.

The other probable reason that Mātua Whāngai was never able to realise its full potential as an alternative fostering scheme is that government departments were simply unwilling to yield territory. It would be dangerous to assume that government agencies do not have a **rangatiratanga** of their own: an underlying view about their own special place in the universe, their own set of underlying values and beliefs, accompanied by the underlying determination to preserve their autonomy. Ultimately, government departments did not want to truly devolve power to Māori in this way. (Workman, 2019: 16)

The development of Māori-led alternative care and welfare structures is not without challenges grounded in postcolonial economic and political history, as well as the material realities produced by this history. Accordingly, it is important to understand that effective autonomous development on this scale was not solely prevented by Pākehā ignorance and intransigence. However, the absence of sociological imagination, real political will and resource commitment from the settler state to develop this capacity has been a perpetual obstacle. Currently, there are glimpses of a quantum shift, as discussed in Chapter 7 of this book.

Internal dissent and practice innovation

It is difficult to definitively disentangle the influences that contributed to child protection policy and practice development over this volatile decade. Te Tiriti o Waitangi-centred land rights protests of the 1970s were driven by the consequences of colonial dispossession. Grievances were articulated by a new wave of so-called 'Māori radicals', who were often vilified in populist discourse. However, social justice for Māori was also supported by a broad left-liberal political constituency. The polarising and politicising effect of the 1981 Springbok tour and the discriminatory law-and-order crackdown associated with the conservative National Party governments of Robert Muldoon also left a legacy of protest and civil agitation for social change. Social workers were not immune to the tide of anti-racist sentiment that was swirling around them by the mid-1980s.

Some saw these issues as symptomatic of a broader crisis within the social work profession. There was mounting pressure on the DSW to move away from professionalised individual casework and the 'centralised, bureaucratised' model of welfare (Barretta-Herman, 1990). As suggested in Chapter 3, neither the 'friendly visitor' nor the 'forensic investigation' models of practice were likely to deliver the preventive practice that many social workers aspired to.

According to Garlick (2012: 104–7), the early 1980s witnessed a period of generalised disruption within the Social Work Division, with agitation for a more community-centred approach (exemplified by the development of a Community Services Unit in 1982), decentralised decision-making, a weakening of hierarchy and a changing of the managerial guard. Professional differences and theoretical disagreements became more overt. Relatively poor pay and high workloads also led to the loss of experienced staff and an appetite for industrial action. There was something of an intangible mood for reform, though the preferred formula for change was less coherent, arguably reflecting the 'mood' of the country at large in these years.

It is also worth reflecting on the fact that this inchoate 'movement' for reform within state social work was not wholly generated by a new salvo of educated and socially aware practitioners. The notion of a wide, if administratively ponderous, role at the nexus of private troubles and public issues continued to influence the professional identity of statutory social workers into the 1980s. As discussed in Chapter 3, state social work derived its formative rationale from the egalitarian ideals of the welfare state (Brodie et al, 2008). In this sense, a degree of challenge to the inequalities embedded in the status quo was wired into the moral and ethical foundations of statutory social work (Hyslop, 2013b; Parton, 2014b).

This orientation sits in stark contrast to the tightly enforced 'apolitical' ethos of current statutory practice. As will be discussed in Chapter 5, state social work was largely divorced from this wider practice vision in the neoliberal blizzard of the 1990s. However, the critical legacy of social work as the 'social profession' located within a structurally unequal society is difficult to completely eradicate. To a degree, it is reproduced within the social work education system and through the experience of applied practice (Hyslop, 2013b). A socio-political analysis that exposes the social determinants of child maltreatment sits uncomfortably with practice directed to forensic investigation and protective intervention. This disjunction creates tensions that continue to drive contemporary debate about social work in child welfare (Featherstone et al, 2014).

Productive ambiguity

Underlying ambiguity can be discerned in the following policy statement attached to a comprehensive set of DSW child abuse guidelines from 1988. This guidance attempts to meld a child protection focus with the commitment to anti-racist policy and practice embedded in the PtAT report of 1986 (see Chapter 5, note 2), with lessons derived from an influential independent report into the death of a child:

The whole field of child abuse is fraught with different points of view which, in the context of NZ society, has as much to do with a clash of cultures as much as anything else.

There is clearly no suggestion that child abuse of whatever kind is acceptable. Indeed, it is patently unacceptable, but there is nonetheless a need to see the issue as a direct consequence of the economic, social and cultural mix which inevitably influences the behaviour of families, whanau and family groups. (DSW, 1988)

Despite the controversial reference to the concept of cultural relativity, this is an unusually frank recognition of some of the frictions that bedevil child protection. Decentralised authority and the less tightly controlled practice regime of the time allowed for some degree of internal dissent and for innovation at the local level. The visibility of unequal outcomes for Māori fuelled grass-roots agitation for change. This is not to say that internal dissent was necessarily rewarded or without personal and professional cost.

Women against racism

Perhaps the most influential example of the groundswell of concern over institutional racism can be found in a document prepared by a group of nine women employed by the DSW in Auckland and motivated by feminist, anti-racist politics – the Women Against Racism Action Group (WARAG) report of November 1984:

Our working premise is that the Department [of Social Welfare] practises institutional racism. We do not mean that all staff uniformly hold racist opinions. We do mean that the institutional framework of the Department – staffing, training, legislation and policies – reflects a relentlessly Pakeha view of society, which oppressively and systematically discriminates against the interests of consumers and staff who are Maori and Pacific.

The philosophical baseline of this group is a feminist, anti-racist one. As feminists we are committed to changing the power structure that oppresses both women and people from other cultural groups. We work in a collective way using consensus decision-making. Our anti-racist stance recognises that we benefit from living in a racist society, and that we have a responsibility to work for change within our organisation. (Women Against Racism Action Group, 1984: 1)

A comprehensive anti-racism programme for the DSW was urged, with a particular focus on recruitment and promotion to address glaring disparities between the ethnic composition of staff and service recipients, for example: '78% of the children and young people in the institutions in the Tamaki-makau-rau area are Maori and pacific people. 25% of staff are Maori or pacific people' (Women Against Racism Action Group, 1984: 16).[2]

This piece of principled advocacy was a significant catalyst for the more wide-ranging inquiry and reform process that followed. A 1985 report by the DSW's newly established Māori Advisory Unit endorsed and extended this critique:

> The Māori Advisory Unit argued that the Department of Social Welfare's 'bureaucratic model' was 'inappropriate' and did not 'adequately cater to the needs of Māori people'. Endorsing a 'structural biculturalism', it recommended the implementation of a 'concept of whānau and community development' based on the 'decentralisation of power and resources' to whānau and community groups. This criticism from a cultural perspective was in accord with other criticisms of the Department's services, particularly that its hierarchical and centralised structure had become increasingly untenable as the Department had grown in size, and that it had become distanced from community perspectives and local needs. (Garlick, 2012: 113–14)

The sentiment behind these initiatives developed something of a life of its own in the struggles of day-to-day practice, with increasing resistance to institutional placements and out-of-family foster care, and support for the matching of 'culturally appropriate' workers with service users. Partly in response to the influence of Mātua Whāngai and an influx of Māori staff, social workers began to practise informal models of whānau resolution and decision-making long before the family group conference (FGC) model was formalised.

For a brief time, in my own experience, leading up to and immediately following the enactment of the CYP&tF Act, the ideal of socially just child protection practice appeared to be within reach. The lynchpin for policy and practice reform was provided by the 1986 PtAT report.

PtAT (day break)

It is difficult to overstate the significance (both historically and in an ongoing sense) of this report for child protection in Aotearoa. PtAT made a dramatic impact, though its promise was not realised as it might have been. The vision of this document continues to resonate like an unfulfilled promise, in much the same way as Te Tiriti o Waitangi has done in a broader sense. As sketched in this chapter, it was located within a complex confluence of change drivers; it contained a set of ideas whose time had arrived.

The PtAT report of 1986 (published as a handbook in 1988) (Ministerial Advisory Committee, 1988) is a historic place marker in the evolution of statutory practice and of social work in Aotearoa more generally. It offered an ambitious template for systemic social change based on a bicultural partnership. There were, and continue to be, constitutional barriers to implementing this vision within the confines of a unitary liberal state. The devolutionary implications of the report also left it open to partial capture by the 'smaller state' family and community responsibility agenda associated with the neoliberal political turn. Nevertheless, it was a far-reaching and now iconic landmark, which refuses to stop speaking into the present.

Kim Workman (2019: 18–19), who was involved with the Review Committee in an advisory role, offers the following insight into the power of the process:

> It was an extraordinary experience. I can't recall a more comprehensive consultative process since then. The public hui were well publicised and well-attended – they were a draw card for iwi and Māori. Te Rangihau's mana ensured that Māori felt safe speaking about the Department of Social Welfare, and treatment of children and young people, and that the hui would be held in accordance with tikanga Māori. People were free to express their frustration and anger, to shed tears and share their stories. The casual observer might have concluded that it was not much more than a cathartic opportunity for participants. But there were also moments of insight, and the articulation of ideas and thoughts, which Te Rangihau and the Committee were able to ultimately transform into workable policy.

As a member of the Advisory Committee, it seems that the Director General of Social Welfare, John Grant, was swept up in the collective charisma of the distinguished advisory group, particularly the chair, **Ngāi Tūhoe kaumatua** John Te Rangi-Aniwaniwa Rangihau. Grant was moved by the power of the message transmitted through the consultation process, and, more importantly, so were most of the social workers within the DSW:

> The evocative realization was that racist social work practice actively contributed to intergenerational alienation and creeping cultural genocide. It was the fall-out associated with this message that most affected the shape of the 1989 Act. Social workers responded creatively to the challenge well before 1989. With the zeal of those converted to a 'new truth' social workers began involving extended family in all key intervention decisions. (Hyslop, 1997: 62)

PtAT brought the voices of disenfranchised Māori to the ears of the public service establishment. The report and the consultative process that informed it have taken on a narrative mystique of their own with the passage of time.

A powerful message of racism, cultural alienation and disempowerment is woven throughout the text:

> Like a litany of sound – Ngeri – recited with the fury of a tempest on every marae and from marae to marae came the cries: '*Their child care processes are undermining the basis of Maori society or have already done so*'. ... '*Rendered children and parents helpless a great cost to racial, tribal and personal integrity*'. ... '*Maori people being allowed to look after themselves – to be given back their own welfare.*' (Ministerial Advisory Committee, 1988: 21; italics in original)

The core message of PtAT is spelt out in Recommendation 1, which calls for an overarching 'policy objective' aimed at aggressively removing the imposition of dominant cultural norms:

> *To attack all forms of cultural racism in New Zealand that result in the values and lifestyle of the dominant group being regarded as superior to those of other groups, especially Māori, by: (a) Providing leadership and programmes which help develop a society in which the values of all groups are of central importance to its enhancement; and (b) Incorporating the values, cultures and beliefs of the Māori people in all practice developed for the future of New Zealand.* (Ministerial Advisory Committee, 1988: 9; italics in original)

Recommendation 2 set out the means to this end: a global 'operational objective' to prevent racist practices and outcomes:

> *To attack and eliminate deprivation and alienation by: (a) Allocating an equitable share of resources. (b) Sharing power and authority over the use of resources. (c) Ensuring legislation which recognises social, cultural and economic values of all cultural groups and especially Maori people. (d) Developing strategies and initiatives which harness the potential of all its people, and especially Maori people, to advance.* (Ministerial Advisory Committee, 1988: 9, l; italics in original)

These are strident demands: eliminate deprivation and alienation; create an equitable distribution of resources; and share power and authority!

It may appear to be a semantic distinction, but the aforementioned recommendations were directed to 'the Government for the development of Social Welfare policy in New Zealand' (Ministerial Advisory Committee, 1988: 9). As it was, the report was accepted and adopted by the DSW. However, the elimination of racial inequality by elevating the 'values, cultures and beliefs' of Māori people to an equal footing, and allocating an 'equitable share of resources' for this purpose, required change of a greater magnitude: constitutional and structural reform that channelled authority and resources to Māori.

In other words, this vison invites a practical and conceptual problem. As Poata-Smith (2002) has argued, colonisation has not simply involved the imposition of generic Pākehā culture, though cultural assimilation was clearly a powerful tool in the naturalisation of the 'modern' settler state. More fundamentally the colonial project involved imposing the twin foundations of liberal capitalism, that is, a legal system that guaranteed individual property rights, especially to land, and the establishment of the capitalist form of economic development, which requires the extraction of private profit from commodified labour:

> In the context of Aotearoa, British settlement brought a people with a distinct method of economic and social organisation into contact with an indigenous population who possessed a radically different mode of ensuring their subsistence. It brought together two societies that were built upon conflicting modes of production, social practices, and cultural ideologies. (Poata-Smith, 2002: 58)

This is not to denigrate the intentions of the PtAT report or the ongoing pragmatic need to find mechanisms to restore Māori autonomy. However, it is important to be clear that cultural concessions alone were unlikely to address material inequalities. There are also indications within the report that the authors were aware of the complex relationship between material and cultural deprivation:

> While mindful of our terms of reference we nevertheless believe that most of the socio-economic difficulties Maori clients have with the Department are a reflection of the socio-economic status of Maori in the community. In proposing a Maori perspective for the Department, we cannot ignore the lack of a Māori perspective in the community at large. (Ministerial Advisory Committee, 1988: 17)

Similarly, the historical appendices to the report clearly associate settler state policy with the systematic destruction of a way of life based on bonds of kin-based reciprocity and communal identity: 'Those early Pakeha power brokers knew exactly what they were doing. It was summed up by the distinguished 19th century politician Sir Francis Dillon-Bell when he said, "The first plank of public policy must be to stamp out the beastly communism of the Maori"' (Ministerial Advisory Committee, 1988: 57).

PtAT also emphasises the problem of 'dependency', which is a malleable term that is open to political interpretation and manipulation: 'We have been confronted with a Maori perception of issues which are deeply rooted and structural, issues which combine to produce an Aotearoa in 1986 in which Maori people are overwhelmingly in a state of dependency – mokai in their own land' (Ministerial Advisory Committee, 1988: 17). Reliance on the liberal capitalist state due to a lack of political autonomy, material resources and independent means of subsistence is one way of understanding the concept of dependency, for example, dependence on unskilled work and low wages. Reliance on government assistance, particularly income support, but also housing, health, education and wider social services, is another way of viewing dependency. These are politically contested constructions.

From the late 1970s, neoliberal political rhetoric attacked the welfare state as an impediment to freedom, enterprise and independence. Dependence on the state, particularly 'benefit dependence', is cast as sapping the moral fibre, work ethic and self-respect of the labouring classes. Too often, it was this latter take on the nature of dependency that influenced the application of PtAT in practice: responsibility was gladly returned to whānau Māori, but the means to fulfil obligations were seldom provided. In the same vein, socially liberal attitudes to cultural expression are not inconsistent with the 'free' functioning of capitalism.

In the bigger political scheme of things, a move by the state to divest itself of direct service provision was ushered in by the Labour government of 1984. This climate provided the opportunity for Māori organisations to assert varying forms of independence, though there were embedded fishhooks:

> By 1986 the process of devolution was increasingly seen as a necessary option for Maori and this idea was given momentum with the release of Puao-te-ata-tu by a Ministerial Advisory Committee. The report, for the Department of Social Welfare, argued unequivocally for public institutions to adopt effective bicultural policies giving Maori communities the power to direct and allocate resources presently controlled by the state. Consistent with Labour's broad direction, the report was vehemently opposed to the central development and delivery of services and programmes and supported the role of tribal institutions in this process rather than central government. (Poata-Smith, 2002: 251)

Much of the content of PtAT speaks to intent and principle. The most significant practical means of ensuring accountability to a bicultural vision entailed the setting up of local community/Māori committees to monitor the work of DSW district offices and residential institutions, under the umbrella of a new Social Welfare Commission.

Detail on the functions and scope of these district executive committees (DECs) is light, apart from reference to community membership and cross-accountability to local interests and tribal authorities. These committees also included local directors of the Social Welfare and Māori Affairs Departments as members, and reference is made to the funding of local projects in consultation with tribal authorities. As it transpired, this experiment in shared governance was short-lived. As discussed in Chapter 5, the dual accountability and Māori/community delegation model that the DEC system implied was anathema to the centrist managerial agenda that came to dominate public service restructuring in the 1990s.

However, PtAT did herald lasting transformation for child protection practice in the form of the CYP&tF Act. In relation to child protection, the report makes the following statements:

> At the heart of the issue is a profound misunderstanding or ignorance of the place of the child in Maori society and its relationship with whanau, hapu, iwi structures. (Ministerial Advisory Committee, 1988: 7)

> The guiding principle in the current legislation is that the welfare of the child shall be regarded as the first and paramount consideration. There need be no inherent conflict between that and the customary preference for the maintenance of children within the hapu. The current principle is seen in practice as negating the right of the group to care for its own or to be heard in the proceedings. (Ministerial Advisory Committee, 1988: 29)

The concept of children fundamentally and irrevocably belonging to a family group had a profound influence on the 1989 legislation.

Legislative reform

Review of the Children and Young Persons Act 1974 commenced in 1983 under National Party Minister Venn Young. A ministerial statement released in December of that year reads as follows: 'A complete review of the Children and Young Persons Act is well advanced and is proposed for passing by Parliament next year, the Minister of Social Welfare, Mr Venn Young, said today' (Young, 1983). Despite the confidence expressed about the pace of law reform, a close reading of this document reveals some of the competing concerns already at play:

> Mr Young said the need to review the legislation has been highlighted by reports over the past 18 months on social welfare institutions by the Human Rights Commission and Archbishop A.H. Johnson, and on Youth and the Law in a Multicultural Society by the Race Relations Conciliator, Mr Hiwi Tauroa.
>
> The major amendments proposed will also take into account recommendations of the National Advisory Committee on the

Prevention of Child Abuse, which are aimed at reducing the incidence of child abuse, improving the detection of many cases, the prevention of any recurrence. (Young, 1983)

For many engaged observers, these imperatives were fundamentally oppositional: the more intrusive and risk-focused lens of a child-centred multidisciplinary approach to child protection was likely to exacerbate the abusive and overtly racist outcomes that were being uncovered within the state care system. Effectively, the minister was attempting to ride two horses at once. This increasingly difficult stance was maintained by the incoming minister, Ann Hercus, during the 1984–87 term of Labour government.

Immediately following the 1984 general election, Hercus embarked on an extended review of her own, setting up a working party in August and a public discussion document in December. Draft legislation was developed in July 1985 and refined over the following 12 months. A bill was not introduced into Parliament until December 1986. Much of the consultative process was facilitated by 'the Department' – accessing the views of social workers and related interest groups.

Archival records evidence some of the mixed currents at work. Although the basic premise of a multidisciplinary focus was widely condoned, at least initially, concerns about the disempowerment of social workers and the absence of 'as of right' family input into decision-making were expressed with some force. There were also expressions of support for the statutory involvement of community panels representing local cultural perspectives and family interests.

Formative iterations of the bill referred to community committees as a diversionary mechanism, seen perhaps as an invigorated version of the largely ineffective children's boards associated with the 1974 Act. The notion of some form of statutory community consultation was a nod towards concern about unbridled professional authority. In turn, social workers expressed unease about the practical difficulty of multiple accountability mechanisms.

Minister Hercus's working party contained no Māori representation, which, according to Workman (2019: 16), was 'seen by Māori, given their increased concerns, as a deliberate snub'. As suggested, motivation to address discriminatory processes gained increasing purchase among DSW staff. To the minister's credit, this combination of external and internal pressure culminated in the establishment of the Ministerial Advisory Committee, which produced the game-changing PtAT report.

Although this decision clearly had far-reaching implications, it appears to have been envisaged as a separate process to the legislative reform programme. The terms of reference are generic and do not specifically refer to legislative change: 'The task of the Maori Perspective Advisory Committee is to advise the Minister of Social Welfare on the most appropriate means to achieve the goal of an approach which will meet the needs of Maori in policy, planning and service delivery in the Department of Social Welfare' (Ministerial Advisory Committee, 1988: 5). It is difficult, in hindsight, to see how child welfare law reform and the issue of Māori well-being could be maintained as parallel processes. The aims of Māori-centric reform and the desire for a professionally centred multidisciplinary approach to expert child protection were inevitably set on a collision course. As we shall see, the lessons within this history were largely ignored in the recent politicised reform processes between 2011 and 2015 (Hyslop and Keddell, 2019).

Legislation for whānau empowerment

Despite rising resistance, the drive for a multidisciplinary focus did not lose all momentum until after the general election of 1987. With Ann Hercus's resignation from Parliament, new Minister Michael Cullen facilitated a resolution consistent with the messages represented in PtAT. In September 1987, he pushed for a redraft of the bill introduced to Parliament in December 1986. A new working party, a fresh round of consultation with Māori and select committee submissions from Māori and Pasifika interest groups eventually resulted in a legislative framework strewn with references to the centrality of family/whānau in statutory child protection and youth justice processes.

The energy and vision of Chief Social Worker Mike Doolan was also critical to the final shape of the CYP&tF Act in relation to moving from a 'welfare/ care' to a 'justice/community' focus for the resolution of youth offending. The separation of youth justice practice from child protection in terms of procedure, principles and judicial oversight led to a significant reduction of Māori young people entering state care. Separate but comparable youth justice and care or protection FGCs became the central decision-making vehicles for the new legislation. Essentially, the child protection FGC is designed to give the (extended) family group the opportunity to propose plans to resolve child safety concerns, though final authority remains vested in state social workers and, ultimately, the judicial system.

The medical/paediatric lobby were predictably displeased with this outcome after years of advocacy for a power shift towards expert multidisciplinary teams in child protection practice. The following extract from a *Dominion Sunday Times* newspaper article in September 1988 illustrates something of the power struggle sitting behind the later stages of the law reform process:

> The debate between Plunket executives and the department is old and bitter. ... Dr Geddes says every culture makes paramount the protection of children. Dr Hassell says departmental representatives mounted a campaign to Maori and Pacific Island groups effectively saying, 'This

is not going to let you have your say, so you don't like it, do you?' ...
The revised bill is to be introduced shortly and seems set to retain
the department's executive authority. (*Dominion Sunday Times*, 1988)

This outcome appeared to signal more than a victory for the status quo
and to potentially herald a sea change in state social work. However, other,
more complex economic and political currents were swirling beneath the
surface, as we shall see in Chapter 5.

5

Revolution from above: the neoliberal turn

The roller coaster ride begins

Garlick's (2012) history of organisational changes within the state welfare system documents a roller coaster of structural reform from the mid-1980s. This process was generated by theoretical and practical tensions that have influenced (and been influenced by) continuous swings between centralised administration and more localised frameworks, including various hybrid arrangements. Garlick locates child welfare and protection services within shifting perceptions of the appropriate role for the state in managing social problems and promoting well-being. Although his account is avowedly apolitical, it illustrates the way in which ideological currents have impacted on the preferred mandate, structure and operation of state services. Child protection policy and practice is clearly connected with the managerial and accountability mechanisms deemed appropriate to the political visions of the day.

Implementation of these visions has seldom taken account of the consuming and resource-intensive realities of child protection social work practice (Hyslop, 2009). It is trite, but essentially accurate, to say that the intent of the CYP&tF Act – and, by extension, the mandate of PtAT – was increasingly distorted and frustrated by a lack of resourcing in an overstretched practice climate. In turn, this climate was shaped by competing priorities and conflicting ideological currents.

The reformist drive of the CYP&tF Act can be broadly aligned to socially liberal elements within the 1980s' Labour Party in Aotearoa, as opposed to the interventionist social conservatism of previous National Party governments. However, notions of community devolution and family responsibility also found political traction beneath the umbrella of neoliberalism, which came to prominence from the mid-1980s. In fact, the former provided a convenient ideological Trojan Horse for the latter. While many social workers saw the new legislation as an opportunity to redress the individual fallout from social and racial injustice (Hyslop, 2007), at a deeper level, the trajectory of practice reform was influenced by a global and local shift in economic and political power – a restoking of the engine of capitalism (Harvey, 2005).

The welfare state was remodelled within the rubric of economic rationalism, leading to the privatisation or contracting out of government services, as well as the creation of quasi-private bodies such as Crown companies and state-owned enterprises (Kelsey, 1995). The 'residual' delivery of direct state services was increasingly subject to audit and control – maximising 'bang for the buck' by mimicking a business-like 'production efficiency' model (Schick, 1996). Within this environment, the material support that was required to make the 1989 Act work was reframed as a drag on family autonomy, effectively, a misguided means to tackle the debilitating scourge of dependency.

The references to Māori dependency within the text of PtAT lent themselves to this politicised interpretation: excessive welfare state assistance, as opposed to the interaction of colonisation and capitalism over time, was the source of Māori social distress. This substitution of symptoms for causes is a persuasive, if often disingenuous, feature of neoliberal socio-political analysis.

Turning the political screw

Just as changes to statutory social work do not occur in a vacuum, so the implementation of new policy directions is inevitably influenced by wider material circumstances (Garrett, 2018). In the 1990s, working-class whānau Māori were asked to do more for themselves at the same time as government policy generated greater relative deprivation. The opening up of the Aotearoa economy to the winds of the transnational market entailed the removal of protective tariffs and production subsidies, and associated legislation to reduce the collective bargaining power of the trade union movement.

The dislocation of working-class life that this economic prescription generated was mirrored in the experience of workers in the industrial cities of the UK and US, and across the Western world, as manufacturing moved to the cheap labour markets of the Global South (Bourdieu and Ferguson, 1999). This transformation impacted most acutely on the unskilled end of the labour market, so that Māori were disproportionately penalised:

> Following the 1987 crash, at its worst, New Zealand had sustained unemployment of 10.5% in 1992. … However, Māori unemployment at the same time was 26%, with Non-Māori unemployment, including Pasifika, at around 7–8%. … Mainstream Aotearoa New Zealand shifted the pain of its restructuring from itself to the Māori population and, to a growing extent, to its Pasifika population. (Eketone, 2020: 37)

When the cumulative effect of the benefit cuts imposed in doctrinaire Finance Minister Ruth Richardson's 1991 budget and the policy of 'market rents' for state housing are added to the equation, it is obvious that the early 1990s was a time of increasing poverty and hardship for many Māori:

> We were not supported or comforted by the Government as we went through this 'Hidden Depression', instead, at the very height of the crisis, we were punished by a cynical National government that hit us with the 'mother of all budgets' that funded tax cuts through a 20% reduction in unemployment, sickness and solo parent benefits. It is interesting that benefits that were dominated by Pākehā, namely National Superannuation, were left mainly intact. (Eketone, 2020: 37–8)

This was the wider economic and social context within which whānau were asked to assume responsibility for children and young people in, or on the verge of entering, the state care system.

The business of state social work

The shape of things to come was foreshadowed from the mid-1980s. In 1987, early in the second term of the Labour government, an administrative review recommended that the DSW replace its emphasis on casework skills with a community services model:

> The indirect funding of community services was increasingly embraced as a solution to the Department's many and varied problems with social work. It seemed a way to develop services that were more 'culturally appropriate' and consistent with the principles of decentralisation, devolution, and greater participation by the community in both policy-making and the provision of services. (Garlick, 2012: 120)

However, this review also argued that decentralisation and delegation 'should be implemented alongside "clear performance expectations and measures of accountability" ... urging the Department to reassert control over its internal operations through the monitoring of performance' (Garlick, 2012: 124).

The conceptual separation of service delivery from policy responsibility presumed that control could be exercised through tight systems of auditing and inspection. Rose (2001: 33) argues that this approach is associated with a deeper shift in the methodology of governance in late modern times:

> The powers once accorded to positive knowledge of human conduct are to be transferred to the calculative regimes of accounting and financial management. And the enclosures of expertise are to be penetrated through a range of new techniques for exercising critical

scrutiny over authority – budget discipline, accounting, and audit being three of the most salient.

As the neoliberal noose tightened under the 1990 National government, the state increasingly looked to exercise a more limited and tightly monitored level of operational delegation, principally through a process of competitive contracting.

Devolution reframed

As explained, PtAT did not simply identify gaps in the cultural awareness and responsiveness of staff. The most significant structural recommendation proposed a limited form of direct participatory democracy. Iwi and community representatives were to have direct oversight of and input into the operation of DSW offices and institutions through local committees reporting to a Social Welfare Commission (Recommendation 3 of PtAT) (Ministerial Advisory Committee, 1988: 9). This role involved the monitoring of service quality and input into service development. It was a move towards direct democracy, community accountability and partnership. This soon came to be regarded as an inconvenient commitment and was quietly 'disappeared'.

Community committees were established, but potentially challenging matters of role definition and pathways to meaningful participation were not effectively confronted and resolved. At first glance, this resistance may appear puzzling given the rhetorically wholehearted acceptance of PtAT. However, the abstract concept of community empowerment and the reality of reform within an overburdened professional bureaucracy are different propositions. Implementation of this scheme was delegated to the local level, where it was not well resourced and not necessarily well understood.

There is a perennial gulf between politically driven policy imperatives and the capacity for operational change in public sector bureaucracies. The misguided assumption that state social work systems, which can barely cope with existing work, can hit the ground running with expanded functions while resolving the practice tensions that arise from large-scale change has often hampered effective reform (Kemp, 2020). The 'core' work of child protection, youth justice and care services essentially proceeded along a separate track from the functioning of DECs, and there was no systemic imperative for this to change. The child protection interface with community occurred through the new statutory requirement to consult with care and protection resource panels – a tangible residue of the multidisciplinary practice model.

There were also growing political and policy tensions between the devolutionary spirit of the mid-1980s and the top-down efficiency focus of the late 1980s. Under the State Sector Act 1988, chief executives were charged with managing the performance of public sector bodies. The Public Finance Act 1989 required the expedient management of financial inputs to maximise the efficient production of outputs purchased by the government. The relatively 'soft biculturalism' of the DECs model was a long way from the concept of self-determined iwi/community social services, but it proved to be too inclusive for a neoliberal 'devolution' of tightly defined and costed services.

A challenging and potentially resource-intensive commitment to a degree of shared service monitoring, planning and development was ill-suited to a shift to the cost-effective delivery of predetermined outputs (Garlick, 2012: 125). In relation to the development of social work, these ideological fault lines are evident in a key document produced by the Principal Social Worker Unit (1989) to coincide with the passage of the 1989 Act: 'Te Ara Hou – The new path'.

Forks in the new path

The 1989 DSW social work development plan (Te Ara Hou) (Principal Social Worker Unit, 1989) is explored in some detail in the following discussion. Close examination reveals some of the challenges within the vision of the legislation and prefigures some of the political and ideological contradictions that undermined the new dawn. This document represents something of a high-tide mark in operational commitment to PtAT and bicultural practice. There was expansive talk of devolution, locally driven initiatives and the active participation of social workers in the process of practice development. However, there were also countervailing messages folded into the narrative.

The following commentary summarises the policy and practice directions set out in page 4 of the document. The plan endorsed the 'principles' of PtAT, for example, the need to understand the place of the child in Māori society, to move from institutional care to community placements, and to 'maintain or re-establish the child within whānau/hapū/iwi structures'. It was recognised that radical practice change was required to achieve this aim, especially in 'supporting and facilitating family decision-making'. A need for 'more people with appropriate skills and experience to deal with Māori families and children' was acknowledged, which sat in tension with the need to retain existing staff who were leaving the DSW in large numbers at the time. It was noted that training for all staff 'must have regard to cultural processes and Māori aspirations'. The plan also envisaged a narrowing of the distance 'between "professional" and "cultural" practice viewpoints', though there was little reference to what this might entail, that is, why these positions are seen to be distinct and what the challenges to bridging this gap might be.

Te Ara Hou presented a serious, if superficial, commitment to the recognition of cultural difference and the capacity of family, particularly Māori, to care for their own. The plan effectively illustrated some of the limitations of biculturalism, particularly within an ascendant climate of managerialism and fiscal austerity. The wider implications of the message contained in PtAT were not adequately processed. The apparent assumption was that cultural capacity would provide a panacea for problems affecting the clients of the DSW. Clearly, cultural understanding and respect are of central importance to good practice, but it was naive to assume that this initiative could provide a complete response to the complex issues of child protection and youth offending, and the socio-economic disparities that drive unequal outcomes.

Although whānau-centred practice appeared to have prevailed over a multi-professional model, this contest was, as we shall see, far from over (Connolly and Doolan, 2007: 6). As the 1990s unfolded, state social work was reframed by an economic and political transformation of a very different order:

> The spectre of racist practice drove the eventual acceptance of a 'whanau', as opposed to a 'professional centred' model for the 1989 legislation (Hyslop, 1997). This was a time of great optimism within the ranks of statutory social workers. For a period at least, one key paradox was resolved; the micro framework of practice could be aligned with the big picture of colonial injustice in Aotearoa/New Zealand, or so it appeared. Suffice to say that, like a Prague Spring, the bicultural idealism of the 1980s was run over, and severely disabled, by a more powerful ideological freight-train: the economic rationalism of the 1990s. (Hyslop, 2007: 6)

The incompatible logics of neoliberalism and 'genuine' biculturalism that emerge from a close reading of Te Ara Hou are a signpost to trouble ahead. The heart of the plan was described as 'the direction to offer bicultural social work services which are consistent with the Treaty of Waitangi and Puao te Ata tu' (Principal Social Worker Unit, 1999: 3). On the other side of the ledger, where the money was apportioned, state sector reform delivered shrinking resources and an evangelical commitment to business-focused managerialism. This agenda severely disrupted the beat of the new heart.

Empowerment and efficiency

Te Ara Hou conflated devolution to iwi with the contracted delivery of government services. Mātua Whāngai positions were to be seconded to iwi authorities or absorbed into mainstream social work roles given that the programme would become a 'way of working for all staff' (Principal Social

Worker Unit, 1999: 4). While it was accepted that this reorientation would require a significant degree of service development, it was also stressed that 'economic downturn' had generated increased social service demand and reduced the resources available.

A greater focus on the roles and responsibilities of service managers was signalled, in order to ensure 'effective and efficient' services within tightly defined contractual arrangements. This efficiency paradigm inevitably generated a focus on control rather than innovation. Strategies for the new social work path were encapsulated in three bland bullet points:

• Raise the standard of social work practice so that it is consistent with the principles of Puao-te-Ata-tu.
• Improve the quality of social work services management.
• Deliver an effective and efficient social work service. (Principal Social Worker Unit, 1999: 7)

As the cliche goes, it does not take a rocket scientist to see the potential contradictions. The 'new Act' required a significant level of material resourcing and social work support to enable and sustain whānau-centred resolutions – the kind of support and development initiatives envisaged in the Mātua Whāngai programme. The concept of empowering families, particularly poor families with high-needs children, was not consistent with the quasi-private sector model of cost-efficient production that was adopted across government services from the late 1980s:

> Current reform of the public service is changing the definition of the business of government departments and also changing the process by which financial allocations are made. Under the new system Cabinet will decide what outcomes it wants from its policies, and Chief Executives then negotiate the 'outputs' each department will deliver in order to achieve the outcomes. (Principal Social Worker Unit, 1999: 9)

Te Ara Hou aspired to devolutionary/locally administered service development within a tight system of central monitoring and control: 'It is intended that from 1991 regional and district managers will have authority to negotiate the extent to which services are delivered directly by social workers or indirectly by funding tribal iwi and community groups' (Principal Social Worker Unit, 1999: 9). A lengthy list of 'corporate tasks' and time-framed 'corporate measures' composed in business model 'corporate-speak' were set out. Ironically, it was also blandly recognised that resources were insufficient to meet current service demand. Accordingly, broad service priorities were selected, and local districts were tasked with planning how these priorities would be met. As with whānau-centred practice, this is an illustration of the 'empowerment without resources and devolution without executive authority' strategy that came to dominate the 1990s.

State social workers are often charged with failing to deliver the vision of PtAT. To a significant extent, it could also be argued that too many social workers kept the faith long after the script was translated into something quite different by a minimalist neoliberal state:

> At the level of casework intervention, the expectation that wider kin groups would assume care of their children was enforced, but the resources needed to successfully discharge this responsibility were often withheld. Over time, this process of demanding responsibility with minimal social assistance has frustrated the intent of the legislation and has, paradoxically, provided the justification for a retreat from the vision of whānau empowerment (Hyslop 2017). (Hyslop and Keddell, 2018: 4)

The struggle to resolve these tensions contributed to the variable, and often poor, quality of service received by those who were constructed as the clients of the state child protection system. Although social workers are well versed in the art of social mediation, positioned as they are between those in need and those with power, some contradictions are irreconcilable.

Practice on the ground

The desire to develop bicultural practice infiltrated office routines and practice processes throughout the 1980s. This intent took varying forms, such as 'culture group' activities, the inclusion of Māori language and the use of **karakia** and **waiata** in formal meetings. Māori motifs were incorporated into workplace design and signage. Staff often adopted the popular Māori-language greeting – '**kia ora**' – to answer the telephone. Many of these actions can be interpreted as tokenistic or even 'colonising'. There was certainly an element of opportunism. For example, I can recall several Pākehā managers, with little in the way of previous links to Māori, opting to wear large bone or pounamu adornments.[1] Excessive demands were often placed on Māori staff to deliver advice or performative cultural expertise (Sorrenson, 1996).

However, to be even-handed, the trappings of biculturalism were easier to realise than the substance, and a passionate commitment to improved cultural understandings and responsiveness was made by many staff. This energy translated into innovative practice in the immediate post-1989 Act environment. As a Pākehā social worker, I had the privilege of providing supervisory support to a team of district office social workers who took responsibility for child protection notifications in relation to Māori children.

Resolution through meetings with extended family without recourse to the more formal FGC process was the preferred practice.

This model of Māori practice teams dealing with Māori 'cases' became relatively common and persisted into the early 2000s in some offices. Although guided by the same legal and practice framework, the practice of rōpū Māori and/or Pasifika teams potentially allowed for a higher level of engagement and trust in situations of risk and family stress. This is not a simple equation, as shared ethnicity can also create a greater level of expectation, which places another layer of demand on worker energy and integrity.

In my experience, state social workers initially pursued the spirit of the new legislation zealously. Although guided by the notion that Māori should and could care for their own, practice methods and outcomes were inconsistent. Initially, social workers were criticised for providing overly generous financial support to whānau, such as transport and accommodation expenses for significant numbers of family members to attend planning meetings. In concert with the economically rationalist turn, a minimalist practice approach was imposed from the early 1990s.

The presumption that children must be returned to family care also resulted in poor outcomes at times, particularly in multi-stressed situations where whānau relationships had been disrupted for some time. The notion that children are best nurtured within their family group was translated into a convenient belief that the transitional and/or therapeutic needs of children would be 'naturally' provided for by parents, grandparents or other whānau caregivers who were not necessarily well prepared for this task.

One of the more significant pragmatic outcomes of PtAT followed from the recommendation that eligibility for the Orphans' Benefit should be extended to cover situations akin to customary whāngai arrangements for the care of children within their wider whānau/hapū networks. In practice, this mechanism was often utilised by social workers to secure the placement of children with grandparents or other related carers when there were concerns about the capacity of parents or the safety of children. On the one hand, children could be supported without the need for care status or oversight. On the other hand, the Unsupported Child Benefit was paid at a lower rate than traditional board payments and the state was absolved of further responsibility.

The philosophy of family empowerment came to be interpreted as avoidance of state responsibility in various ways, including pressuring family members to seek legal orders under the Guardianship Act to secure the safety and security of children when parents were thought to be inadequate. Leaving whānau to resolve problems that are beyond their resources is, of course, not an emancipatory project. Sometimes, in situations of high risk or need, it is necessary for social workers to exercise authority so that the empowerment of whānau can be supported. This reluctance to intervene can also mean that when intervention does occur, it is crisis-driven and disproportionate.

In hindsight, it is hardly surprising that the imperative to avoid responsibility where possible became a dominant driver in statutory child protection practice as the 1990s wore on. The growing political expectation of family autonomy, in combination with rapidly escalating demand and reduced resources, created a perfect storm. Over time, the conflation of whānau empowerment and minimal intervention led to the placement of high-needs children in situations that were often not well planned or supported. As we shall see in relation to the recent Modernising Child, Youth and Family Expert Panel (EP, 2015) review process, the problems that this sort of 'wing and a prayer' practice generated, particularly repeat notifications and placement breakdown, were eventually interpreted as evidence that the vision of the legislation was fundamentally flawed. The genesis of this libellous turn of events is discussed in Chapter 6.

Professional guidance

Child protection practice is a demanding and skilled role undertaken by social workers organised in teams and subject to supervisory oversight. Practice procedures with decision thresholds and alternate pathways based on clinical assessment can obscure the many complexities of this work. Accumulated 'professional' practice knowledge drives practice outcomes to a much greater extent than processes of reform or reorganisation generally recognise (Hyslop, 2009; Ferguson, 2018a, 2018b; Kemp, 2020). Although the system of practice was changed by the CYP&tF Act, the need for specialist knowledge and careful, accountable practice remained.

According to Garlick (2012: 133): 'the Act reduced the function of the social worker to "assistant, facilitator, or coordinator", and restricted the Department to "an enabling role, and perhaps confined it even further as a referral agency or service purchaser"'. However, within this relatively circumscribed ambit, some onerous – at times, life or death decisions – are made in child protection work. Appropriate decision-making can often be a delicate balance. It is influenced by a wide range of dynamics, including service demand and shifting organisational priorities (Keddell and Hyslop, 2019).

An influential set of practice guidelines issued in late 1988 sought to consolidate some key messages in relation to child protection practice (DSW, 1988). In part, this information was developed in response to an independent 1987 review into a tragic death in Auckland: 'The death of a child report (dangerous situations)'.[2] Retrospective practice errors are not difficult to identify, as attested to by the plethora of practice tragedy reviews internationally over the last 40 years. Significantly, given the ethos of the times, it is the shortfalls in cultural understanding that are emphasised in this practice memorandum.

Garlick (2012: 131) is a little more candid about the flavour of this report in the following summary comment:

> The need for a more culturally appropriate service, the report argued, had been 'accepted but without any follow through', resulting in an 'atmosphere of paralysis' amongst staff. It found a 'causal web' linking 'inappropriate front-line decisions with inadequate monitoring, shortfalls in staff levels, a lack of training programmes, a lack of confidence by groups or agencies to challenge DSW decisions on whether abuse was occurring'.

These new practice guidelines recognised the need for a multidisciplinary approach and a nod is given to the work that had gone into developing this orientation. A range of decision-making approaches were presented, but the clear preference was for family conference models. The associated narrative explained the draft bill emphasis on final decision power resting with expert consultants or child protection teams, and described the way in which this emphasis was eclipsed by PtAT.

The professionally challenging detail of how a whānau empowerment lens could be melded with a child protection mandate was the issue that really needed addressing. Although the guidance provided does not confront this central challenge as directly as was needed, the practice information that is presented is commendable. The complexity of the social work role is acknowledged, including the potential for 'dangerous dynamics' and the risk of both over- and under-intervention.

Key procedural steps are outlined in relation to information gathering, assessment, consideration of options, decision-making and review. Detailed processes are set out in relation to 'investigation' planning, specifically, 'sighting' the child and assessment in terms of risk, needs and strengths. The guidelines go on to delineate situations of particular risk and to document elements of key 'knowledge' for child protection, including types/forms of abuse and some discussion of risk indicators. There is a separate detailed section dedicated to the management of child sexual abuse.

The focus is on responses to reported incidents of child abuse, which is not unusual for systems of child protection in the Kempe forensic tradition. The main impact of this official guidance resulted from a set of five key procedural steps that were subsequently posted on site office walls throughout the country:

1. Is the child safe now?
2. Do not work alone.

3. Record, record, record.
4. Least intrusive intervention consistent with the safety of the child.
5. Get help for yourself. (DSW, 1988: 23)

There were some serious unforeseen consequences of this guidance that can be explained with reference to the wider picture.

Political and organisational distortion

In the context of rising demand, a focus on the immediate safety of children within an incident-based investigative frame often fuelled or justified a minimalist approach to practice. This was seriously exacerbated by the politically orchestrated practice climate of maximised throughput: the rapid processing of notifications to the point of closure and no real mechanism for review, barring re-notification. On the shop floor, the officially sanctioned mantra was abbreviated to 'minimal necessary intervention'.

In this climate, the question 'Is the child safe "right" now?' was not difficult to answer in the affirmative in the absence of attention to wider patterns or stresses, and with little or no capacity to provide supportive social work assistance to high-needs families. Ironically, an initiative designed to increase child safety in the child protection system had the opposite effect in practice. This is a 'too often repeated' consequence of attempting to improve practice systems without taking adequate account of the influence of countervailing organisational and policy drivers (Kemp, 2020).

The production model of practice demanded a strict hierarchical process of accounting for the time social workers spent in 'producing' the services that the government was paying them for, so that the efficiency of this process could be measured. Child protection practice management by way of commercial production analogy was a fundamentally flawed process. The varied functions of child protection practice, such as investigation and assessment, FGC work or service to courts, were divided up into discrete sub-outputs and assigned numerical codes. For a brief period in the early 1990s, social workers were required to record exactly which categories of work they were engaged in delivering. I remember irreverently 'inventing' these data for every unit of five minutes or more across the working day. It was a process that had very little correspondence to the reality of a hyperactive multitasking practice environment. It did, however, add something to the increasingly surreal flavour of triage child protection work.

It is difficult to overstate the dysfunctional nature of the practice environment up until the later 1990s (Hyslop, 1997, 2007). Escalating demand pushed the available resources to the front end of immediate safety assessment and intervention. Site offices guarded their geographical boundaries fiercely, often looking to transfer 'cases' whenever possible. Office teams also tended to become defensive, closed and isolated. Youth justice and child protection teams disputed responsibility when young people's needs fitted both categories. All of this was a natural organisational response to unreasonable demand.

Further, other organisations broadly concerned with services to children and young people, such as education and mental health, also became increasingly siloed, being focused solely on the efficient delivery of the core business they were contracted to supply. It was, as suggested, a wicked cocktail of production pressure and expedient practice; in this context, whānau empowerment was often equated with practice decisions that Horatio Nelson would have been proud of (!!).

A systemic problem

Along with the wider income support and community welfare functions of the state, social work has been subject to myriad reviews over the past 30 years, with varying levels of political motivation and impartiality. In Aotearoa, and across the anglophone world, the travails of statutory child protection have prompted a variety of policy shifts over time. As illustrated in Garlick's (2012) account, successive governments have endeavoured to develop solutions for the perceived failings of the system. Many of these exercises have focused on the optimal structure for the provision of statutory practice:

> Between 1986 and 1991, the Department of Social Welfare's Social Work Division was restructured no fewer than four times before being separated out as a 'business unit' of DSW in another restructuring in 1992. The greater operational autonomy of the New Zealand Children and Young Persons Service [NZCYPS] did not herald a new era of stability: NZCYPS was restructured in 1994, and again in 1996, when it was renamed the Children Young Persons and their Families Service. Just a few years later, in January 1999, the Service merged with the Community Funding Agency to become the Children Young Persons and their Families Agency. In October of that year, it was given independent status as the Department of Child, Youth and Family Services. That department was restructured in 2000, 2002 and 2004 before its merger with the Ministry of Social Development (accompanied by another restructuring) in 2006. (Garlick, 2012: 9)

Numerous other reporting exercises have examined the appropriate direction and/or preferred priorities for child protection social work, including practice reviews prompted by deaths of children in care or otherwise 'known' to the system. State social work was subject to a near-continuous process of review between 2011 and 2015, culminating in a stand-alone Ministry of Children (Oranga Tamariki [OT]) in 2017 (Hyslop and Keddell, 2019). The future of this arrangement is hotly contested at the time of writing, as canvassed in Chapter 7 of this book.

The 1992 'business-unit' restructuring referred to earlier was a significant ideological realignment of the DSW, in that it:

> embodied the principles of the state sector reforms, which distinguished between managerial accountability for outputs and political accountability for outcomes and emphasised operational efficiency and accountability. The Department was comprehensively reconfigured. Two decades earlier it had been conceived as providing all New Zealanders with a broad range of intersecting welfare services underpinned by centralised planning. Now its three discrete units were to deliver – as cheaply as possible – a modest safety net of essential services to only the most disadvantaged. (Garlick, 2012: 145)

The creation of a separate enterprise specifically dedicated to the practice of youth justice and care or protection under the 1989 Act coincided with a ministerial review into the early operation of the legislation. The Mason Review (Mason, 1992) was critical of the DSW's lack of transparency and of staff competence, highlighting procedural shortcomings such as the failure to consult with care and protection resource panels. It recommended a refocusing on the child protection task and suggested the first of many subsequent adjustments to the whānau-centric focus of the Act, specifically, that the original principle, which stated that the interests of the child would take precedence when there was a conflict with the interests of the family, should be amended to clearly restate the paramountcy principle – that the interests of the child should be the first and paramount consideration. Judge Mason also delivered the following portentous message:

> If the Act is not generously supported in terms of personnel and funding, it will fail. Resourcing the Act is an expensive business but the consequences of not doing so will be even more expensive. In human, social and economic terms our New Zealand community, long-term, will reap the rewards of a generosity of spirit and pocket. (Garlick, 2012: 154)

As explored in earlier commentary, this was not the road that was taken. Rigid expenditure limits were imposed on FGC outcomes, and all interventions were costed to tight financial plans.

Child protection revisited

A complex mix of generative forces saw public and media concern about child abuse rise throughout the 1990s. The structural adjustment process of privatising state services, tight contracting with third-party providers and the imposition of business-style accountabilities on direct services effectively meant that less support was provided to families in need. As suggested, whānau Māori were expected to step up to their 'cultural responsibilities' and care for wider kin in this hostile administrative climate. On top of this, the imposition of market forces in terms of higher rents for state houses, job losses and benefit cuts generated widespread social suffering.

The burden of economic reform fell disproportionately on those with the least material and social capital, as it inevitably does in deregulated capitalist economies. In this context, it is very likely that the incidence of child maltreatment increased. The increased visibility of poverty and associated symptoms of family distress also tends to raise the rate of child welfare notifications from allied health and education professionals. Finally, in combination with intense media scrutiny, a series of reviews into the deaths of children beginning in the 1990s raised challenging questions about the capacity of the system:

> According to NZCYPS practice manager Craig Smith, these 'painted a stark picture' of 'patterns of practice and organisational failure', including: 'Lack of clarity about statutory role, poor or absent supervision, breakdowns in communications between workers, sites and interagency, inadequate recording, an incident focus with failure to recognise abusive patterns, an inadequate knowledge base, an unstable organisational context, information-gathering with little analysis or assessment and failure to protect.' (Craig Smith, quoted in Garlick, 2012: 176)

In an increasingly overwhelmed bureaucratic environment, an approach of minimal necessary intervention had translated into incident-focused and triage-driven practice. I have suggested that this orientation arose out of practical necessity. However, as Bradley (1997) observes, this necessity arose from the policy settings adopted by the state. Bradley (1997: 3) contrasts the potential for an 'empowerment approach', involving a more equitable distribution of resources 'and non-exploitive relationships between people', with the reductionist approach that was adopted:

> This occurs by targeting the most serious abuse notifications and reducing the level of risk to individual children and young people through using minimum intervention strategies. Whanau, hapu and

iwi wellbeing is not advanced through this practice approach. Success is based on how well the method was adhered to rather than the extent to which the client's welfare and well-being was promoted.

Within this schema, tragic events did prompt systemic changes in terms of tighter prescribed liaison with the police in cases of serious abuse and the incorporation of a formal risk estimation system (RES) template into the computerised assessment and intervention recording process from late 1996.[3] Although such instruments have their limitations, particularly the narrow focus on the risk posed by individual 'perpetrators', they do encourage wider consideration of abuse recurrence and severity.

Risk rating tools are best used as part of wider systemic assessment processes, with appropriate attention to family strengths and possibilities (Salomen and Sturmfels, 2011). They also do little to prescribe the most effective form of intervention or assistance in any given risk situation. More importantly, in a compliance-focused environment, timely completion of the administrative process becomes the dominant practice measure. From my own experience, the supervisory question became 'Have you completed the RES for the purposes of case sign-off?', rather than 'How useful was the exercise?'

Much of the nature of child protection social work is conditioned by the practice environment. The workplace context of long task lists, the continuous balancing of home visiting with recording, meetings and consultations of all descriptions, unpredictable case work crises of varying scales, and the constant expectation to process existing work in order to pick up new work is critical to understanding the hazards and limitations of modern child protection bureaucracies:

> A large helping of irreverence should be included in every social worker's survival kit. Resilience is, in part, a mindset; almost an acquired methodology. I often describe effective practice as akin to the progress of an acrobat along a beam. Within this metaphor is the notion of nurturing the ability to remount the apparatus – falling off goes with the territory. I must have supervised scores, perhaps a hundred or so practitioners over time, who in turn provided services to thousands of clients. I encountered social workers of all shapes and forms. I pondered over thousands of practice strategies, read tens of thousands of case notes, often in my own time – such is the consuming, perhaps compulsive and addictive, nature of statutory child protection. (Hyslop, 2007: 7)

This fast-paced 'hell's kitchen' practice atmosphere may have peaked in the late 1990s, but it has never completely dissipated. Statutory child protection is generally practised against an imperative background of rush and time scarcity. It employs a predominantly female workforce, at least below the supervisory level, and the culture tends to be infused with values of selflessness and sacrifice.

Good systems can provide a healthy balance of challenge and support for social workers, as well as opportunities for careful reflection (Ferguson, 2018a). Office and practice team cultures can shield workers from burnout given that the practically and morally challenging nature of the work is not necessarily well understood outside of the workplace. However, workplaces can also become unhealthy systems, prone to siege mentality and averse to constructive critique (Morrison, 1997).

It is important to grasp the influence of this context of hurry and strife when trying to understand the effect of higher-level policy shifts or changes to operational systems and objectives. As Kemp's (2020) recent research in the South Australian context has highlighted, well-intentioned efforts to reform or improve the safety of child protection systems are often counterproductive, merely adding another layer of work and further compromising professional decision-making. In my view, over time, those in charge of new initiatives and practice developments have seldom appreciated the nature of the beast they are grappling with (Hyslop, 2009). Social work is interactive relational practice, conditioned as much by emotional intelligence as by the completion of task-driven procedures, recording templates or allegiance to idealist practice frameworks (Morrison, 2007).

Shifting policy responses

Since the mid-1990s, political and managerial responses to the challenges of state social work have taken varying forms, sometimes specific to the dynamics of child protection but always coloured by deeper ideological currents. In 1993, an external review concluded that there was insufficient systematic evidence to clearly demonstrate workload increases in state social work. The NZCYPS was significantly reorganised from early 1994 under the watch of then Director General Margaret Bazley, a senior career public servant with a reputation for astute management (Keenan, 1995: 28).

This restructuring exercise resulted in the replacement of social work-experienced General Manager Robyn Wilson with Griff Page, an experienced port administrator. The idea that generic managerial functions are directly transferable to niche public service specialisms is a key part of orthodox neoliberal state sector reform. It is a practice that has resurfaced with a vengeance in the complex contemporary reorganisation of child protection within the current Ministry of Children (OT). An understanding of the minutiae and nuance of practice is seen as having little relevance to the task of managing for results.

As suggested, political and managerial initiatives to redefine practice priorities have seldom taken adequate heed of the constraints imposed by workload demands, resource shortfalls and the conflicting pressures associated with child protection practice. A rebranding to the Children Young Persons and their Families Service (CYPFS) in May 1996 was designed to signal a refocusing on the provision of wider family support-based practice. A merger between the Community Funding Agency and the CYPFS in January 1999 created the Children, Young Persons, and their Families Agency. A new prevention-focused vison – 'early help' – was introduced in mid-1999, which seemed particularly farcical at a time when practitioners were overwhelmingly engaged in crisis-driven triage.

Biculturalism: lost in translation

Margaret Bazley also promoted a recommitment to bicultural practice with the release of an aspirational policy document: 'Te Punga o Matahorua – Our bicultural strategy for the nineties' (DSW, 1994). Keenan (1995) notes that Te Punga was informed by in-house staff consultation and did not have the wider community reach of PtAT. He argues that the stated commitment to Te Tiriti o Waitangi is deceptive because it was rooted in the shallow interpretation encompassed by the Crown's narrow 'principles of the Treaty' approach. This state-sponsored realignment of the meaning of the treaty was arguably an attempt to tame and minimise its potential implications for Māori self-determination: 'As a consequence of these "principles", Social Welfare's commitment to Māori people was in the end significantly diminished' (Keenan, 1995: 30).

More than this, there was a yawning gap between this policy commitment and the reality of practice as I have described it here. Sorrenson's (1996) research into responses to Māori needs in the restructured state sector suggests that local managers struggled to clearly grasp and implement this sort of strategic affirmation. He notes the apparent difficulty 'in translating intensions into actions. There was, for example, significant difference between what was written into major organisational documents such as planning papers or mission statements and what actually occurred in day to day practice' (Sorrenson, 1996: 122–3).

The following excerpt from an interview with a local manager may mask a deficiency in individual commitment, but it also appears to speak to a sense of genuine uncertainty, confusion and disillusionment: 'Again, it is like the other one ... it's token. ... It's fairly shallow policy really, with no real desire by the department to follow through on it ... no ... the desire might be there but the ability to do so isn't because of funding and other resources needed' (Sorrenson, 1996: 122). Garlick's (2012: 233) appraisal of a further pledge to advance the interests of Māori in the crisis-saturated state social work environment of the early 2000s speaks volumes:

> A strategy for Māori, 'Te Pounamu', had been published in 2001, but it is hard to reconcile its rhetoric with evidence of its practical impact. Though it described itself as a 'turning point in our history', an implementation plan for this strategy had still not been approved two years later.

This disjunction is graphically demonstrated by the substantive failure to develop the Iwi Social Services envisaged in the CYP&tF Act.

Iwi social services

Alongside the restated commitment to a bicultural practice vision, the DSW also made a commitment to have functioning iwi social services in place by the year 2000. A complex confluence of practical, institutional and political barriers effectively stymied this process. Bradley (1997) highlights the absence of clearly defined (or agreed) standards or procedures for the registration of iwi social services and the default position of potential iwi providers choosing to operate under a more straightforward classification as 'child and family support services'. He argues that the Community Funding Agency set up convoluted approval processes that acted as a 'shield to discourage potential applicants' (Bradley, 1997: 4).

Supposedly ring-fenced funds for iwi development arising from the closure of institutions and disestablishment of the Mātua Whāngai programme did not eventuate:

> In the meantime, funding is weighted at the end of the continuum to support the practice of CYFS's [Child, Youth and Family Services] providing stranger or alternative care to mokopuna (Maori grandchildren). The practice incentive is that these professional caregiving organisations derive an income by providing alternative care for mokopuna instead of the funding being directed to whanau, hapu and iwi well-being through Iwi Social Services or (Maori) Cultural Social Services. (Bradley, 1997: 4)

Despite targets for progress being set and affirmation of the related aim of identifying 'outputs and resources for devolution', in 1999, 'the Department acknowledged that the target of contracting with all 54 priority iwi would not be met, "new models" of service delivery for Māori [had] not emerged, and frameworks for measuring outcomes for Māori were yet to be developed' (Garlick, 2012: 184).

The August 1999 Cox–Irwin Review of Iwi Social Services Strategy strikes a bemused note in the following description of the process: 'a cyclical series of initiatives in policy with a focus on process followed by periods of inactivity, with lack of substantive progress, followed by further initiatives and accompanying faltering of achievement' (Cox and Irwin, 1999: 15). The lack of effective strategic planning was underpinned by a failure to confront and address underlying tensions in the relationship between Māori and the state.

The post-PtAT bicultural commitment was not directed at establishing autonomous Māori institutions; rather, it was concerned with countering the assimilationist past by infusing Pākehā institutions with Māori values. Increasingly, this focus was confined within a centrally controlled business model paradigm. By the mid-2000s, the situation was still far from satisfactory. Doolan (2005: 27) summarised progress as follows:

> Iwi Social Service organisations exist, few of whom act as independent statutory authorities as the law permits, and there is no effective geographical network of them. No Cultural Social Services organisation exists at all. This seems, on the face of it, a significant failure of legislative intent. There is no doubt that CYFS has devoted considerable effort to this issue, but the results are not encouraging.

At the risk of oversimplification, the root problem appears to be the same conflict of interest and perspective that has always troubled the relationship between Māori and the settler state: questions of power and authority and the efforts of successive governments to fit a square peg into a round hole, specifically, in this instance, to confine Māori social service aspirations within a top-down contracting framework:

> It seems unlikely that the designers of the statute introduced the provision for Iwi Social Services with the intention of having such organisations behave in the same way as the state. Indeed, the very essence of the vision of Puao-te-Ata-tu and the Act is that Iwi Social Services will act differently, providing services that are nested in the values, customs, and beliefs of Māori. (Doolan, 2005: 31)

At the level of strategic governance, the crux of the problem has not changed. Regardless of political complexity, it is necessary for the policy implications of rangatiratanga to be meaningfully negotiated with Māori, as opposed to the platitudinous repetition of treaty commitments in strategic plans. As discussed in Chapter 7, this challenge has raised its head once again in the contemporary furore about racist practice outcomes and the need for meaningful devolution to Māori. Chapter 6 explores the political genesis of this current crisis of legitimacy.

Cycles of crisis and review

Limits of the efficient production state

Weaknesses in the Aotearoa model of state sector reform became widely apparent from the mid-1990s. A narrow focus on the core business of separate government departments undermined intersectoral cooperation. It also tended to obscure the public ownership interest in state services. These issues were highlighted in an influential report prepared for the State Services Commission and Treasury by American public economist Allen Schick (1996). While politically sympathetic to the aims and intentions of market-driven reform, this report highlighted the way in which a preoccupation with short-term efficiency had undermined strategic capacity (Schick, 1996: 53). Efficient 'output' delivery needed to be tempered with a focus on desired 'outcomes'.

The Strengthening Families (SF) programme from 1997 was a response to the silo effect of the efficiency paradigm. It aimed to promote client-centred dialogue and service integration for families with needs spread across a range of services. Independent coordinators were charged with convening SF meetings to facilitate inter-agency dialogue and cooperation. There are echoes here with the more recent children's teams approach envisaged by the 'White Paper' on vulnerable children's reforms discussed later in this chapter.

Organisational capacity was a barrier to implementing the SF project at the practice level. The scheme relied on the assumption of intersectoral cooperation without any allocation of personnel resource (beyond the coordinator positions) or any increase in local agency funding. State agencies were all stretched to capacity and, as with the child protection team initiatives of the 1980s, any serious exercise of coercive authority in situations of risk fell, by default, to statutory social workers.

Labour's social development agenda

It is important to contextualise the developing saga of 'crisis, review and reorganisation' within the broader economic and political milieu. The late 1990s were witness to something of a turning point in the doctrinaire 'more market/less government' agenda associated with the first decade of the neoliberal turn. However, neoliberalism was adapted and modified rather than abandoned in the three-term period of Labour-led government from

2000 to 2009. The political notion of a 'Third Way' transitioned mainstream anglophone 'Labour' parties into a stance closer to the traditional 'centre' of liberal politics (Chatterjee, 1999). It was accepted that the working-class population needed to adapt to the new disciplines that flowed from economic globalisation and that the state had a role in supporting and encouraging this accommodation.

Much of the policy agenda of the Helen Clark Labour-led governments mirrored the politics of New Labour in the UK (Hyslop, 2017). The social policy function of the state had been relegated to pariah status within the dogmatic market primacy ethos of the 1990s. Aspirational planning enjoyed a renaissance in the 2000s, with an expanded role for the Ministry of Social Policy, which became an independent organisation after the dismantling of the DSW.

The raft of strategic policy documents produced in this period tended to be preoccupied with goal setting and sector coordination in line with the strategic objectives of government. It appeared that the production of these documents served as a proxy for the development and resourcing of social programmes – stated policy agendas served as a cypher for tangible outcomes. The funding of new programmes or the expansion of old ones, as in the case of the Family Start high-needs parent support programme or the Social Work in Schools (SWIS) initiative, tended to be cautiously implemented and evaluated.

In a comparable vein, the Department of Child, Youth and Family Services (CYF) produced a range of operational planning papers in relation to the achievement of results in key areas set by the government. The jargon-filled business plans of this period seem to effortlessly span the contradictions that flow from the competing aims: applying practice tools, monitoring practice quality, recommitting to PtAT and promoting partnerships and community leadership while working harder to keep children within families and placing them outside of the family more effectively.

'Social development' was the umbrella label applied to Aotearoa's version of the Third Way model. It focused on the broad notion of social exclusion as a function of an unproductive economy, as opposed to the 'old' Labour analysis which recognised inequality as a function of capitalist economics (Lunt, 2010):

> In retrospect, the 'social development' agenda adopted by the three-term Labour-led coalition administrations (1999–2008) represented something of a holding pattern. Third-way rhetoric contained little reference to the redistribution of wealth and the pre-eminence of competitive globalised markets was accepted as a fait accompli. There was some account taken of the need for supply-side adjustments to make people work-ready. (Hyslop, 2017: 1808)

As per the line of critique developed by commentators in the UK (Featherstone et al, 2014; Parton, 2014a), it can be argued that the populationist approaches that informed Third Way thinking paved the way for more punitive policy responses, particularly to the underclass poor. The focus on identifying groups in need of targeted enablement shifted to a focus on disciplining the recalcitrant when subsequently adapted to the politics of the centre-right, specifically, in Aotearoa, the social investment ideology of the three-term National-led governments from 2009 to 2017 (Hyslop and Keddell, 2019).

The Brown review and new directions

Historically, across anglophone 'report and investigate' child protection systems, inquiries into child deaths have tended to document similar practice shortcomings and to propose similar remedies. However, efforts to address these issues through interagency cooperation, practice monitoring, procedural compliance and safe practice guidance have not provided the desired remedy. Kemp (2020: 241–2) argues that an inability to grasp the applied practice roots of child protection often leads to counterproductive solutions:

> As has been discussed in this thesis, practice must be contextualised organisationally, politically and socially, and it is within these realms that powerful social forces push solution finding in child protection in a direction which is antagonistic to the very idea of applied practice. With the centrifugal forces of neoliberalism, New Public Management and risk aversion, what rises to the top is not (as so often proclaimed) a renewed trust in practice wisdom, judgement, discretion and experience, but a sustained belief in the safety of standardised, proceduralised, simplified and sanitised responses.

The June 2000 report of the Office of the Commissioner for Children into the death of James Whakaruru said little that had not been said before. CYF was criticised for a lack of both 'professional' child protection awareness and cultural expertise, that is, for failing to take protective action or develop supportive whānau-centred solutions. The following is taken from the executive summary:

> The investigation found that poor interagency communication characterised the professional work with James and his family. Agencies worked without reference to each other and ended their involvement, assuming that other parts of the system would protect James. Some workers seemed unaware of the indicators of a child at risk or did not appreciate the role they needed to play to ensure his safety and wellbeing.

There was little if any attempt to engage culturally appropriate services, or to address the situation in the context of wider whanau, hapu and iwi. (Office of the Commissioner for Children, 2000: 1)

This report coincided with a period of heightened public anxiety over, and media exposure of, alleged practice shortfalls in relation to the deaths of several other children. Escalating notifications meant that 'cases' were triaged, with many left unallocated for long periods. Investigations were often superficial and 'closure-driven'. Perceptions of crisis led to a ministerial review of child protection procedures, commissioned from Judge Michael (Mick) Brown. Brown's (2000) criticisms were substantive and wide-ranging, recognising that under-resourcing had resulted in reactive and crisis-driven social work. The report located the genesis of this situation in the competitive business model approach of the previous decade and recommended a return to a participatory community framework consistent with PtAT:

According to Brown, the 'efficiency drive' of the 1990s had broken down the interface between government agencies, and the limited funding available to community organisations had led to a competitive approach which had inhibited co-operation and interaction. Brown argued that the public responsibility for care and protection should be more widely distributed; CYF needed to 'share the load' and co-operate more with other agencies, particularly in carrying out the non-statutory aspects of child welfare work. He urged the government to revisit the Puao-te-Ata-tu report, consider re-establishing the participatory mechanisms that had been set up in response to it, and evaluate the role, effectiveness and reporting lines of Care and Protection Resource Panels. (Garlick, 2012: 229)

The minister responded with the launch of a fresh development strategy under the banner 'New Directions'. According to Garlick (2012: 220), Minister Steve Maharey maintained that targeted social spending could produce economic benefits and that enhanced community relationships could release entrepreneurial energy and develop social capital. This communitarian emphasis on an idealised role for civil society also resonates with the liberal heritage of charity and neighbourly help as substitutes for state services and programmes, for example, the 'Big Society' thinking later associated with the Conservative politics of David Cameron in the UK (Parton, 2014a). Minister Maharey favoured the concept of strengthening communities as opposed to merely strengthening families. This became the preferred direction of travel for CYF in the early 2000s.

Under the 'New Directions' package, a funding injection aimed to support a focus on longer-term outcomes for children and families. This initiative included spending on staff competency, training and partnerships with non-government organisations (NGOs). However, the gap between policy rhetoric and operational reality continued to assume Shakespearian proportions. As indicated, the operational arm of CYF had little capacity to manage the kind of transition that was envisaged. As it was, the immediate challenge of responding safely to the sharp 'high-risk' end of practice inevitably generated a reduction in the quality of service to children and young people in state care:

> Two years into the change programme, the influence of many of the New Directions projects remained confined to head office; those intended to significantly change social work practice had failed to bear fruit. Though it was the centrepiece of the New Directions strategy, progress on a project to implement a 'strengths-based, outcome-focused' approach to social work was slow. By late 2001 there was a design proposal, a project plan, and a report on best practice models and tools – but more than a year later, little further had happened, and New Directions was behind schedule. (Garlick, 2012: 223)

In 2003, a further 'First principles baseline review' (Ministry of Social Development, 2003) coincided with revelations about more child deaths and apparent practice errors. This review argued that the objectives and responsibilities of CYF were too wide and ill-defined, and identified that strategies to resolve earlier deficiencies in workload management and high-risk responses had led to further systemic problems:

> Much of this variability, the review argued, could be attributed to the pressure CYF was under to minimise the number of unallocated cases and improve the timeliness of investigations, which had led managers to privilege quantity over quality. Not only did this reinforce the perception of front-line staff that the organisation did not value quality social work practice, it also risked additional pressure through renotifications. Because of the volume of work, more time was being spent on investigation, at the expense of other areas of social work and with a cost in morale and staff turnover. (Garlick, 2012: 235)

A focus on priority outcomes, service quality, improved information systems and organisational capability was recommended, and considerable corporate effort was made to streamline systems to this effect.

Strategic responses to risk and overload

From mid-2004, CYF began to develop the concept of community/non-government social service organisations providing direct or delegated assessment and intervention services in situations of lower prima facie risk. Practice strategies of this nature were developed in similar jurisdictions overseas (Waldegrave and Coy, 2005). In part, such initiatives provide a means of managing excessive demand. However, the notion of partnered or differential response is also informed by the idea that NGO social services are better able to develop relationships of support and trust, particularly in situations of need rather than acute risk. The CYP&tF Act was subsequently amended to allow for the development of differing assessment pathways in response to incoming reports of concern to the National Contact Centre (Hanna, 2008), and a formal operational 'differential response model' was rolled out in 2008.[1]

There are challenges with differential response models in terms of funding, interface management and the tendency of risk and need to be fluid and intertwined. In addition, the post-intake management of notifications can be uncertain given that families are under no obligation to engage with services offered by community agencies. However, this initiative did reduce statutory workload. CYF was merged with the Ministry of Social Development in 2007, partly as a way of rationalising corporate activities and sharing expertise in system development. The other strategy for managing overload from the later 2000s involved tighter managerial scrutiny of site-specific performance measures and regional or national oversight of casework practice in situations deemed high-risk in terms of safety or organisational credibility. At the 'care' end of the practice continuum, efforts were made to move children from foster-care situations to stable long-term guardianship arrangements. Associated concerns with vulnerability, child-centred practice and early permanency were to be a harbinger of things to come.

The child protection system underwent further lengthy, disjointed and highly politicised processes of review under National-led governments from 2011 to 2015 (Hyslop and Keddell, 2019). The 'transformational agenda' outlined in the final report of the Modernising Child, Youth and Family Expert Panel (EP, 2015) did not settle the matter by a long chalk. Debate over the appropriate direction of child protection reform in Aotearoa continues to rage into the third decade of the 21st century.

Moral panic and populist politics

The trajectory of the reform process came to be associated with a rejuvenated neoliberal/neoconservative agenda for the management of problem populations and, more recently, with a subsequent backlash regarding the racist consequences of this policy turn. The initial genesis of this extended period of review arose from populist political responses to media-driven public anxiety generated by a series of child deaths through the mid-2000s. The parallels with comparable events in the English setting are clear.

However, in Aotearoa, a series of tragic events related to Māori children was linked to the demonisation of a class of morally threatening, brown-skinned beneficiaries: 'Between 1989 and the present, the racialised child protection narrative has transformed from a focus on the damage done to Māori children by state violence to the cost visited upon the state and wider society by dangerous families' (Hyslop, 2017: 1809). This discursive turn to a punitive focus on an undisciplined underclass was arguably the starting point for the contemporary political rhetoric around 'our vulnerable children' and 'our' most vulnerable citizens. Significantly, the site of this vulnerability is generally associated with individual and family deficit rather than economically generated social suffering. An agenda for inclusive capitalism is seen to have a duty to reform the threatening and afflicted.

The target of fear and loathing was explicitly racialised. Hackell (2016) explores the political dimensions of the fantasy of a 'savage' Māori underclass, arguing that this construction operated as a convenient means of concealing the inequalities produced through neoliberal political economy. She highlights the media frenzy following the death of the Kahui twins as follows:[2]

> A clear parallel can be drawn with the Baby Peter Connolly furore in England: The Government was able to appear to respond decisively to the child abuse case 'that had traumatised New Zealanders' ... while at the same time narrow the operational focus of child protection agencies away from recognition of the multiple and complex causes of child abuse towards a more singular focus on policing welfare populations. (Hackell, 2016: 869)

Provan (2012) links this popular politics of disgust and punishment to the fragility and centrality of liberal Pākehā nationalism in Aotearoa.

Ontological insecurity: Māori mothers and Pākehā identity

Provan's (2012) doctoral research offers a provocative critique of the drivers of Pākehā nationalism. She argues that the history of colonial dispossession that underpins contemporary middle-class Pākehā privilege (and subliminal guilt) is constantly repressed through the reproduction of benign, depoliticised cultural mythology: 'This endlessly unstable system haunts the nation, an uncanny reminder of the rift on which the nation is founded. The notion of a unified nation is constantly destabilised, rendered endlessly uncomfortable' (Provan, 2012: 121). By applying this psychoanalytic lens to a range of non-fiction texts, such as television programmes, advertisements, opinion columns, editorials and letters to the editor, Provan (2012) identifies the way in which the search for a simple and comfortable national 'Kiwi' identity is inevitably undermined by the shadow of a violent colonial past, with all of its disturbing ties to contemporary inequality – a continuous Freudian repression of the irrepressible:

> Within Pākehā nationalism, a nostalgic vision of a unified, innocent, childlike nation is used as a defence against undesired knowledge of national disunity. National discomforts, which are generated by the impossibility of repressing the nation's history, are projected onto those assigned an abject position in the nation. As a result of this process of projection, mediated by the association of national identity with childhood and home, the fantasised figure of the 'bad Māori mother' emerges as the ultimate uncanny element within the nation. (Provan, 2012: 4)

Provan (2012: 33, 42) connects the vehement demonisation of women whose children have died from abusive injuries with an existential need to restore and preserve a banal, sanitised nationalism. The concept of projected anxiety provides a powerful analytic tool when applied to the central place of the 'abused Māori child' in state responses to the 'national' issue of child protection. This psycho-symbolic linkage goes a long way towards explaining the zealotry associated with the child protection reform process from 2011 to 2015.

Critical appraisal of the way in which child abuse tragedies were represented in the popular press in the mid- to late 2000s reveals the dominant construction of child abuse as a 'Māori problem' (Provan, 2012: 204). In the same breath, these crimes against 'our children' are perpetrated by an 'other' who has no place in our wholesome nation. Provan (2012: 186) characterises severe child abuse as a uniquely 'nationed' crime, specifically developing the connection between vehement expressions of revulsion and the aberrant place of Māori in an imagined Pākehā nation:

> I will explore the ways this projection of abjection, of filth, of death-bringing, is particularly cast onto Māori women, or onto a terrifying fantasy of the Māori mother. I will highlight the way in which all of these accusations are at play in the cases of Māori women whose partners kill their children. From this, I will examine the way in which the cluster of accusations against these women betrays, beyond disgust at violence against the helpless, a deep anxiety about the nation. The image of the 'bad Māori mother', the 'mother who failed to protect', carries with it, I will argue, all that is uncanny, 'un-homely' within the nation, everything that should be hidden that continually comes to light. Ultimately, I will argue that 'the mother who failed to protect' stands accused of failing to protect Pākehā from knowing about all that

is unwanted within the nation, about all that prevents the fantasised 'homelike' nation from being possible. (Provan, 2012: 188–9)

Populist print media of the time was prone to eugenic rhetoric, while dismissing issues of poverty and systemic racism. Colonisation is particularly unspeakable because of the ontological threat that it poses to idealised New Zealand nationhood. This anxiety is projected onto the folk-devil image of the Māori mother. As demonstrated in the following discussion of the extended National-led child protection reform process, Provan's analysis resonates in the dismissal of an association between poverty and child abuse, and in the emotive appeal to embrace all of 'our vulnerable children' to the bosom of a mythical and comforting middle New Zealand.

Green and White Papers

The review process(es) under National Ministers Paula Bennett and Anne Tolley, respectively, can be clearly demarcated. The initial Vulnerable Children (VC) reform process was rapidly followed by the Modernising Child Protection (MCP) exercise (Hyslop and Keddell, 2019). The VC reforms began with a wide-ranging cross-sectoral Green Paper discussion document that included consideration of the socio-economic stresses impacting on family life in Aotearoa (Ministry of Social Development, 2011). However, the resultant White Paper (Ministry of Social Development, 2012) was a far narrower and ideologically confined piece of work. The simplistic and politically populist position of 'getting tough' on child abusers is overtly signalled by Minister Bennett in the Foreword to the White Paper report: 'Though I acknowledge the pressure that financial hardship puts on families, that is never an excuse to neglect, beat, or abuse children. Most people in such circumstances do not abuse their children, and I cannot tolerate it being used as a justification to do so' (Ministry of Social Development, 2012: 2).

An overriding emphasis on individual responsibility is clearly disconnected from any consideration of the structural factors that may impact upon family well-being and parenting capacity. A limited range of preconceptions about the child protection system in Aotearoa and the changes needed to enhance child safety informed the White Paper project:

However, the notion that 'something must be done' is seldom a successful reform platform if causation (the nature of the problem to be addressed) is not adequately delineated. In this case, despite extensive evidence to the contrary, the problem of child abuse was simplistically connected with 'bad' individuals who could be 'caught' through increased surveillance. According to this logic, a solution could be achieved through extensive safety checking of the professionals working with children and the use of data modelling to identify families at risk. (Hyslop and Keddell, 2019: 103)

The legal framework generated from this project (the Vulnerable Children's Act 2014) is primarily concerned with protecting children by developing the capacity to identify and catch 'abusers' through enhanced workforce surveillance and communication between agencies. Although there was a shift of focus in the subsequent MCP exercise, there are also significant points of ideological commonality. There is little or no recognition of the complex relational craft of applied social work practice in child protection (Hyslop, 2009). If anything, the VC reform package backgrounds social work, emphasising the detection and policing role of statutory practice. Two significant assumptions are implicit in the following excepts. First, child abuse is perpetrated by 'different' and dangerous others, not good ordinary, decent, 'everyday Kiwis' like 'us': 'Better and smarter use of the information government already holds can help us focus on children who are really vulnerable, reducing the chances that a child in need will be missed, or that an everyday family will be incorrectly labelled as being at risk' (Ministry of Social Development, 2012: 11). Second, state social workers are associated with the spectre of authority, being an enforcement agency that the recalcitrant can be reported to: 'Where parents refuse to participate in the process, and where concerns are sufficient to indicate that children may be in need of care and protection, the option of referrals to Child, Youth and Family will remain. Parents will be made aware of this possibility' (Ministry of Social Development, 2012: 64).

As will be explained, the change of political emphasis to a specific social investment frame of reference in the MCP Expert Panel review was a significant revisioning. However, both exercises are consistent with a broad neoliberal agenda, albeit with an overlay of moral conservatism. As argued in the introductory chapters of this book, the perennial liberal analysis of individuated cause and effect has consistently dominated social policy in the settler state of Aotearoa.

Vulnerable children

The VC reforms were influenced by racialised moral panic and informed by medico-scientific understandings of individual pathology, diagnosis and cure. The 'problem' of child protection is associated with the shortcomings of social work and the risk posed by a dangerous group of people. The systemic problems that directly resulted from policy confusion, misguided managerial prescriptions and under-resourcing are rendered invisible in this analysis. The underlying issue of rampant social inequality is not regarded as relevant:

As suggested, the White Paper pays minimal attention to the socio-political context of child protection. Specifically, there is no analysis of the relationship between the suggested group of dangerous families and the socio-economic form within which this apparent underclass is produced. The influence of social inequality – the structural reasons for the increasingly unequal distribution of material and emotional hardship – is absent from the text. (Hyslop, 2013a: 7)

The White Paper is also politically constructed in less blatant ways. Economically generated social suffering resulting from inadequate income, crowded and substandard housing, deprived neighbourhoods, food insecurity, and associated emotional and relationship pressures are all backgrounded, apart from references to the importance of paid work and the ever-present danger of benefit dependency:

> Material hardship and financial stress could, for instance, be constructed as unifying concepts in relation to child vulnerability rather than simply recorded as a minor sub-heading amongst a list of contributing factors. Anti-social behaviour, criminality, addiction and mental health issues, are all disproportionately prevalent/visible amongst the economically disadvantaged. (Hyslop, 2013a: 7)

The White Paper also generated the idea of future children being taken from parents when a previous child has been removed: 'there is an expectation that the child will be removed from the care of the parents, unless it can be shown that this is not in the best interests of the child' (Ministry of Social Development, 2012: 8). This authoritarian assumption resulted in an amendment to child protection law, popularly referred to as the 'subsequent child provision(s)'. It alters the standard of proof for child removal and flies in the face of fundamental social work precepts about equality of rights and the innate capacity for humans to develop and change their behaviour.

Finally, the White Paper repeatedly refers to the desirability of 'evidence-based' programmes and practices. This is a reductive approach concerned with efficiency and effectiveness. It is superficially persuasive, but it conceals the way in which 'evidence' is applied creatively in the engaged and interactive 'doing' of social work in child protection practice. This is clearly captured by Munro (2011b: 92) in her critical review of child protection in England:

> In practice the application of evidence involves a flexible/discretionary matching of intervention to the needs of clients in their particular circumstances: Here it is used in the broader sense of drawing on the best available evidence to inform practice at all stages of the work and of integrating that evidence with the social worker's own understanding of

the child and family's circumstances and their values and preferences. It is 'not simply a case of taking an intervention off the shelf and applying it to a child and family'.

The ascendancy of evidence-based practice is not unrelated to the context of neoliberalism, managerial measurement and the standardisation of practice (Grey and McDonald, 2006; Pease, 2010):

> Selective recourse to scientific research highlighted the detrimental consequences of abusive experiences and the importance of identifying and combatting adult pathology, while downplaying extensive research concerning the socio-contextual contributors to child abuse ... VC policy reform focused on cooperation and information sharing among professionals engaged with children's services, including a loosely coordinated (and still active) 'children's team' initiative, formal safety check vetting of 'the children's workforce' and the requirement for agencies working with children to develop more robust abuse recognition and reporting policies. (Hyslop and Keddell, 2019: 103)

In something of an oppositional, or at least 'parallel', process, the Office of the Chief Social Worker and the Public Service Association published a carefully researched 'Workload and caseload review' (Office of the Chief Social Worker, 2014): 'This document identified the way in which longstanding issues with workload and workforce capacity in a neoliberal managerial context were detrimentally impacting the ability of the organisation to meet demand driven by an exponential rise in notification rates' (Hyslop and Keddell, 2019: 104). Some demand management strategies were generated through this exercise, notably, a tightening of notification acceptance criteria, particularly for emotional abuse. Although it reduced intake levels to the state agency, there were downstream consequences because the NGO sector and the fledgling children's teams initiative was not resourced to respond to the resulting transfer of service demand.

Social investment

I have argued that the centre-left, 'Third Way', Labour-led governments of the 2000s put a brake on the crude business model agenda of the 1990s. The three-term National-led governments (2008–17) reshaped and reinvigorated the neoliberal agenda. This time a much more sophisticated analysis was applied to the production of social services, the targeting of outsider groups and the measurement of efficiency and effectiveness. The social investment approach is consistent with a more advanced and nuanced conception of governance which recognises that marketisation needs to be actively enabled and steered by central government – that 'markets' must be made. Risk and responsibility are privatised to an extent, but the state remains active – a facilitative spider within a complex web. In Aotearoa, this agenda intersected with a desire to forcefully remoralise an imagined recalcitrant section of the population – the same moral drive that animated 19th-century approaches to the poor within the political logic of liberal capitalism.

The 2015 report of the New Zealand Productivity Commission policy think tank – 'More effective social services' (NZPC, 2015) – is replete with the language of accountancy and micro-economics, reflecting a reductionist understanding of the human condition and the social world. The social investment paradigm, as developed in the Aotearoa context, envisages the role of the state through an economic and 'business case' lens of analysis. For all the apparent sophistication, social investment analysis rests on a very narrow, individualised, commodified and marketised view of social well-being, where services 'aim to improve the wellbeing of clients by broadening access to the things in life they value (or by removing barriers to accessing these things)' (NZPC, 2015: 39). The underlying reasoning is akin to classical liberal economic theory, with its assumption that life is naturally about self-interested actors maximising their access to desirable goods in a competitive society.

People are perceived as innovative and flexible market players across the lifespan (Sugarman, 2015). Neoliberal subjectivity is predicated on the idea that people are required to invest in themselves as marketable commodities – to achieve self-responsible well-being. However, within this ideological frame, the report recognises that 'people, for many reasons, fail to make good choices or fail to take advantage of private markets' (NZPC, 2015: 238). Failure to make an 'optimal investment' may result from poor choices, lack of family support, insufficient saving or lack of access to capital. These market imperfections, or market access blockages, legitimise a role for the state.

Social investment is a potentially misleading descriptor for the concept at hand. Counter-intuitively, it is not about 'investing' in service development to improve the long-term capacity of social assistance programmes or the well-being of people in receipt of services. Concepts from the insurance industry inform the logic of the model, particularly the key analytical tool of calculable forward liability. The emphasis is on the mitigation of downstream costs to taxpayers incurred by the 'poor outcomes' attributed to 'failing' individuals and families. Once the need to reduce future costs is accepted as the goal of welfare policy, it follows that the most expensive section(s) of the population must be targeted for remedial intervention. Accordingly, the focus is on fixing the failing poor; a formula eerily reminiscent of the late 19th century (Welshman, 2013; Hyslop, 2016b; Cummins, 2018).

A central flaw in this economically reductive analysis is the presumption that once the current crop of high-cost individuals is effectively 'fixed', the future pool of disadvantaged people will reduce. The social investment paradigm implicitly draws on the notion that poverty is reproduced within a specific group of families. This naive and politically loaded idea is dressed up as self-evident because of the obvious correlations between poverty, ethnicity and social suffering in Aotearoa. In this way, like all hegemonic ideology, social investment is presented as natural and self-evident, both as politically and scientifically rational and, in perhaps the most authoritative sense, as economically rational. Any measure of critical engagement with the exploitative nature of capitalist economic and social relations is missing from the agenda. In fact, the underlying theoretical position has its ideological roots in eugenic ideas that connect poverty and disadvantage with individual behaviour, attitude, morality and capacity (Gillies et al, 2017; Flanagan, 2018).

The social investment schema is, in my view, explicitly ideological. It imports the punitive shadow that has always haunted liberal politics into a neoliberal economic frame. It functions as a 'common-sense' screen discourse, obscuring the economic drivers of inequality. In this world view, the notion of cyclic disadvantage and intergenerational dependency is perceived to be nested in individual, family and community deficit. The structural realities of relatively unregulated capitalism are conveniently rendered invisible. Centralised state services are also seen as potentially crowding out market remedies, 'natural' civic responsibility and voluntary community assistance as per the idealised vision of liberal community (NZPC, 2015: 104).

The application of this ideologically saturated approach to social services generally, and to child protection in particular, is examined in the following discussion of two very significant policy documents produced in 2015: the aforementioned 'More effective social services' (NZPC, 2015); and the final report of the Modernising Child, Youth and Family Expert Panel (EP, 2015). These exercises were both chaired by the same conservative economist and tend to assume that social services are best understood (and structured) as transactional economic exchanges.

'More effective social services' (NZPC, 2015)

The narrative of this report begins with the somewhat disingenuous gambit that the government does not know what causes poor outcomes and that there is beneficial scope for greater privatisation of service provision. There is a fundamental adherence to the value of direct or proxy price mechanisms in determining the nature and quality of human exchange. Social services are conceived as existing within an underperforming market, though it is recognised that there are differences from purely commercial markets. Direct 'purchasing' or 'commissioning' of services is seen as a means of harnessing the innovative and 'agile' qualities of private or third sector providers. A variety of social service marketisation models, drawn mainly from UK precedents, are canvassed (NZPC, 2015: 150). Contracting for outcomes is one suggested way of controlling desired results without necessarily prescribing the means of delivery.

It is also asserted that new social service business models could be supported by the more effective deployment of data analytics, enabled by the broad data sets available to the state. Linkage of these data sets is said to better position providers and commissioners to 'demonstrate the value-added from services both on average and for particular clients. Commissioners of services will be able to match service levels to client characteristics and set prices according to the cost of providing effective services for different types of clients' (NZPC, 2015: 204).

The report also proceeds from the position that the objective of social services is to effectively support individuals to resolve the problems in their lives and that the current system is not delivering this outcome:

> Some New Zealanders are particularly disadvantaged. The Commission has come to the view in this inquiry that the current system is not working at all well for these people. The Commission believes that a different approach is needed to support them to improve their lives. To not change could condemn them and their children to a continuing poor quality of life, and continue to inflict large costs on the rest of society through both negative impacts on others and the high costs of government services that 'pick up the pieces'. (NZPC, 2015: 1)

Responsibility for disadvantage is located at the level of the individual while also being attributed to an identifiable subgroup of the population.

Targeting the expensive and irresponsible

This report contains unmistakable resonances with the long history of identifying a subclass of the poor as the source of social ills. A list of social problems or deficits – domestic and sexual violence, poor educational achievement, reimprisonment, even damp and inadequate housing – is associated with this recalcitrant section of the population:

> Data made available to the Commission suggests that outcomes such as these tend to occur together for a relatively small number of the most disadvantaged individuals and families. Further, a large proportion of the costs to government of healthcare and social care, income support, corrections services and police services are linked to these disadvantaged individuals and families. The 10,000 highest-cost clients of the social services system are each expected to generate lifetime budgetary costs

of $500,000 or more, involving a total cost of $6.5 billion. (NZPC, 2015: 3)

It is further asserted that 'there are over 900 clients that will cost the system $1 million over their lifetimes' (NZPC, 2015: 55). Although this narrow method of framing social inequality, and the solutions that it begs, is naive sociologically, it is superficially persuasive and very attractive politically (and economically) within a neoliberal policy frame. There is a token effort to broaden the concept of causation beyond a behaviouralist lens, but this is essentially limited to the role of family, community and individual lived experience: 'Social services are only one influence among many that determine people's outcomes. The relationships between influences and outcomes are complex and often not fully understood. Other important influences include family, friends and community, work and colleagues, and early physical and social experiences' (NZPC, 2015: 4). The report goes on to conceptualise four distinct classes or 'quadrants' of social service users, in much the same way that Charles Booth classified the poor of London in the 1890s.

Quadrant D and future welfare liability

Those in quadrants A and B are said to be able to navigate the system to meet their needs for the most part, though they should be empowered to exercise their own market choices in terms of services required, while those in quadrant D lack the capacity to 'extract' enough commodified support to 'turn their lives around':

> For these people (and for some of those in quadrant C), accessing the services they need, in the form that they want, and when they want, can be extremely difficult and frustrating. Too often needs go unmet, opportunities for early intervention are missed and disadvantage perpetuated. For taxpayers it often means the fiscal cost of the system escalates as people re-enter the system at a later date at more costly intervention points – such as emergency units and prisons. The human costs are extremely high for these clients, their children and wider society. (NZPC, 2015: 3)

The exact membership of quadrant D is a little nebulous, though they are regularly referred to as 'these people' – differentiating them from the client mainstream. It is suggested that traumatic experience is a common distinguishing feature. Trauma is a pervasive concept in contemporary approaches to social disadvantage. It carries notions of individuated causal experience, suggesting the need for therapeutic remedies while backgrounding structurally generated inequality: 'Yet client choice is not appropriate for some services or clients. These include services involving the coercive power of the state and where people experiencing psychological trauma or acute physical trauma receive services. These people would generally fall in quadrant D' (NZPC, 2015: 3). It should not be surprising that the application of an economic, as opposed to a critically informed political or sociological, lens to the challenges of social service provision in an inherently unequal society adopts 'investment and insurance tools to prioritise clients and services and selects interventions based on expected reduction in future welfare liability (FWL)' (NZPC, 2015: 15).

Dedicated navigators with the capacity to deliver or purchase the necessary services are proposed as the key to uplifting those in quadrant D. The overriding focus, in the good liberal tradition, is the scourge of benefit dependency and the panacea of paid employment (NZPC, 2015: 226). Reliance on poorly paid and insecure work is not a form of dependency; it is a marker of freedom. The political economy that informs this report is captured in the following excerpt:

> Effective social services will not only improve the wellbeing of clients, but also reduce the likelihood that clients will remain on benefits for a prolonged period. ... Policy and operational changes associated with the Government's Investment Approach in the 2013/14 year resulted in an estimated reduction of $2.2 billion in FWL. Evidence shows that long-run human capital is an important driver of labour productivity, which in turn in is a key driver of long-run economic growth and incomes. (NZPC, 2015: 24–5)

The reduction of long-term benefit dependency was, after all, the first of ten public service result areas promoted by the National-led government. The report explicitly acknowledges its ideological kinship with the Welfare Working Group of 2011, which recommended a more aggressive and targeted approach to high-cost beneficiaries: 'The report proposed that the welfare agency would "be held accountable for improving work outcomes for people of working age at risk of long-term welfare dependency and reducing the long-term costs of welfare dependency (as measured by the forward liability)"' (Chapple, 2013: 57). The banality of the language disguises the coercive sanction system that was applied to those in receipt of income support:

> The actuarially determined forward liability of the benefit system reduced from $76.5 billion to $69.0 billion in the year to 30 June 2014. Taylor Fry (2015) attributes $2.2 billion of the $7.5 billion reduction to 'better than expected performance over the year – as a result of policy and operational changes over the year that influenced the benefit dynamics' (p.3). (NZPC, 2015: 73)

It was no coincidence that the Expert Panel that recommended the reorganisation of state social work along similar ideological lines was led by Paula Rebstock, a conservative economist and former chair of the Commerce Commission, who also chaired the Welfare Working Group.

Whānau Ora and commissioning

Significantly the Whānau Ora policy initiative is offered as a positive example of the commissioning approach to social services. This programme has functioned well at a distance from government, though it has been subject to significant political steerage. Whānau Ora is something of a special case because it descends directly from earlier Māori initiatives designed to promote autonomy through harnessing the collective strength of Māori social structures. In this sense, it is the utility of the practice model itself and an alignment of political opportunities that has generated a successful outcome.

Whānau Ora became a flagship policy of the Māori Party, which was formed after Tariana Turia resigned from the Labour Party in 2004 'in response to the government's introduction of the Foreshore and Seabed Act (2004) which removed the ability of Māori to test their claims to areas of the foreshore and seabed by vesting ownership in the Crown' (Smith et al, 2019: 512). The Māori Land Court had raised the question of a Māori common law claim to customary title to the foreshore because ownership rights had not been extinguished or transferred to the Crown. This created a shrill storm of mainstream Pākehā concern, and the government moved to pre-empt this possibility.

Many Māori saw this defensive reaction as another colonial land grab. Arguably, such ruptures in the liberal political veneer reveal the real basis (and the real power distribution) of the relationship between the Crown and Māori. Ironically, the beginnings of the Whānau Ora initiative were born of a confidence-and-supply agreement between the Māori Party and the conservative National Party in 2008. As Harris (2007) has illustrated, this background is important because it illustrates the connection between Whānau Ora and the wider context of creative (sometimes opportunistic) Māori struggles for self-determination and a resource base to build from. As will be explored in Chapter 7, aspirations for an independent Māori child protection system are linked to this heritage, and some of the key players, or their intellectual heirs in the Māori world, continue to be at the forefront of this process.

The programme has subsequently established a positive record as a whānau empowerment social service approach. It rests on a coherent philosophical base that is firmly rooted in Māori values and practices. It is also heir to the aspirations of whānau development expressed in the vision of PtAT and the practice aims of the Mātua Whāngai programme:

Whānau Ora has achieved early gains for its intended beneficiaries and has succeeded in engaging whānau who were not connected to mainstream social services, or for whom the fragmentation of existing services had led to poor outcomes. Connecting Māori service providers and wrapping support around whānau have helped to overcome this fragmentation, while Whānau Ora 'navigators' have proved successful in building trusting relationships with whānau. (Smith et al, 2019: 506)

Whānau Ora is predicated on an appreciation of whānau (as a multigenerational kinship group) as the fulcrum of development, as opposed to the centrality of individual rights and freedoms found in the liberal tradition. Where individual advancement is the target of intervention, it is understood as a means of strengthening the collective.

Rickard's (2014) study of iwi social services in the Ngati Porou **rohe** on the East Coast of the North Island reminds us that hapū and iwi social programmes have operated on similar principles since well before the official state endorsement of Whānau Ora. However, the 'devolution to those best suited' commissioning model can enhance opportunities for Māori to provide social services to their own people on their own terms: 'While the implementation of Whānau Ora is likely to have little impact on the substance of social services provided by iwi and Māori organisations, it does have the potential to significantly boost the ability of organisations to deliver these services effectively and affordably' (Rickard, 2014: 116).

The notion of 'intervention' is also backgrounded in Whānau Ora practice. Although the philosophy is consistent with the minimisation of state dependence, the route to self-reliance is associated with the exercise of autonomy, consistent with community development theory (Bhattacharyya, 2004). Whānau determine their own needs and priorities, and are provided with resources to give effect to specific plans. Support is provided by 'navigators', who engage cooperatively with whānau. This role entails the development of trust through deep engagement, empathy, respect and healing, as opposed to disengaged professionalism. This is influenced by the Māori sense of connection and continuity through time: you cannot fix some and leave others behind without consequences.

As touched on, the devolutionary contracting environment of the 1990s offered a degree of synergy between the desire of the state to privatise services and promote economic self-reliance, and Māori aspirations for self-determination:

Whereas the state saw the development of Māori health providers as an opportunity for Māori to develop an economic base through partnerships in the health and disability sector … Māori saw an opportunity for self-determination and an ability to deliver services to their people that were better aligned with their own customs and world views. (Smith et al, 2019: 506)

Whānau Ora is very much a product of this symbiosis. Smith et al (2019: 507) rightly identify that the durability of this programme also owes much to the energy, integrity and perspicacity of its political champion, Tariana Turia:

> In political terms, Whānau Ora should also be seen as a story of strikingly successful policy entrepreneurship, in which a committed politician, Dame Tariana Turia, and her colleagues seized a window of opportunity to devise and implement an approach capable of delivering major social value impacts for Māori whānau. The fact a policy approach explicitly designed around Indigenous concepts, practices and values was established within a political environment that had proved itself to be indifferent to Māori initiatives at best, and outright hostile at worst, is remarkable.

Funding and service procurement was devolved to three non-government commissioning bodies from 2014, with strategic oversight from a group comprised of Crown ministers and iwi leaders:

> In 2014, funding was devolved to three independent non-governmental commissioning agencies: Te Pou Matakana (North Island), Te Pūtahitanga o Te Waipounamu (South Island) and Pasifika Futures (Pacific peoples). Strategic leadership was provided by the Whānau Ora Partnership Group of six ministers of the Crown and six iwi members nominated by the iwi chairs forum. (Smith et al, 2019: 515)

The momentum developed through this process has fed, in part, into mounting dissatisfaction with the service delivered to Māori by the statutory child protection system (as discussed in Chapter 7).

Expert Panel

The drivers of political decisions are not always transparent or easy to discern. The decision by new Minister Anne Tolley to pull back from the implementation of a model of individuated abuse prediction and intervention based on big data analytics is a case in point (Ballantyne, 2019). Tolley also initiated the Expert Panel process, with its focus on solving the problems of the state care system. The escalating numbers of historic claims for abuse in state care, as well as the difficulty of keeping a lid on this process through closed and confidential processes of redress, may have also been an undeclared influence. The state initially took an obstructive, legalistic stance to these claims:

> The State's redress processes, including the Crown's approach to civil claims, have been overly focused on the financial implications to the State, rather than on providing satisfactory compensation to survivors and ensuring their wellbeing. The Crown has vigorously defended claims in court, while government agencies have developed alternative, out-of-court claims processes that survivors describe as protracted, lacking transparency, inconsistent and full of hurdles. The resulting financial settlements are also inconsistent. Rehabilitation, such as counselling, medical treatment, and employment training, is inadequate. (Royal Commission of Inquiry into Historical Abuse in State Care and in the Care of Faith-Based Institutions, 2020: 16)

It is apparent that the final report of the Modernising Child Youth and Family Expert Panel (EP, 2015) resulted from a predetermined reform exercise. Essentially, data compiled through the 'review' process was slotted into a preordained conceptual framework. As acknowledged in the 'More effective social services' report (NZPC, 2015), these exercises were not unrelated. In terms of the shared social investment agenda, they were singing from the same ideological songbook:

> The inquiry is not taking place in a vacuum – the Government is actively pursuing a range of initiatives to improve social services in line with its Better Public Services priority. The initiative to trial social bonds, MSD's community investment strategy and the external expert panel for modernising Child, Youth and Family are examples. (NZPC, 2015: 33)

The Expert Panel report relied heavily on the social investment schema applied in the Welfare Working Group report. At times, the problem of child abuse is explicitly conflated with the supposed intergenerational transmission of the forward cost associated with 'benefit dependency'. The 'outcomes' for children and young people within the statutory care system are a major preoccupation within the Expert Panel report:

> Regular reviews of the contemporary care system in New Zealand have been undertaken, but not one has produced sustained positive changes in the lives of our vulnerable young people. In April 2015, the Minister for Social Development established an Expert Panel with a mandate to determine how to tackle this most pressing issue that faces contemporary New Zealand: How can we transform the lives of our vulnerable children once and for all? (EP, 2015: 3)

Orchestrated input from a selected group of care-experienced young people was central to the review process. Historically, the child protection system has an abysmal track record in terms of medium- to long-term outcomes for children entering state care, for example: experiences of 're-abuse'; the insecurity occasioned by placement with multiple caregivers; and discharge at the age of 17 with few skills and resources for independent living.

The Expert Panel made some far-reaching and progressive recommendations for reform in this area. In subsequent legislative amendments, the jurisdiction of the Youth Court and the minimum age for exiting care were both raised to 18, and significant ongoing support for transition to adulthood was enabled. A semi-autonomous Young Persons' Advocacy Group was established, and the oversight responsibility of the Office of the Children's Commissioner was extended. However, in other ways, conceptualising CYF as a failing care system rather than an overloaded and under-resourced statutory social work system led to extremely problematic outcomes.

Vulnerability and love

As exemplified in the foreword to the final report of the Expert Panel, the narrative is interspersed with recurring references to the self-evident truth that secure and loving care provides the best-possible outcomes for children: 'The solution this review found is that our most vulnerable children have the best chance of leading a full and happy life if they live within families that give them life-long, stable, loving relationships and if they belong to communities which cherish them' (EP, 2015: 3). The draconian implication sitting behind this saccharine tautology is that inadequate homes need to be made stable and loving, and that if this is not possible, children need to be permanently placed in homes that do comply with these criteria. In the context of child 'abuse', in all its complex manifestations mediated by inequality, poverty and social distress, this prescription is inevitably a recipe for discriminatory outcomes in terms of class and ethnicity.

The Expert Panel report recognises that the existing care system is damaging for children and seeks to resolve this by making early permanent arrangements for long-term care. A child-centred system that places the well-being of children at the centre of policy and practice is proposed. This is ultimately another 'motherhood and apple pie' mantra. It signals a significant departure from the central message of PtAT and the CYP&tF Act that children's well-being cannot be considered outside of their need and right to belong to whānau.

These tensions are not overtly confronted in the text of the report. Rescue mentality foster care is not seen as the source of long-term problems, provided that the care system can be fixed. The predictable outcome that more Māori children would likely come into permanent care away from immediate family is not acknowledged.

The concept of vulnerability is central. 'Vulnerability' is a flexible term that is used here to demarcate a specific section of the community – effectively, a subgroup of the poor. Poverty and related social disadvantages in terms of housing, education and health are gendered, raced and classed in Aotearoa. As with the Productivity Commission, there is no connection made between vulnerability and the wider economic structures that deliver graphically unequal life experiences for children (Rashbrooke, 2013). Family environment is perceived as the sole locus of social suffering:

> The definition of vulnerable children is those children who are at significant risk of harm now and into the future as a consequence of their family environment and/or their own complex needs, and young people who have offended or may offend in the future. Currently around 230,000 children under age 18 may experience vulnerability at some point during their childhood, and around six out of 10 of this group are likely to be Māori. (EP, 2015: 7)

The notion of early decisions about long-term care outside of immediate family is reflected in the first of six objectives for a child-centred system: 'Ensuring that children have the earliest opportunity for a loving and stable home.' The other part of this formula is the concept that children need to be healed from past family-centred trauma to enable productive lives, as expressed in objective 4: 'Helping children to heal and recover.'

Since abuse and neglect are damaging (and expensive) experiences, it is recommended that the law be amended to support 'the objective of life-long, stable, and loving care from the earliest opportunity' (EP, 2015: 156). In my view, the lineal 'rescue and heal' focus in this approach radically oversimplifies the complex, socially structured experiences of children born on the wrong side of the economic tracks (Featherstone et al, 2014). The socio-economically embedded nature of the child protection system is not addressed by this orientation, but it is very effectively concealed.

Remedies

Historically, lack of support for the onerous job of fostering children has contributed to the difficulty of providing stable out-of-family care. New Zealanders are urged to step up to the task, not only of providing stable and loving homes, but also of providing wider support to 'our' vulnerable children. There are a variety of wishful and idealised references to the whole of New Zealand, presumably middle-class New Zealanders (but possibly including whānau Māori), to contribute to this imperative. For the most part, this seems to be conflated with destigmatising the care population. Very little is provided in the way of concrete actions, which is not surprising given that it is such a nebulous and strangely naive concept – the idea that the systemic problems of child maltreatment and social inequality can be resolved by middle New Zealand somehow extending its inclusive, conservative, communitarian 'Kiwi' identity (Provan, 2012).

Early support and timely alternatives

The Expert Panel report argues that too many children have been re-abused in family or extended family care post-involvement with CYF. This analysis is accurate, but it is also more than a little superficial, and it is applied deceptively. The Expert Panel was not particularly interested in looking into why this had come about because solutions had already been determined. As illustrated throughout this book, the whānau-centric vision of the 1989 Act was not realised, but this was not because it was flawed conceptually; rather, the overriding problem was that it was not resourced materially. This is consistent with the warning about the dire risk from under-funding that was articulated in the 1992 Mason Report (Mason, 1992).

In the 1990s and through the 2000s, the practice of minimalist social work in a resource-scarce environment led inexorably to children being placed with, or returned to, family without the necessary supports and services being put in place. A national managerial system of 'traffic light' reports that rated and compared site office performance against measures of throughput and timeliness contributed to a compliance culture divorced from practice quality, apart from the containment of risk (Hyslop, 2017).

The answer provided by the Expert Panel is a time-limited period of intensive support for families with children at risk of harm, followed by alternative arrangements to secure a stable and loving family if sufficient parental improvements are not made:

> This involves early and intensive support to give birth families the best opportunity to provide the love and care their children need, applying transparent and effective decision-making to identify those circumstances where this is no longer possible, and where necessary, taking timely action to identify alternative arrangements for children so they can develop relationships in a loving, stable family. This is of primary importance as ultimately this is what helps children to have happy childhoods, be resilient, develop a sense of belonging and identity, and to grow into flourishing adults. (EP, 2015: 8)

A transparent 'shape up or lose your children' stick-and-carrot approach is clearly suggested, in conjunction with the idea that bonds between children and birth families will be retained post-removal:

> Where the family is unable to make the changes required in a timeframe that meets the needs of their child, it is important that alternative arrangements are made for the child to form stable loving relationships at the earliest opportunity.
>
> This means that the decision to continue working with a family to care for their child, or to find an alternative home for that child, needs to be taken in a considered way that is consistent with the age of the child. Planning for a permanent relationship outside the family home should start early, and often at the same time as continuing to support the family to become strong. (EP, 2015: 81)

Retaining a productive relationship through this kind of authoritarian intervention is more than a little idealistic in my experience. Significantly, state social workers are not perceived as providers of ongoing assistance to whānau. In part, this may have arisen from the Expert Panel's collective ignorance of social work practice systems, but it is more likely related to the envisaged role of social workers as direct brokers and purchasers of services.

State child protection social workers have 'traditionally' performed direct work with children and whānau after FGCs or under family/whānau agreements. Essentially, the Expert Panel's perspective is that where intensive support (which will not necessarily be provided by social workers) is not 'successful', permanent placement outside the birth family is required. This is seen as both child-centred and in the interests of minimising future cost to the state.

The 'purchase' of early support or 'prevention' services is conceived in the same terms as the Productivity Commission prescription:

> Where prevention services are required, they will be delivered through strategic partnerships with other agencies, iwi and community organisations, including the ability to directly purchase services on behalf of vulnerable children and their families from other agencies. The future department would have a market-making role to create the capability and capacity in the market for the services that deliver prevention outcomes. (EP, 2015: 8)

Notions of commissioning and market-building also echo the neoliberal schema of the Productivity Commission:

> The department will not significantly expand its in-house delivery, but instead build the capacity, capability and supply of services with

community and iwi to meet children's needs. It is communities and iwi who are closest to families and can bring the connections, support and care required to support vulnerable children. Where services do not yet exist, such as specialist services to address the impacts of trauma, the department will commission these and play a market building role. The use of evidence-based monitoring of outcomes will help create a learning system to improve the quality of services commissioned and available. (EP, 2015: 11)

Members of the Expert Panel came with little or no direct knowledge of contemporary state social work. This was presumably regarded as an efficacious arrangement. Within the text, social workers tend to be subsumed under more generic references to 'workers', 'staff' or 'professional practitioners'. The report emphasises the importance of practitioners from diverse disciplines working with children and families. This is reminiscent of the multidisciplinary wave of the early 1980s.

Attributing blame and reframing social work

When social workers are mentioned, it is in relation to the new knowledge, skills and competencies they will be required to master in areas such as 'direct purchasing' and awareness of 'trauma' (EP, 2015: 142). As will be discussed in Chapter 7, this lack of attention to the central role of day-to-day, on-the-ground, state social work practice came back to bite as the managerial vision of the Expert Panel was implemented after 2015 (Hyslop and Keddell, 2019). Lofty visioning and an associated prescription for resource-intensive centralised managerialism either failed to foresee or simply ignored the child rescue furore that this policy prescription was inevitably building towards.

The Expert Panel report also features an apparent blurring of correlation with causation, in that historical involvement with CYF is repeatedly associated with detrimental social outcomes for children. This is extended beyond destructive care experience to suggest that CYF contact per se is a source of social disadvantage:

New data on long-term outcomes reveals higher rates of early parenting and subsequent involvement with child protection for mothers with a history of childhood contact with CYF. Women with some level of childhood contact with the agency were nearly three times more likely to be parents before the age of 25, and as parents were three times more likely to have a child referred to CYF. (EP, 2015: 42)

A plethora of poor and costly outcomes is equated with CYF involvement, including a connection with child/youth mortality. Predictably, the most repugnant link appears to involve that cardinal sin against the neoliberal creed: benefit dependency. By association, the demons in this story are young, underclass, Māori women:

> Of children born between 2005 and 2007 and known to CYF by age five:
> - 39 percent had mothers who had been receiving a benefit for more than four out of the last five years preceding their birth, and 60 percent had a primary carer who was receiving a benefit at the time of their birth.
> - 37 percent had a parent who had a criminal conviction in the five years prior to the child's birth.
> - 69 percent had parents where there was a family violence incident attended by Police in the five years prior to the child's birth, and
> - 36 percent had parents who were known to CYF as a child. (EP, 2015: 44)

CYF contact is also taken as a proximal measure of childhood vulnerability. Rather than being recognised as a complex, socially configured function of liberal capitalism, vulnerability is conceived to be an individuated condition – a 'thing in and of itself'– that is exacerbated by the state social work system. The prescribed cure lies in an investment approach to social services. This emphasis minimises the wider social determinants of child maltreatment and the complex bias mechanisms that afflict 'notify and investigate' systems (Keddell, 2014):

> The overall prevalence of contact with CYF provides a benchmark for the size of the population who might be vulnerable at some point during their childhood. Using this historical benchmark, we estimate there are about 230,000 children and young people currently under age 18 who might experience vulnerability at some point during their childhood. Around six out of 10 of this group are likely to be Māori. Based on what currently occurs, it is estimated that one quarter of this group will require intensive support and a statutory response at some point in their childhood. (EP, 2015: 41)

This stilted analysis amounts to an inversion of cause and effect: contact with the statutory social work organisation does not generate social disadvantage; 'vulnerability' isn't a virus, though referrals are linked to systemic social inequality. Similarly, statutory social work does not cure disadvantage and it is not designed to do so.

In the Expert Panel's view, disadvantage is reproduced across generations in failing families. Love is the answer; ultimately, a coercive love directed at a certain element within the population, mirroring Parton's (2014a) more aggressive 'muscular turn' in English child protection. Systemic structural inequality is not perceived as the problem. As predefined for this exercise, the key problem is that 'a person who had contact with CYF as a child is more likely to require benefit system support as an adult, and for people already receiving a benefit, this is a significant risk factor in terms of long-term benefit dependency' (EP, 2015: 161).

Social investment

There is, then, a disconcerting conflation of child maltreatment, the operation of CYF agency in Aotearoa and the issue of financial cost incurred by the state through income support transfer payments to entitled families. These things are drawn together in an elaborate, and, in my view, ideologically and politically constructed, argument:

> Within an already vulnerable group of young benefit recipients, the average benefit system lifetime cost for these clients is 40% or $47,000 higher than those with no history of contact with CYF. This equates to approximately half of the estimated lifetime cost for this age group, at approximately $6 billion. This figure is limited to the future cost of young people in the benefit system receiving employment services, income support and supplementary assistance; but currently excludes all other government costs across CYF, Corrections, Education, Health and Social Housing. Where the child or young person's first contact with CYF occurred early in their life, the total lifetime benefit liability increases substantially compared to benefit recipients who had no contact with CYF as a child or young person, when controlling for other factors. (EP, 2015: 161)

For all the talk of stability and love, praise for the wisdom of the care-experienced Young Peoples' Advisory Group, and exhortations for all New Zealanders to contribute to meeting the needs of vulnerable children, the bottom line is about reducing future costs:

> In the future, growing up in a loving and stable family must become the norm for New Zealand's vulnerable children, and the future system must be organised to support this. The future system is not a social welfare system but a cross-sector social investment system, drawing on the capability of professionals, the community and, most importantly, New Zealand families to enable children to have happy childhoods and grow into flourishing adults, and to reduce the over-representation of Māori within the system. (EP, 2015: 10)

As argued, the idea of fixing one family at a time effectively turns a blind eye to systemic socio-economic causation. More importantly, it assumes that an identifiable group of child-abusing families inflict trauma and reproduce social disadvantage. Essentially, social workers are charged with intensively intervening with the children of 'quadrant D', as per the Productivity Commission designation. If this is unsuccessful, the plan becomes overtly eugenic. Children are to be removed into the care of stable and loving families in order to prevent the transmission of abuse, trauma, disadvantage and the downstream financial costs. All of this is justified by good economic sense and the needs of the vulnerable child:

> Experience with other liability models suggests an aspirational target to reduce the forward costs of maltreatment and vulnerability by 50% over a generation is ambitious but achievable with concerted leadership and investment. This translates to an indicative overall liability reduction of 20% over five years, once the new operating model is in place. The achievement of this overall indicative target and the target to reduce the over-representation of Māori would require the forward liability associated with poor outcomes for Māori children to reduce by at least 25–30% over the same period. (EP, 2015: 171)

Among other things, it is argued that a reduction of the costs associated with repeated notifications will follow from a timely, once-and-for-all approach to intervention (EP, 2015: 162). Orwellian references are made to the development of an actuarial model and a feasibility study which suggests that measures for the calculation of individuated future liability could be developed by means of a well-being framework. A further scoping study is recommended.

Māori commissioning and control

The basis of a whānau-centred approach to child protection was clearly being seriously undermined in the child-centric discourse that framed the Expert Panel process. This generated significant opposition across a range of stakeholders. The alternative approach offered to Māori within the report contains contradictions that continue to play out in fierce contemporary debate about the future shape of statutory child protection in Aotearoa.

The Expert Panel envisaged a central planning, coordination and governance agency, with the resources to develop (rather than practically deliver) the services envisaged within the new system. This is justified in terms of the need to be accountable to families in need of services, that it, the provision of a 'single point of contact'. The critical role of a strategic central agency is described in various ways as 'leading the system' or 'holding the investment'.

Vulnerable Māori children are a special area of focus in this exercise. After all, Māori children are hugely over-represented regardless of the lens that is applied. The following excerpt illustrates the racially skewed nature of the system (And there is that benefit-dependent Māori mother scarecrow again!):

> For example, Māori children born between 2005 and 2007 were four times more likely to have a mother who had been dependent on a benefit than non-Māori children born in the same period.
>
> Importantly, the over-representation of Māori children and young people increases with the extent of involvement with CYF. About five out of every 10 referrals to CYF are for Māori children and young people, yet Māori make up six out of every 10 children and young people in care. (EP, 2015: 43)

Accordingly, a higher target of cost saving is pitched for Māori than for the general population: a 25–30% reduction in forward liability in five years (EP, 2015: 56). The intent to preserve and foster connections to culture and identity where children are cared for outside of whakapapa is expressed. There is mention of the need for Māori caregivers, which is another refrain reminiscent of the early 1980s. In what appears to be a deafening piece of tokenism, provision is made for dedicated Māori representation on the proposed Social Investment Board that will oversee the new model. Some degree of power sharing with iwi in service planning is proposed. It is suggested that partnerships with Māori organisations will facilitate more effective 'preventive' work in community settings, though the notion of strategic partnering inevitably begs the question of who controls the strategy. It is further envisaged that iwi may take up a range of direct statutory roles at some indeterminate point in the future – effectively, at the master's pleasure.

The aftermath

A separate Ministry of Children (OT) was established in 2017.[3] Many of the service coordination functions of the Ministry of Social Development were migrated to the new ministry. In recent times, the model of partially devolved practice that the Expert Panel report envisaged has generated an unprecedented expansion of centralised management, control mechanisms and development projects.

Interested readers of the final report were introduced to the concept of the 'tranche', used to describe the orchestrated step-by-step rollout of a complex reform process. The 'management-speak' associated with tranche description is difficult to decipher:

The focus of Tranche One is delivering initial changes across the range of services for children and families and establishing the building blocks of the future operating model. This is an intensive phase in which progress must be made on multiple fronts: planning, design, and delivery. It is important that this tranche establishes the momentum for change and credibility of the change programme with the participants of the system. (EP, 2015: 180)

This seems to imply the application of significant resources and organisational energy to bringing various key stakeholders into line with the restructured system. Tranche Two is more focused on the wholesale design and delivery of the social investment model, though the language is equally impenetrable:

The focus of Tranche Two is delivering the full set of changes required to deliver the future experience for children, young people and their families. This tranche tackles more complex changes that require a longer lead time for design and development, and tackles those services in the system that are more entrenched and require fundamental culture, mind-set and behavioural change across the sector and/or within the department workforce. During this tranche, the Transformation Programme will be fully integrated into the future department. It is likely it will continue to operate as a change programme with representation on the leadership team. (EP, 2015: 185)

The Expert Panel placed a lot of stock on the development of overarching practice frameworks to shape the nature and quality of practice, both within the central organisation and within other state services involved with vulnerable children. It is suggested that this umbrella would be supported by common technical tools to help identify vulnerability and head it off at the pass: 'Guidance and training in common tools would be provided by those who regularly engage with vulnerable families (including doctors, nurses, teachers, Police, social housing providers and others)' (EP, 2015: 77). Six years on from this report, it does not seem that tangible progress has been made with developing a cross-disciplinary assessment framework. As will be canvassed in Chapter 7, much of the Expert Panel vision has imploded, or exploded, in recent years – despite the best efforts of a highly efficient and resource-intensive corporate communications regime.

7

Building a new paradigm

Political location

We are at a critical juncture in relation to the trajectory of the child protection project. The outlook is contested, in the same way that the function of state-sponsored child and family welfare practice has always been disputed. In my view, the future design and development of policy and practice requires a critical analysis of the relationship between child protection and the wider system of liberal capitalism in the settler state of Aotearoa. To some degree, this process is unfolding as this concluding chapter is being penned. There is, as there seemed to be in 1989, an opportunity to construct a world-leading and socially just child protection system. There is a great deal of work to be done but recent developments signpost a possible pathway to this objective.

The foregoing chapters have demonstrated the way in which responses to child and family welfare have been politically configured over time. The ideological rubric of liberal capitalism has tended to set the discursive parameters within which the problem of child maltreatment is defined (Duncan, 2004). Child protection is enmeshed with the relations of power inherent to this economic and political system. It is also connected with related socio-economic disparities that intersect with class, gender and ethnicity. Common-sense understandings about the genesis of social inequality and the relationship between poverty and child protection have shifted as liberal political orthodoxy has moved across the liberal spectrum, from laissez fare capitalism, to the welfare state, and back again. Themes are persistent and recurrent: 'Since its earliest incarnations, social work has been inextricably bound up with poverty and with the complex and contradictory attitudes towards people living in poverty that have characterised social policy since the late 19th century' (Warner, 2015: 46).

The fact that damaging structural inequalities are systemically reproduced within the capitalist model of development is an uncomfortable truth for governments across the liberal spectrum. The children and families who come to the attention of the child protection system are drawn predominantly from the frayed and precarious edges of the working class. This insecurity is a function of the economic system, and it is perennially reframed as a problem of individual failing and family morality. It is time, in my opinion, to move beyond this illusion. This does not mean that parental harm to children should be ignored, but it does mean that the problem must be better understood and responded to.

Relative social deprivation impacts unevenly on Indigenous people in settler societies. Accordingly, whānau Māori receive disproportionate intervention from the state child welfare system. Transformational policy design and practice delivery needs to provide services that work for Māori. This involves addressing the economic drivers of inequality, systemic racism and unresolved issues of power, authority and Māori autonomy in Aotearoa (Potter and Jackson, 2017).

Social work in the state

The social workers who implement child protection policy are inevitably entwined with the machinations of the state. Shifts in policy emphasis across the child protection–family support continuum are determined by the government of the day, though, as we have seen, implementation and resourcing has seldom matched the rhetoric of expansive policy agendas. There has also been some historical impetus for progressive developments and resistance to racist or otherwise discriminatory practices from within the professional workforce given the left-wing leanings associated with social work education and professional values.

The expressions of internal organisational dissent and local autonomy possible in the 1980s would likely be considered treasonable in the current environment. In contrast to the social work development plan of 1989, centrally planned, monitored and evidentially evaluated innovation has been seen as the realm of centralised bureaucracy in the recent past. In recent decades, the critical voice of state social workers has been reined in and the locus of resistance has shifted to the external community of practice, particularly Māori stakeholders.

This separation of policy and practice development from the operational realities of OT has followed from tighter organisational regulation and, in part, from a reconfiguration of statutory social work; processes of labour in terms of the determination of risk and intervention options have become increasingly prescribed, though the standards set out are not necessarily met. In the current system, as shown in the spate of recent inquiries discussed in this chapter, the gap between the florid aspirations of Wellington bureaucrats and the messy experience of reactive practice on the ground have become ludicrously wide; state social work with multi-stressed whānau does not happen in a corporate boardroom.

Politics and professionalism

Social work is politically situated, but it is also an interpersonal undertaking. The implementation of policy prescriptions has seldom, if ever, taken adequate account of the complex and resource-intensive realities of engaged child protection practice. In this sense, the relationship between political intent and practice realities has often been lost in translation (Hyslop, 2009). The interactive communication at the heart of applied practice sits awkwardly alongside the efficient delivery and measurement of outputs and outcomes, which has come to dominate public service design over the last three decades. This is ironic in the sense that engagement and trust are essential for effective social work.

The related question of professionalism (and who defines it) is also critical for contemporary social work. As well as providing a place to stand alongside more established occupational disciplines, notions of specialist diagnostic skill and packages of intervention informed by technical expertise have also distanced social workers from service users. The associated 'science-informed' approach, in concert with funding mechanisms designed to measure and reward cost-effective 'best' practice, disguises the socio-structural dimensions of social suffering (Pease, 2009).

There is a long (and ongoing) history of associating the residual poor with the reproduction of social failure. Practice technologies designed to diagnose and fix individualised social deficits are consistent with this lineage of targeting symptoms rather than causes through an individualised liberal lens. This is graphically exemplified in recent critique of the application of neuroscience to social interventions (Gillies et at, 2017). Brain science has been erroneously deployed as an imperative justification for privatised parenting interventions to enable impoverished women to arrest the causes of poverty in their children. There is an elision of behavioural causation and biological determinism: 'Left aside in the seemingly common sense and straightforward scenario of early intervention to save young brains is the unequal gendered, classed, and raced environment in which parents and children live out their lives' (Gillies et al, 2017: 131–2).

However, where there is power, there is resistance. The socially embedded, communicative nature of social work is a perennial problem when it comes to the commodification and regulation of practice. More specifically, the recent positioning of children and families as sites of trauma to be measured and treated tends to objectify and delegitimise the life worlds of those living at the edges of capitalist society. By contrast, genuine understanding tends to humanise and enfranchise service users:

> Social workers engage clients in exchanging knowledge about their life experiences so that their voices can be heard, and their stories can expose the inadequacy of official constructions of their lives. By supporting the creation of counter discourses social workers assist those outside of their circles to understand the world from client perspectives. (Dominelli, 2004: 38)

This sounds a lot more like the job description of a Whānau Ora navigator than a contemporary state social worker. There is an imperative need for social workers to engage directly and personally with individuals, families and communities in need of support. However, a legacy of mistrust makes this a practically and emotionally fraught undertaking. These tensions play out in the relationship between social workers and the regulatory realm of managerial accountancy and technocracy, where social work has often been regarded as an unruly foreign country in need of discipline, measurement and control (Hyslop, 2009).

This misalignment is reflected in anglophone child protection reform processes, which are often sparked by perceptions of systemic crisis and/or official inquiries into practice tragedies. Such inquiries are apt to provoke managerialist remedies that further compromise the quality of practice. This difficulty is highlighted in Kemp's (2020) painstaking study of the paradoxical effects of reform recommendations in South Australia. Ironically, efficiency-driven processes of compliance management and progress measurement are apt to impact adversely upon engaged communicative practice, even when the development of emotionally competent social work is the intended focus of reform.

The capacity to operationalise our awareness of the relationship between structural inequality and private pain is the unrealised potential of social work. This involves recognising the contradictions of the child protection task and getting past the seductive shorthand of mantras like 'child-centric social work' or the practice of simply compiling deficit-based inventories of cultural well-being. The recent New South Wales review into Aboriginal children in out-of-home care presents a simple, yet profound, message (Davis, 2019), recommending greater transparency and relationship building, more intuition and judgement, and less risk aversion and systemic compliance. It observes that espoused commitments to cultural recognition – high-sounding words on paper – do not themselves facilitate relationships with people and may, in fact, work against real engagement.

Deep echoes

Past constructions of social work and client status resonate powerfully within current debate about the future development of child protection. I have argued that much of this discourse is framed within the confines of liberal individualism. Contemporary notions of practice at both ends of the child protection spectrum – early and intensive intervention – are consistent with the notion of individuals as packages of problem behaviour in need of correction. As Pease (2013: 28) has argued, more progressive practice must, as a minimum, 'avoid pathologizing service users and holding them responsible for problems shaped by structural and material conditions'.

More worryingly, predictive risk approaches based on sophisticated analysis of service population data or the linkage of family dysfunction with the idea of poverty reproduction and future cost (as seen in the 2015 report of the Productivity Commission and the Expert Panel process) are aligned with a sinister history (Hyslop, 2016b). To revisit the dogma of our most august charitable aid inspector, Dr Duncan McGregor, the identification of problem outsiders who pose a risk to 'our' vulnerable children and to the moral boundaries of the liberal creed is consistent with 19th-century notions about the genetic reproduction of 'social parasites'. Perhaps this is the real 'cycle' that needs to be broken in our approach to the reform of child protection.

Problem families

Flanagan's (2018) research into the discourse of problem families in the context of Tasmanian public housing in the early 1970s raises some disconcerting questions in terms of evaluating the common sense of child protection work. The demarcation of a specific group of families as an identifiable subsection of the population is identified as a recurrent theme in relation to how public welfare agencies view service users. More specifically, the idea of classifying and counting problem families connects back to the origins of social science and social work. It is argued that the discourse of the 'problem family':

> has manifested over more than a century as the knowledge that there is a small group of people living amongst us who do not live as 'we' do and that this is a problem requiring sustained public attention. Early discussions of this 'problem' drew attention to the 'submerged tenth' (W. Booth, 1890), sorted them into 'classes' (C. Booth, 1904), talked of 'pauperism' (Ely, 1891; Warner, 1889, 1894) and drew charts of their 'pedigrees' so that the cost they imposed upon the community might be calculated (Dugdale, 1970 [1910]; McCulloch, 1888). (Flanagan, 2018: 684)

In various shapes and forms, all of these 'discussions' are evident in the foregoing chapters, including recent formulations seen in official reports such as the White Paper or the Expert Panel review that frame the problem family as 'an object of government' in child welfare policy and practice.

Flanagan (2018: 686) employs Foucault's (1981) concept of 'commentary': the reproduction of a 'truth' made possible by earlier foundational text. Commentary is 'the repetition of old content which sounds new' (Flanagan, 2018: 687). Flanagan also notes the difficulty of objectively pinning down the parameters of the problem family: that it is often perceived as a social object that is easier to recognise than define; and that the category is related to the perceptions of middle-class welfare workers regarding what is required to lead an appropriately ordered life.

She identifies that the resilient notion of a 'submerged tenth' was coined by Charles Booth of Salvation Army fame, though it is often incorrectly attributed to the social researcher William Booth. This prescription is a reflection of the blossoming Victorian social imagination, that is, the possibility of applying scientific discipline to the problems of the social world: 'The desire for intervention to be made on "scientific" footings loops back to the desire for the "problem" itself to be defined in "scientific" terms. It represents the imposition of the ultimate form of order (scientific method) on this most disorderly of problems' (Flanagan, 2018: 697).

The sort of classification processes leading to open-ended supportive service status for certain high-needs families with state social workers in the 1970s come to mind: 'When inscribed into the case notes, textbooks and datasets of the welfare state, a given "problem family" can be joined to other "problem families", becoming just one example of a "type" and consequently, available for collation, comparison and the accrual of evidence that can be operationalized into intervention' (Flanagan, 2018: 697–8). William Booth's work was foundational in terms of separating population groups and in legitimating the failing poor as targets for rehabilitation. His methodology involved counting and naming, but it was also supplemented by the recording of individualised descriptors: '"Queer character"; "Two elder sons loaf about"; "Good workman but lazy and cantankerous"; "3 school children (1 an idiot)"' (Flanagan, 2018: 697).

Eugenic traces

The identification of multi-problem populations as those in receipt of multiple services is not a new idea, though the sophisticated use of 'big data' potentially enables unprecedented surveillance and intervention. Flanagan (2018: 690) cautions that, unpalatable as it may be, '"problem family" discourse must be considered in its relation to eugenicist discourse if we are to fully understand it'. These constructions are not interchangeable, but they share a common discursive root. Flanagan (2018: 694) argues that the accumulation of individual case data to build a type is common to the designation of eugenic 'pedigrees', which characterise individuals and families as identifiable sites of unsavoury diseases, habits or conditions.

According to Flanagan (2018: 694), such analysis was 'attractive to the emerging professions of psychology, social work and sociology, offering "a rationale, scientific authority, an aura of expertise and objectivity" to those "involved in the new business of social control"':

Inherent to 'problem family' discourse is the thinking of people into categories based upon their transgression of the order of things in the welfare state, categories through which they can be converted into objects and subjects of governmental action. The emphasis is on entrenched, self-perpetuating disadvantage, but 'problem family' discourse crucially also situates the 'problem' within a family, a group of people related to each other through a shared genetic profile. (Flanagan, 2018: 698)

Flanagan's archival research is restricted to a specific period of intervention policy towards the public housing population in Tasmania in the 1970s. Her study gives special attention to the work of Eric Cunningham Dax, an English psychiatrist and influential mental health administrator with demonstrable links to eugenic ideology. Dax had a predilection for citing statistics to demonstrate that problem families used a vastly disproportionate amount of services and generated an unconscionable level of cost in relation to their numbers – effectively, the argument promulgated by the Productivity Commission in 2015.

In my view, it is important to reflect on the associations that Flanagan's analysis suggests when we are considering how best to progress the design of child protection interventions:

It means something when we co-locate disadvantage and a genetic relationship, as we do in the 'problem family'. The boundaries of a single encounter between an individual and a service slip beyond the presenting individual and their presenting issue to encompass parents, siblings and children, and their respective pathologies and service interactions. (Flanagan, 2018: 698–9)

When we contemplate notions of early or intensive intervention – of breaking cycles – it is instructive to consider the 'common-sense' discursive boundaries that inform this thinking, that is, to question why 'problem family' pathology is so often seen as the target and rationale for intervention.

Child welfare inequalities

The findings of the 2013–19 Child Welfare Inequalities Project (CWIP), an extensive mixed-methods programme of research into child protection system contact and outcome inequalities in the UK, have recently been reported (Bywaters and CWIP Team, 2020). Smaller-scale research of a similar nature in Aotearoa, principally undertaken by University of Otago academic Dr Emily Keddell (2020), has produced comparable data in the Aotearoa context.

The CWIP began with the proposition that although inequalities have influenced policy and service development in health and education for many decades, relative deprivation has been largely ignored in child welfare planning and service development. The research programme assembled extensive data from England, Scotland, Wales and Northern Ireland, identifying correlations between Index of Deprivation scores and ranks for small neighbourhoods, and the relative proportion of children placed in state care or on child protection plans: 'Data was analysed in terms of decile (10%) or quintile (20%) bands of deprivation, i.e. from the 10% or 20% most deprived neighbourhoods to the 10% or 20% least deprived' (Bywaters and CWIP Team, 2020: 4).

The quantitative outcome inequality findings are stark, graphically identifying a steep gradient across the UK:

Children in the most deprived 10% of small neighbourhoods in the UK are over 10 times more likely to be in foster or residential care or on protection plans than children in the least deprived 10%. ...

There is a steep social gradient in children's chances of a coercive intervention. Around 55% of children on protection plans or who were looked after lived or came from the most deprived 20% of neighbourhoods. (Bywaters and CWIP Team, 2020: 4, 5)

It is recognised that the relationship between relative poverty and outcomes is a nuanced process involving interactions between the complex factors that contribute to service demand and supply:

Each step improvement in socio-economic circumstances is accompanied by a proportionately similar drop in intervention rates, right across the spectrum of family circumstances. It is not just about poverty, although the material and psychological pressures on family life and relationships associated with poverty are insufficiently recognised. Even families in the second most advantaged decile of neighbourhoods in the UK are more likely to find their children on protection plans or looked after than families in the most advantaged decile. (Bywaters and CWIP Team, 2020: 31)

This analysis refutes the assertion – relied on by then Minister Paula Bennet in her Foreword to the *White Paper for Vulnerable Children* (Ministry of Social Development, 2012) – that poverty is irrelevant simply because all impoverished people do not abuse their children:

Many parents in poverty do not abuse or neglect their children. But poverty makes the task of good enough parenting much harder while greater economic resources provide the opportunity for many and varied solutions to parenting difficulties – from nannies to treats, from private education to security in meeting basic needs for food, shelter and warmth. Poverty can have direct effects on children, such as an inability to provide the basics or buy alternative forms of care, but also indirectly affects parenting through anxiety shame and stigma (Featherstone et al., 2019). (Bywaters and CWIP Team, 2020: 16–17)

With the partial exception of Northern Ireland, analysis of case records indicates that deprivation was not regarded as a target for social work intervention. Poverty was conceived as external to the 'core-business' of child protection, and issues such as 'Income, debt, food, heating and clothing, employment and housing conditions were rarely considered relevant risk factors in children's lives' (Bywaters and CWIP Team, 2020: 38, 5).

Poverty blinkers

There is some profound irony here, in the sense that 'children's services practitioners and managers interviewed and observed in the case studies … described deprived neighbourhoods as the usual sites of practice; streets and areas to which they returned repeatedly' (Bywaters and CWIP Team, 2020: 31). It appears that the dominant risk-saturated construction of child protection legitimises a form of discursive blindness, or a reframing of economic disadvantage as personal inadequacy (McCartan et al, 2018; Featherstone et al, 2019):

> Rather than emphasising poverty as a structural problem, once risk became an issue, poverty was not infrequently framed pejoratively in England and Scotland, through descriptions of communities that lacked aspiration and suffered from generational deficits. At the time of the case studies (2017–19), the language of the 'toxic trio' (a term used to signify the combined presence of substance misuse, domestic violence and mental ill-health within a household) was often used to frame low-income neighbourhoods and their residents in terms of toxicity and the 'problems' that families presented. (Bywaters and CWIP Team, 2020: 37)

Disturbingly, this analysis tracks back to the persistent spectre of the problem family in public welfare. The CWIP found that in England and Scotland, socio-economic burdens were likely to be framed within a blaming and stigmatising multi-problem, 'troubled families' discourse. The 19th-century imagination still sends long tendrils out to capture the sensibilities of modern practice. This association is actively and tacitly justified by liberal political theory.

Implications for reform

This report includes recommendations for child protection reform that are directly relevant to the Aotearoa context. In accord with the stance adopted in this book, it is recognised that child protection, and ideas about social welfare more generally, are constructed within dominant relations of power:

> A social welfare system reflects the society in which it operates: its assumptions, priorities and attitudes to children, parents, and family life. It also reflects the role of the state: how policy is made, the values that underpin policy, the power it exercises over its citizens, how it manages and polices that power and what it counts as success. (Bywaters and CWIP Team, 2020: 1)

It is also recognised that the stakes are high, not perhaps for the powerful, but certainly for the children and families on the receiving end of statutory social work intervention:

> The implications for children's lives are profound. Child welfare inequalities have profound implications for the lives of children and their families. There are growing numbers of young people in the child protection and care systems across the UK. This is likely to continue to feed the prison and homeless populations, teenage pregnancy and parenthood, high rates of poor physical and mental health amongst young people and premature death (Murray et al., 2020), with long term human and societal consequences and costs. (Bywaters and CWIP Team, 2020: 5)

These are, of course, the very associations that the simplistic 'safe, stable and loving homes' at the earliest opportunity panacea promoted by the Expert Panel (EP, 2015) was designed to disrupt. However, within a neoliberal capitalist society characterised by the production and reproduction of deeply classed, gendered and raced inequalities, this prescription is, in my view, akin to mowing the grass and expecting it not to grow again.

The report suggests that it is time to fundamentally rethink and redesign the model of child welfare practice in the UK:

> The scale and reach of inequalities identified make the case for rethinking the focus and priorities of children's social care systems in the UK countries and internationally. More of the same will not reduce inequity in children's life chances. Rather it is likely to continue the negative spiral of increasing investigations, coercive high cost interventions and the separation of children from their birth families, drawing ever more scarce resources away from supporting families and preventing harm to children. (Bywaters and CWIP Team, 2020: 8)

It is argued that the relationship between material circumstances and related family stresses needs to be brought to the fore in front-line practice. In a manner reminiscent of Jones's (1983) emphasis on the disjunction between the social work mandate and the realities of working-class lives, it is proposed that a lack of attention to the challenges imposed by poverty and inequality 'has reinforced a disjunction between families' priorities and service's priorities, and obstructs the development of positive relationships between professionals and families' (Bywaters and CWIP Team, 2020: 6).

The paradigm shift that is recommended is said to necessitate a fundamental change in the way that families living in material hardship are viewed by the state: 'This means changing the narrative about families across governments. Governments should seek to build up support for families rather than stigmatising families as troubled, chaotic or failing, recognising that most parents want to do the best for their children' (Bywaters and CWIP Team, 2020: 56). This would require moving away from the dominant individuated responsibility agenda and a return to building close working relationships with families and communities, providing services connected to 'geographical and identity communities' and the support that is 'recognised as helpful by families' (Bywaters and CWIP Team, 2020: 56).

Inequalities in Aotearoa

Keddell, Davie and Barson (2019) adopted similar quantitative building blocks to assemble comparative data regarding child welfare inequalities in Aotearoa. Using the Integrated Data Infrastructure (IDI) system, a large research database held by Statistics New Zealand, the authors correlated three system contact outcomes – abuse 'substantiation',[1] FGCs and entry into care – with relative poverty 'decile ratings'. Decile ratings are a small geographic area measure of deprivation (New Zealand Index of Deprivation [NZDep]), based on a range of variables: income, homeownership, employment, qualifications, family structure, housing, access to transport and communications. As in the UK studies, a severe 'social gradient' is disturbingly clear:

> The main finding of this study is that there is a substantial social gradient relationship between deprivation and all three types of child protection system contact. The spread of system contact relative to deprivation level is marked. For example, 36% of all substantiated findings, and 28% of all children placed, occurred in the most deprived decile. The size of the differences between quintiles of NZDep were particularly marked for substantiations and family group conferences although a rate more than six times higher was still observed for placement of children in the most deprived quintile compared to the least deprived quintile. (Keddell et al, 2019: 6)

While it is recognised that there are significant differences of scale and that the measures of intervention status or 'severity' are proximal rather than exact, it appears that inequalities may be even starker in Aotearoa:

> In England, a child in the most deprived quintile, compared to the least deprived quintile, was 2.7 times as likely to be a 'child in need' (somewhat comparable to the family group conference point examined in ANZ) and 2.8 times as likely to be in 'out of home care'. ... In Aotearoa New Zealand, the differences are much more marked, with FGC intervention rates 18 times higher for children in the most deprived quintile compared to the least deprived quintile, and placement rates six times higher. This large difference begs the question of why deprivation is so highly associated with system contact, leading to such differing experiences for families, and what should be done to reduce such disparities. (Keddell et al, 2019: 6)

There are a range of possible reasons for such disproportionate outcomes. As I have suggested, poverty is linked with social class and ethnicity – with capitalism and with colonisation. There are also complex issues relating to systemic bias.

Bias and inequality

In Aotearoa, Indigenous children comprise about 25 per cent of the child population but represent approximately 60 per cent of those in state care. In part, this reflects Māori over-representation among the working-class poor and the associated influence of historical dispossession and cultural alienation. Such disparities are routinely reflected across a range of comparative social statistics (Cram et al, 2015). Keddell, Davie and Barson (2019: 6–7) acknowledge the competing factors at play, including likely connections between the prevalence of 'abuse' and the social stressors associated with poverty, lack of access to support or preventive services, and the differential surveillance of poorer communities from the agencies that generate reports of concern.

The operation of bias in professional decision-making is a nuanced area of study; biases can be related to more or less conscious belief systems, cognitive processes, and organisational cultures (Keddell and Hyslop, 2020). A recent mixed-methods study of the practices and perceptions of child welfare social workers employed by statutory and non-government organisations within Aotearoa identified a degree of racial bias in practice, noting that whānau Māori are more likely to be perceived as inherently risky (Keddell and Hyslop, 2019). Among other things, this research looked to shed light on the way in which Māori children are ratcheted more rapidly into the system once notified: 'There is an increasing overrepresentation of Māori children at each stage of progressive contact with statutory services, increasing from 40% of children notified to 60% of those entering the care system [EP, 2015]' (Keddell and Hyslop, 2019: 411).

Respondent social workers were randomly provided with 'case situation' vignettes where the protagonists were assigned either Pākehā or Māori identity. The vignette scenarios were presented at four levels, corresponding to escalating levels of concern. Data analysis revealed small but potentially significant indications of ethnic bias: 'Qualitative perceptions of risk, safety, problem causes, and plan goals were elicited. The quantitative findings showed family ethnicity had a moderate effect on perceptions of risk, safety, and decisions. The Māori family was perceived as higher risk than the Pākehā family and had more decisions made about them' (Keddell and Hyslop, 2019: 411).

Although the threshold and intervention decisions made by social workers are entangled with wider contributing factors, it is likely that practitioner bias is a factor in outcome differentiation for Māori:

> This pattern of findings suggests that despite similar ways of defining risk, safety, problems, and practice aims, practitioners can still differ in their perceptions of the level of risk, as despite these similarities in problem conceptualization, they perceived the Māori whānau as higher risk than the Pākehā family. When combined with a lessened ability to identify safety factors operating in Māori whānau, this may result in heightened intervention for some Māori whānau, especially where concerns are serious. (Keddell and Hyslop, 2019: 418)

Echoing the analysis of Parton (2014a), Keddell (2019: 23) suggests that there are wider indications, such as hospitalisation rates for serious injury, which suggest that the overall incidence of child maltreatment may, in fact, be decreasing. However, the relationship between the actual prevalence of child abuse and how it is reported and responded to has never been straightforward.

Reform, conflict and recurrence

Although most abuse is never reported, child protection is volatile media and political fodder (Warner, 2015). Organisational responses to both demand management and scandal politics can alter practice priorities and the way that notifications are categorised or processed:

> One explanation for the reducing care and protection reports of concern is that those notifications accepted as reports of concern have to meet a higher threshold for acceptance by OT, or that certain types of cases are no longer accepted. ... In a similar manner, the sharp

reductions in substantiations without equal reductions in notifications suggest that the cause is changes in the application of decision-making tools or logics at intake, rather than true changes in the incidence of these types of child abuse. (Keddell, 2019: 22)

Keddell (2019) develops a nuanced account of the child protection practice outcomes delivered by OT in its early years of operation (2015–18). As predicted by many critical commentators, the number of children subject to urgent care proceedings escalated markedly. Much of this is accounted for by a rise in urgent 'uplifts' of Māori babies.

She associates this outcome with a long-standing international trend, at least in neoliberal anglophone contexts, to risk-averse child-focused practice. Similarly, in Aotearoa, the backlash against this outcome can be aligned with a recent turn to rethinking what has proven, ultimately, to be a socially divisive and destructive approach to child protection in increasingly unequal societies (Featherstone et al, 2017).

The discourse of child-focused and trauma-informed early permanency leaked into the fabric of practice sensibility after 2015 (Hyslop and Keddell, 2019). However, the conflicted debates of the 1970s and 1980s have now re-emerged with a vengeance, based on the historical friction between Māori concepts of child and whānau welfare and the liberal ideological precept of the child as an individual unit to be protected from harm. All of this is being played out against a backcloth of systemic social inequality and political contestation.

Escalating Māori baby uplifts

Keddell (2019) documents a steady rise in care numbers since 2013. There are significant subtleties within these figures. First, the overall number of children entering care reduced over this time. However, once in the system, children were less likely to exit care, which is consistent with the logic of decisive intervention and early stability:

Although overall the numbers of children in care have increased, entries to care have reduced 2013–2018 by 10%. Exits have reduced much more sharply, by 34%. Once they are placed in care, they are more likely to stay for longer, pushing up overall numbers in care at any one time. (Keddell, 2019: 25)

Second, entries into care are skewed towards younger children, particularly babies and, more particularly, Māori newborns. The practice of 'removal' by emergency interim order became increasingly entrenched, rising 'from 258 in 2008/2009, to 380 in 2017/2018, while babies entering care by arrangement or agreement declined from 168 to just 60'(Keddell, 2019: 28). The incidence of Māori disproportionality is confronting:

> The largest increases by age 2013–2017 are in children under aged 5–9 at 31%, but the later data on new-borns show an even greater increase 2015–2018 of 33%. Examining the baby increase further shows that this increase is racialised, with the total increase accounted for by an increase in Māori babies removed while other group rates remain stable. (Keddell, 2019: 29)

By way of comparison, the overall Māori rate of newborn removal equates 'to 103 per 10,000 births, compared to the non-Māori rate of 24 per 10,000 births' (Keddell, 2019: 27). Keddell (2019: 27–8) reminds us that 'there was an outcry in England recently due to the rate of baby removals over the last 10 years doubling to 35 per 10,000 births'.

As has been argued throughout this text, these brutal figures reflect the disproportionate positioning of Māori at the bottom of the socio-economic heap, the way in which young Māori women disproportionately carry the burden of poverty and hardship in Aotearoa, and, in recent times, the re-emergence of a narrow child rescue mentality.

Signs of a wind shift

It should similarly be noted that there has also been an increased focus on placing children within extended family settings, which reflects a degree of increased responsiveness to Māori:

> The biggest increase in care type, with a 48% increase 2013–2017, is in the use of family/whanau placements, while non-kin care placements increased by only 5%, and residential placements reduced. However, due to the increase in numbers overall, this translates into a small increase of kinship care as a proportion of all care, from 44% to 53%. This increased use of whānau care may be the reason for the reductions in children moving into 'home for life', that is, permanent foster care with non-kin placements. This number has reduced since 2013, from 417 that year, to 331 in the 2017/18 year. (Keddell, 2019: 25)

As suggested, the thrust of the Expert Panel reforms was not unopposed, particularly by iwi and social sector interests outside of the state system, but also by Māori advisory voices within the bureaucracy. As Keddell (2019: 21) points out, the final shape of the revised legislation is a mixed bag:

In short, the existing tensions in the Act between family empowerment and children's best interests were re-inscribed, with both family and whanau-oriented sections, and those that focus exclusively on the child's rights to protection and best interests. For example, families will be both assisted to, 'at the earliest opportunity, to fulfil their responsibility to meet the needs of their children and young persons' (s4 (d)) but also, where children 'require care under the Act' will be ensured 'a safe, stable, and loving home from the earliest opportunity' (s4 (e) (i)).

In terms of the 'tranched' rollout of the 'modernisation' programme, the early and intensive intervention elements of the proposed package have been very slow to materialise. Changes to the legal framework have also been staggered. In particular, the effect of the recently activated section 7AA requirement to make decisions in partnership with whānau and hapū under Te Tiriti o Waitangi is only now beginning to emerge.

As per the discussion that follows, there are strong indications that the balance may be swinging back to a more whānau-centric focus. As I have argued in this book, statutory child protection is a complex undertaking. Practice development and subsequent implementation is politically generated and contested. Legal and procedural frameworks do not sit apart from this volatile context, and they are also constrained by organisational capacity, managerial commitment and practitioner consciousness.

The more draconian practice developments of recent years have been influenced by an ideological focus on the concept of trauma reproduction and the persuasive notion that all children, as social and economic citizens of the future, have a right to reach their developmental potential as neoliberal market players. As in the English setting, the narrow concept of individuated social justice allows for a punitive stance to be taken with parents who are deemed inadequate and for the structural nature of social inequality to be backgrounded (Hyslop, 2016b, 2017).

It is important to be unequivocal about the negative consequences of recent practice reform. The overtly racist post-Expert Panel practice outcomes evidence a lack of meaningful commitment to the kind of resource-intensive and culturally informed solution building for whānau that Māori advocates have advanced for over 40 years now. These results are clearly consistent with the aggressive social investment analysis proffered by the Expert Panel: the early removal and resocialisation of Māori children as a means of reducing future cost and preventing the intergenerational reproduction of social disadvantage. This thinking is dressed up in notions of individuated children's rights and behavioural science, in the same way that the quasi-eugenic elements of liberal governance have been disguised over time (Gillies et al, 2017).

The geyser blows

In May 2019, concerns about the authoritarian and glaringly incompetent efforts to 'uplift' a newborn Māori baby from her mother at Hawkes Bay Hospital in the North Island city of Hastings sparked a public furore. The mother concerned was supported by whānau and by an articulate midwife who felt that this kind of ham-fisted practice was unwarranted and intolerable. Many of the emotive exchanges between state social workers and whānau/supporters in this situation were video-recorded and later reported by an investigative journalist who was present during key periods of this extended confrontation.

The images and commentary presented on a popular mainstream digital news site brought the harsh reality of OT's without-notice uplift practices into the living rooms of 'middle New Zealand'. This story came to symbolise all that was amiss within the corporate walls of the new-look state agency, begging questions about how and why such practice was condoned, how such decisions were made, and by whom? This event generated a rash of official inquiries into the operation of the state child protection agency.

It also generated an urgent claim to the Waitangi Tribunal concerning the risk of significant and irreversible prejudice arising from OT practice. The claim was accepted in late October 2019, and an extended series of hearings developed around the question of whether policy and practice settings are currently consistent with the principles of the Te Tiriti o Waitangi. The implications of the far-reaching insights arising from this process are discussed at the conclusion of this chapter.

Waitangi Tribunal evidence

Much of the substance and upshot of the inequalities research undertaken by Keddell and collaborators is usefully summarised in a brief of evidence provided to the Urgent Waitangi Tribunal Inquiry – Wai 2915 (Keddell and Cleaver, 2020). First, it is made clear that Māori child protection system disparities intersect with relative deprivation levels. Within this overall pattern, there is also evidence of the 'inverse intervention law' reported by the CWIP in the UK, specifically, that families living in relatively deprived pockets within wealthier areas are likely to attract more intervention than poor families living in generally impoverished areas:

> Regional differences also show interesting patterns. Equally highly deprived children (who are disproportionately Māori ...) in regions with low overall levels of deprivation, have as much as 2.6x the chances of entering care as those in regions with higher levels of overall

deprivation (known as the inverse intervention law – found in other countries too). (Keddell and Cleaver, 2020: para 8)

It is asserted that the dichotomy between greater need versus greater surveillance explanations for system contact (the 'risk bias' or 'need bias' debate) should not be regarded as mutually exclusive:

As Detlaff[2] notes in the US context: 'Despite the body of evidence that exists, those who contend that "disproportionate need" is the primary contributing factor to disproportionality have largely discounted the role of racism or racial bias in child welfare systems and have emphasized the role of poverty and related risks. ... These arguments that frame "disproportionate need" as the predominant contributing factor have led many in child welfare systems to believe that the causes of disproportionality occur largely outside their systems, and as a result, racial disproportionality is to be expected and no action is needed to address it'. (Keddell and Cleaver, 2020: para 15)

The potential for surveillance bias regarding 'famous' problem families is noted. Biases within and between systems can have compounding effects. Police call-outs for family violence, for example, are automatically notified to OT. There is a higher likelihood of Māori being victims of intimate partner violence, and there is evidence that a larger proportion of Māori notifications are classified as requiring further action. Instrumental bias may also be generated by an emphasis on historic 'case' records rather than current circumstances:

An emphasis on 'the history', as contained in case records, at the expense of current, in-depth assessment based on an engaged relationship (as we saw in the Hawkes Bay case) will exacerbate bias because of the weight of history – more Māori are surveilled and have intergenerational whanau histories of system contact. Giving weight to recorded contact in decision-making without up to date assessment, compounds historic inequities. (Keddell and Cleaver, 2020: para 22)

There are also practice variations relating to workload, values, practice theories and the support available to practitioners, which, in turn, can be associated with the practice orientation or culture of site offices:

Site cultures also shape disparities for Māori. At one site we interviewed in our research, we found a strong commitment to family preservation which was linked to both family support values and a sense of community investment by the social workers. Many lived locally, and were Māori and Pasifika similarly to the community they worked in. More efforts were made to engage with whanau and gather information directly from them, and the rates of children in care at that site were low. At other sites, such explicit commitment to family preservation was less obvious in the site culture. (Keddell and Cleaver, 2020: para 29)

As argued within this text, the politicised underpinnings of the two-stage Vulnerable Children/Expert Panel reform process were always likely to impact detrimentally on Māori despite rhetorical assertions to the contrary:

> The direction of these reforms was bound to disadvantage Māori. Neither reform took seriously either the effects of social conditions or biases, or lack of prevention services as key contributors to disparities in the care system. Our child poverty rates remain high, housing is in crisis, and the NGO and Iwi social service sector is notoriously underfunded. Oranga Tamariki has only recently begun to engage in provision of what are now called 'intensive intervention' services. Both reforms played to political concerns about high profile child deaths, despite the fact that the vast majority of families referred to Oranga Tamariki are struggling with a range of social pressures and issues, rather than the demons presented in child death cases on the front pages of the news. (Keddell and Cleaver, 2020: para 35)

It should be added that an emphasis on 'forensic' child protection within stressed and risk-averse bureaucracies can become overly focused on gathering evidence of danger at the expense of working with families to reduce the possibility of harm. The inquiry processes to date, as canvassed in the following discussion, bring together many of the challenges that have confronted child protection practice in Aotearoa over time.

Practice review

An internal review, instigated by OT and published on 5 November 2019, documented a raft of errors with the management of the specific Hastings 'uplift' situation (Oranga Tamariki, 2019). Practice decisions were found to have been based on historical records rather than an impartial appraisal of current circumstances. Information consistent with the initial assessment was accepted without the required scrutiny, and contrary evidence was disregarded. Opportunities to work constructively with the whānau to provide support and develop strengths were not pursued.

The early permanent removal logic of the Expert Panel reform process was clearly on show, and the practice orientation was essentially skewed towards this predetermined outcome. An older child had previously been taken from the family, and this decision was used to provide justification for the chosen practice path. No FGC was held (though a referral was made) and the family were not visited. Family members and non-government services involved with the family were not involved in case-planning processes.

As well as exhibiting many of the classic elements of decision bias, the case also contained many of the perennial ingredients consistent with racist and oppressive state social work: a young and relatively powerless Māori family with challenging past experiences that were used to underscore risk rather than point to the need for social and community support. The 'buzzword' of 'past trauma' was equated with future harm. The construction of the unborn baby as 'the client' appears to have justified a very limited focus on meaningful engagement with whānau. The expedient dynamic of the situation was reinforced by key staff vacancies and a site culture that emphasised 'decisive and timely decision-making to facilitate stable and permanent care as early as possible, especially for babies' (Oranga Tamariki, 2019: 37).

There was evidence of poor understandings of the law and practice. Attitudes to the parents and potential whānau caregivers appear to have been influenced by the 'subsequent parent' legislative provisions, though the legal threshold was not met. The internal practice review also noted the wider systemic normalisation of 'without-notice' applications for interim custody. This process effectively removes the opportunity for whānau to respond to information placed before the court until a later date, so that removal occurs without challenge.

Remedies

OT climbed down from initial denials once the 'casework' practice was scrutinised and undertook to back away from the default use of interim custody applications. The following excerpt is taken from an official statement attributed to then OT Chief Executive Officer (CEO) Grainne Moss in response to the subsequent Ombudsman's report (Boshier, 2020), which exposed systemic issues within the ministry:

> Oranga Tamariki introduced system and practice changes in November 2019 following its own Hawke's Bay Practice Review, which addressed a number of the issues identified in the Ombudsman's Report, says Ms Moss. These changes included:
> Unless there is a clear need for action to protect a child from immediate and imminent danger, all interim custody order applications are made 'on notice' to ensure the family is given the opportunity to have their say before the judge makes a final decision. (Oranga Tamariki, 2020)

Given that this is the legislated test for recourse to these orders, the organisation was essentially undertaking to desist from breaking the law. There were also assurances of greater practice oversight in future. It is difficult, however, to place a lot of faith in tighter top-down compliance measures in relation to practice reform in statutory child protection systems. Such mechanisms are often counterproductive, reinforcing the sort of 'ritualised' practice that can detract from thoughtful, creative work with whānau (Hyslop, 2009). This area of well-supported and supervised discretion is at the heart of skilful child protection work in my experience – practice that is inclusive, respectful and strengths-based without being blind to risk and harm.

OT was, naturally, inclined to frame the 'Hawkes Bay Case' as an exceptional example of poor practice that the organisation was willing and able to address. As we shall see, subsequent inquiries, particularly the review undertaken by the Ombudsman and ex-Principal Family Court Judge Peter Boshier, begged to differ.

'He Take Kohukihuki': a matter of urgency

In short, Boshier's (2020) report – 'He Take Kohukihuki' – clearly demonstrates that the Hastings uplift scenario was a long way from an isolated or anomalous incident of system overreach. In many ways, this measured review is damning. The practice of OT social workers is described as unreasonable, and compliance with the statutory legal mandate is clearly identified as inadequate. Examination of a sample of 74 cases of children uplifted by way of 'without-notice' orders revealed excessive practice variability, poor understanding of the law and delayed, reactive decision-making:

> I found the outcome in many of these cases was that decisions for **pēpi** were being made late and without expert advice or whānau involvement. I also found that urgency and the need for without notice applications were created through the Ministry's lack of capacity to follow its own processes in a timely and effective way. (Boshier, 2020: 20)

A disturbing lack of engagement with whānau is evidenced in the routine absence of **hui ā-whānau**, formal FGCs or even basic home visiting:

> I found that urgency was created through the Ministry's inaction and lack of capacity to follow processes in a timely and effective way. As a consequence, parents were disadvantaged – first, by not having an opportunity to respond to the allegations or challenge the information

relied upon by the Ministry before their pēpi were removed, and second, by having to challenge orders after they were made, and when the parents were vulnerable because they were either heavily pregnant or had just given birth. (Boshier, 2020: 174–5)

It is fair to say that the extent of gaps in practice identified, as well as the obvious disregard of the rights of whānau to due process and natural justice, surprised even established critics of OT practice. This report concludes by offering ongoing oversight and review by the Ombudsman's Office as a means of assuring that recommended changes are adequately progressed.

Ko Te Wā Whakawhiti

Boshier's (2020) report was preceded by 'Ko Te Wā Whakawhiti, it's time for change' (Whānau Ora Commissioning Agency, 2020). This was a Māori-initiated inquiry under the umbrella of the 'Whānau Ora Commissioning Agency, with the support of the South Island Commissioning Agency Te Pūtahitanga o Te Waipounamu and under the guidance of renowned Māori leadership' (Whānau Ora Commissioning Agency, 2020: 11). Although the Hawkes Bay uplift debacle was the catalyst, this response was clearly informed by sentiment that had been building for some time, as well as by a political agenda for Māori independence with a much longer lineage.

The process was supported by established Māori interests via the Iwi Chairs Forum and driven by a 'who's who' of Māori in relation to the politics of social development. Given the links to the Whānau Ora structure, the inquiry inevitably had some predilections for this model of service provision. However, be that as it may, the inquiry clearly stamped the authority of Māori leadership on an agenda to disestablish the current system of statutory child welfare, especially for Māori, and to develop a new service 'for, by and with' Māori.

The inquiry adopted an inclusive approach to information gathering, accessing the voices of those with lived experience of alienating practice, testimony that is seldom reported in official narratives:

Whānau from all around the **motu** shared their stories of loss and struggle, and the hurt and suffering caused when **tamariki** and mokopuna had been ripped away. Even more heart-wrenching was hearing what happened in the aftermath of an uplift; whānau feelings of hopelessness and depression. Yet these same whānau found the strength to stand up and be heard, to share stories that were often deeply personal and raw, and to come together with other whānau around the country to make change. (Whānau Ora Commissioning Agency, 2020: 11)

The Ko Te Wā Whakawhiti report provides a useful summation of the historical relationship between the developing child welfare system and Māori, much of which coalesces with the content of this book. A turning point in authoritative integration policies is traced to the 1961 Hunn Report (Hunn, 1961):

> The Hunn report proposed a raft of policy initiatives to encourage and speed up the process. Hunn argued that Māori who resented the pressure to conform to 'the Pākehā mode of life' needed to understand that this was an inevitable consequence of becoming modern: 'It is not, in fact, a Pākehā but a modern way of life, common to advanced people ... not merely white people – in all parts of the world.' (Whānau Ora Commissioning Agency, 2020: 28)

Modernity and capitalism are not synonymous, but they are inextricably entangled (Hyslop, 2012; Casassas and Wagner, 2016). This insidious doctrine of integrating the non-compliant into the disciplinary programme of liberal capitalist modernity justified the escalating 'removal' and attempted 'resocialisation' of neglected, abused or otherwise maladjusted children within the state care system. As discussed in Chapter 3, this agenda created a painful legacy for whānau Māori.

A 'school of hard knocks' approach has often been delivered to the children of the poor. Overall, the care system in Aotearoa has a grossly disturbing underbelly, which is currently subject to a Royal Commission of Inquiry into Historical Abuse in State Care and in the Care of Faith-Based Institutions. In an interim report published in December 2020, the commission estimated that the staggering figure of 250,000 children were abused in care between 1950 and 2019 (Royal Commission of Inquiry into Historical Abuse in State Care and in the Care of Faith-Based Institutions, 2020). Institutional abuse was routinely visited upon working-class children, particularly Māori.

Much of the discomforting history (Stanley, 2016) of abuse in state care is predicated on the inability of children to be heard within the confines of adult power systems. There is a significant recent history of abusive practices in national residential institutions. Through the 1990s and into the early 2000s, scores of young people were abused and intimidated at the Whakapakiri Youth Programme on Great Barrier Island. The conditions of the camp and the culture of the programme were such that this was entirely predictable, while warning signs and frequent disclosures were steadfastly ignored. The placement was convenient for 'difficult' youth, and it is hard not to conclude that a lesser standard of human rights was accorded to these children of the para-proletariat.

Concerns recorded in the Ko Te Wā Whakawhiti report in relation to the capacity of OT staff, and the institutional support provided to enhance their practice, are not encouraging and not unfamiliar:

Oranga Tamariki social workers who participated in the Māori Inquiry highlighted unacceptably large caseloads, an organisational bullying culture, issues of burnout, and issues of social workers' own health and wellbeing problems. Based on whānau interviews, there also seemed to be a shortage of Māori social workers, or that whānau ended up with non-Māori social workers who they felt weren't culturally competent or couldn't relate to. (Whānau Ora Commissioning Agency, 2020: 59)

Predictably, whānau reported receiving more accessible 'trust-based' support from Whanau Ora 'navigators' or Māori providers.

Suggested way forward

This inquiry concluded that the existing system failed to harness the potential capacity of whānau to find and develop their own solutions:

The overwhelming and consistent message that the current State care and protection system simply does not work for any of the stakeholders involved – tamariki, whānau, care-givers, social workers or other **kaimahi** – was reinforced throughout the submissions, and pointed to a complex systemic mix of inadequate political representation, political bias, and adverse policies. The effects of service fragmentation and sectoral competition, inadequate and siloed funding systems, faulty sub-contracting and one-dimensional deliverables, was underpinned by the reliance of Western knowledge systems over **Mātauranga Māori** understanding, and **Kaupapa Māori** practice. (Whānau Ora Commissioning Agency, 2020: 67)

A staged change process centred on three action points is recommended:

1. A strengthening of whānau capacity to deal with the current system, including the provision of 'wraparound' support, particularly for wāhine Māori (Māori women).
2. A structural analysis and review of OT, including: 'A) Review to inform: Legislative reform; accountability by Crown for best outcomes for Māori; Māori data sovereignty; adherence to Te Tiriti O Waitangi. B) Review uplift practices, particularly criteria for uplifts, with a view to abandoning "uplift" as a legitimate intervention. Revised practices and procedures, at a bare minimum, must look to reduce the harm caused by whakapapa trauma, and optimally, support the fundamental and customary rights of tamariki Māori'.
3. A building on the call from whānau for 'by Māori, for Māori, with Māori' solutions for long-term sustainability. The long-term vision for whānau

well-being is for robust and sustainable change that is ultimately driven by whānau priorities and world views. This long-term systemic change is based on Māori decision-making, collective Māori endorsement, integration, workforce development and sustainable funding. It includes the voices of whānau Māori with lived experience at all levels of decision-making and builds on collective Māori endorsement (whānau/hapū/iwi/ **hapori**) and political momentum.

The Ko Te Wā Whakawhiti report pulls no punches in mapping the contours of a totally redesigned child protection system, where resources are reallocated for 'high quality whānau centred kaupapa Māori services in every rohe of Aotearoa' (Whānau Ora Commissioning Agency, 2020: 72).

The Office of the Commissioner for Children's review(s)

In June and November of 2020, the Office of the Commissioner for Children also produced a two-part report on questions raised by the removal of Māori infants from parental care by the state: 'Te Kuku O Te Marama' (TKOTM). The focus of this review process was framed as follows: 'what needs to change to enable pēpi Māori (0–3 months) to remain in the care of their whānau in situations where Oranga Tamariki–Ministry for Children is notified of care and protection concerns?' (Office of the Commissioner for Children, 2020a: 6). Significantly, this reporting exercise mirrors the process and findings for the Ko Te Wā Whakawhiti Māori inquiry.

Te Kuku O Te Marama: Part 1

Following the lead of Ko Te Wā Whakawhiti, TKOTM set out to access and listen to the voices of whānau. The question of who controls the narrative has always been critical to statutory child protection and, in a broader sense, in relation to the history of Māori and the state (Hibbs, 2005). The experiences of families on the receiving end of statutory practice, particularly high-stakes interventions such as child removal, are usually confined to case-note records assembled by social workers. For all intents and purposes, the official version of practice becomes 'the' authorised story. Whānau accounts of practice in these circumstances are delegitimised by the ascription of such subaltern labels as belonging to the uneducated, immoral, emotionally traumatised and any number of similar deficit categories.

The first part of the TKOTM review foregrounds stories from whānau, mainly mothers, with recent experience of child removal and/or significant involvement with the process of statutory child protection in Aotearoa. The report articulates the pain, anger and confusion suffered by those on the receiving end of coercive statutory intervention, and, to a degree, brings this suffering into the public domain. Glaring discrepancies are highlighted between the managerial artefacts of OT practice – high-level policy commitments and espoused practice standards – and the accounts shared by informants.

Whānau reported an absence of respectful engagement and trust, as evidenced by exclusion from decision-making processes. OT social workers were described as lacking commitment to the possibility of change, short on empathy and overly focused on calculating past deficits. Māori mothers were concerned about a lack of meaningful support, unclear concerns and shifting goalposts. They felt that their context and life stories were disregarded. They wanted social workers, preferably but not necessarily Māori practitioners, who had some awareness of their worlds – workers who could stand alongside them rather than pass judgement.

I am not saying that these accounts are gospel. They are, however, indicative of how the child protection arm of the state is understood and experienced by those in most need of successful assistance. There were specific stories about the execution of unnecessarily traumatic uplift practices and of the court system being held over as a threat to ensure behavioural compliance. Feelings of being punished for being a victim of violence or past life challenges were shared, in keeping with the extreme child-centric mindset that the mother is merely a vehicle for child well-being. Some of the practice criticisms aired are deeply disturbing: threats around the consequences of criticising OT via social media; being goaded to return to substance use so that children will be taken; or threats of baby removal to encourage a pregnancy termination.

Te Kuku O Te Marama: Part 2

The current Children's Commissioner, Andrew Becroft, initially expressed some confidence in the capacity of the post-Expert Panel reform process to deliver quantum change in statutory child protection and youth justice practice. However as the reality of reform hit home and as the inquiry process unfolded, Judge Becroft arrived at the point of calling for a much more radical transformation and urged the government to transfer outright authority to Māori. The following unequivocal statements are taken from the introductory comments that preface Part 2 of TKOTM:

> Our statutory care and protection system is one place where the issues of colonisation, modern day racism and systemic bias clearly collide with te ao Māori. It is here, day by day, that tension is played out – to the detriment of far too many generations of Māori people. (Office of the Commissioner for Children, 2020b: 7)

> Our call, and the key recommendation in this report, is for a total transformation of the statutory care and protection system. By that

I mean nothing short of a 'by Māori, for Māori' approach and a transfer of responsibility, resources and power from the state to appropriate Māori entities, as determined by Māori. (Office of the Commissioner for Children, 2020b: 6)

The immediate rationale for the inquiry – an escalation in baby 'removals', particularly of pēpi Māori (Māori babies) – is illustrated with the following statistical breakdown:

Over the past six years (to June 2019), an average of 265 babies, of which 171 were pēpi Māori, were taken into state custody each year, and the trend over this period showed planned (with notice) removals have declined while urgent (often without notice) removals had increased overall. While the numbers may seem small, the immediate and intergenerational impact on the 64% pēpi Māori and their whānau, hapū and iwi is immense. (Office of the Commissioner for Children, 2020b: 16)

It is also acknowledged that this practice has been scaled back since the Hastings 'event' and associated practice review, though the numbers remain disproportionate: 'the year to June 2020 showed a decrease in decisions made to remove babies under three months into state custody (153 total babies, of which 54% were Māori), while reports of concern remained stable' (Office of the Commissioner for Children, 2020b: 16). More broadly it is apparent that the system continues to produce and reflect unacceptable inequalities:

Inequities are seen for tamariki Māori of all ages in the care and protection system. As at June 2019, 69 percent of the children in state custody were tamariki Māori (4,420 out of 6,429). In 2019, pēpi Māori aged 0–3 months were taken into state custody at five times the rate of non-Māori babies (0.67% compared with 0.13%). (Office of the Commissioner for Children, 2020b: 24)

The second report drew on a wider process of interviews with whānau, midwives, community support workers and OT practitioners themselves. In many ways, the argument developed, and the evidence assembled, is compelling.

A litany of troubles

This report identified that whānau, particularly young mothers, were disrespected – their views were ignored or disregarded. Distrust of state social workers was found to be engrained in historical experience and reinforced by contemporary interactions. Social workers were perceived as punitive and lacking in compassion for mothers pre- or post-birth. The critical significance of whakapapa was overlooked, and no real time was spent getting to know whānau. An overriding desire for radical change is highlighted.

FGCs were experienced as oppressive and often predetermined, rather than empowering, processes. Social workers were perceived as overloaded, unresponsive and preoccupied with 'tick-box' procedures. A misguided child-centred focus was said to obscure the wider needs of whānau and their capacity to build solutions with the right resources and encouragement. This is contrasted with the positive assistance received from community-centred Māori support and advocacy services. Participants identified implicit and explicit racism within the system, with whānau experiencing discrimination because they were Māori: 'Whānau described a care and protection system dominated by Pākehā values, practices, and ways of being. They said what Oranga Tamariki sees as appropriate and necessary for tamariki to be happy and healthy is based on an individualistic worldview, incompatible with Māori perspectives and values' (Office of the Commissioner for Children, 2020b: 45).

OT staff

For the most part, data provided by OT staff are equally disconcerting. They talked about reliance on historical records in the absence of time to build relationships. Site staff 'said social work practice that works best for whānau often happens despite Oranga Tamariki systems and policies rather than because of them' (Office of the Commissioner for Children, 2020b: 38). A widening focus on 'risk' was described, alongside inconsistent practice between, and even within, site offices. Interestingly, given the espoused high-level commitments to cultural responsiveness, staff 'reflected that there is little clarity within Oranga Tamariki about how they are expected to work in partnership with whānau Māori, or iwi and Māori organisations' (Office of the Commissioner for Children, 2020b: 43). OT staff also identified elements of institutional racism, over 30 years on from PtAT. The organisation was described as complex, insular and inflexible – essentially, not designed to support whānau.

Conclusions and recommendations

The report concludes that state child protection in Aotearoa has shifted too far towards child rescue:

Statutory social work practice focuses on child rescue of pēpi at the expense of family support New Zealand's statutory care and protection system aims to strike a balance between protecting the physical safety of children and keeping children within their whānau, hapū, iwi or family group. A recurring theme identified in our review is that the current system places too great an emphasis on removing children from families when there is risk of harm, and not on actions to reduce risk from occurring. (Office of the Commissioner for Children, 2020b: 81)

It is recognised that efforts have been made to improve services, but it is very clear that progress is inadequate. Beyond the burning need for systemic change, it is identified that the service is not delivering on its fundamental obligations:

The information shared with us in our interviews, as well as the findings of Oranga Tamariki file review and the Ombudsman's report, all demonstrate that in many cases, minimum social work standards are not being followed and current legislation is not being upheld. This is despite the legislation, practice guidance and professional standards currently in place. Immediate and ongoing harm is being caused by current poor practice. This must stop now. (Office of the Commissioner for Children, 2020b: 83)

Immediate changes are suggested, bearing in mind that devolution to Māori is the imperative destination. Recommended urgent practice changes include 'having independently facilitated Family Group Conferences, ensuring assessments are based on current (not only historic) information, and stopping hospital removals of pēpi' (Office of the Commissioner for Children, 2020b: 18).

A raft of suggested legislative change is also set out. Among other things, it is suggested that the subsequent child provisions that impose a lesser set of rights on parents who have already lost children to state care should be repealed and that the fast track to permanency provision – 'safe, stable and loving homes at the earliest opportunity' – be amended. It is argued that adherence to the Te Tiriti o Waitangi should be embedded more firmly in the legislation to enable the exercise of **tino rangatiratanga**.

The report recommends that government enables a sweeping Māori-driven process of transition:

where Māori lead the transition from a system dominated by state intervention to approaches where whānau, hapū and iwi are the decision makers in all areas relating to the wellbeing of pēpi. This requires the state to honour Te Tiriti o Waitangi and relinquish power and resource to its Treaty partner to determine themselves what system, services and supports are needed for pēpi and their whānau.

Honouring and embedding Te Tiriti o Waitangi into this approach will enable an equal relationship between the government agency and iwi and hapū Māori and support the vision of Māori to exercise tino rangatiratanga in all matters relating to the care of their pēpi. (Office of the Commissioner for Children, 2020b: 108)

The text concludes with a reference to PtAT: 'We believe these steps will lead to the new daybreak that has long been envisioned by many – the realisation of tino rangatiratanga through Te Tiriti o Waitangi, and a future where Māori can achieve their own **moemoeā** for their pēpi, tamariki and **rangatahi**' (Office of the Commissioner for Children, 2020b: 112).

Discursive gaps

In summary, the TKOTM report(s) make a clear and compelling case for the urgent devolution of child protection social work in Aotearoa to iwi and Māori social service organisations in a manner and form best determined by Māori themselves. Although this is a challenging proposition, it is potentially a pathway to a much-improved service because of an enhanced capacity to build appropriate trust-based solutions with whānau.

The second report identifies the umbrella issue of entrenched socio-economic disadvantage but sees this as beyond the control of the child protection system. The historic (and contemporary) harm that has flowed from colonisation and the imposition of Pākehā/Western belief systems upon the social world of Māori is recognised, and it is argued that more of the same will not bring the change that is needed.

This is essentially where the political/structural analysis of this report ends. Although the repeal or amendment of the provisions of the Oranga Tamariki Act that have facilitated the early removal of pēpi Māori from their parents is urged, it is not acknowledged that these provisions were the direct result of a process of reform driven by a 'tough on abusers' and 'tough on those who cost the state money' neoliberal political agenda informed and justified by the ideology of social investment.

Further, as argued and exemplified in this book, a specific strand of liberal ideology that justifies dismissive and punitive approaches to the underclass poor has coloured the child protection project since its origins in the late 1800s. Liberalism is the political vehicle that underpins capitalist social relations. Capitalism produces and reproduces inequality systemically. The disproportionate representation of Māori on the relatively impoverished margins of the working class is a function of both historical dispossession and the needs of capital (Poata-Smith, 2002). In this analysis, colonisation is not simply about the imposition of generic Pākehā culture, though this process and the racism that accompanies it is a large part of the problem;

it is also about the enforcement of a specific socio-economic system – liberal capitalism.

He Pāharakeke, He Rito Whakakīkanga Whāruarua

The pre-publication report of the Waitangi Tribunal – Wai 2915 ('He Pāharakeke, He Rito Whakakīkanga Whāruarua') was released in early May 2021 (Wai 2915, 2021). It heralds an opportunity for a significant reformation of the child protection project in Aotearoa, especially for Māori. In my view, somewhat ironically, a reform analysis based on the discriminatory Māori experience of child welfare practice also signals the potential for a more just state welfare system for all children and families in Aotearoa.

The Waitangi Tribunal essentially takes a 'rights-based' approach to the relationship between the state and Māori, interpreting the implications of the reciprocal rights and obligations that flow from Te Tiriti o Waitangi. As a legally constituted judicial body, the Waitangi Tribunal considers claims with reference to understandings of Te Tiriti o Waitangi that have been clarified over time, specifically, precedent developed through past claims hearings and settlement recommendations. In summary, the Waitangi Tribunal is concerned with questions of sovereignty, authority, harm and redress.

The report recognises that disparities for Māori are rooted in colonial dispossession and in a 'failure by the Crown to honour the guarantee to Māori to the right of cultural continuity embodied in the guarantee of **te tino rangatiratanga**' (Wai 2915, 2021: xiii). In other words, 'indigenous people have a right to a particular way of life', which is protected by the promise of Te Tiriti o Waitangi; the Crown's failure to uphold this right is linked with 'hostility to the promise itself' (Wai 2915, 2021: 12), in that 'efforts to assimilate Māori to the Pākehā way – is perhaps the most fundamental breach of the Tiriti/the Treaty and its principles' (Wai 2915, 2021: xiii).

Although, the deliberations of the Waitangi Tribunal are concerned with justice for Māori within this specific framework, intersections between Te Tiriti o Waitangi obligations and the economic and political drivers of racism are implicit and unavoidable. When considering the duty of the Crown to actively protect Māori interests, the Waitangi Tribunal report accepts that racist outcomes have arisen from structural drivers, as well as factors internal to the OT system:

> Active protection means recognising that Māori parents struggling in poverty have an equal right as citizens to meet their children's needs as do the better-off in society. Active protection means recognising that the vast majority of whānau in contact with Oranga Tamariki are not out to harm their tamariki, but they may have ongoing needs that place stress on the whānau. These include factors such as

poverty, poor housing, poor mental health, substance abuse, intimate partner violence, or children with high needs. Growing inequality and the disparities in child protection, education, justice, and health that result are not the inevitable outcomes of individual choice. They are substantially the outcomes of legislation, policy, and economic settings about which a society has choices. Active protection requires substantive changes designed to address these structural conditions. (Wai 2915, 2021: 20)

Logically, in my view, it clearly follows that the discriminatory and detrimental outcomes associated with the children of the proletarian poor in disproportionate contact with the state child protection system are also in need of a new child protection paradigm centred on the active pursuit of social and economic justice. This is not to say that Māori do not have a separate and urgent claim to social justice in this context; they do, and this is what the Waitangi Tribunal found. The report essentially recognises that justice for Māori will not be achieved within a liberal Pākehā system.

In addition to socio-economic inequalities, it is recognised that there are significant internal drivers that compound institutional racism. This is captured powerfully in the following excerpt from the report: 'Johnny Apatu, a witness providing evidence in support of claimant Rex Timu, notes that "we [Māori] are the living result of that racism … every Māori person knows what racism feels like"' (Wai 2915, 2021: 51). The Crown, in the evidence provided by CEO Gráinne Moss, conceded that 'structural racism is a feature of the care and protection system which has adverse effects for tamariki Māori, whānau, hapū and iwi' (Wai 2915, 2021: 175) and asserted that efforts to partner and engage with Māori were beginning to bear fruit.

Nevertheless, the Waitangi Tribunal upheld claimant concerns that a range of factors inherent to the operation of OT contribute to profoundly unequal outcomes for Māori in the statutory child protection system. These factors can be summarised as issues related to Crown authority and control: legislative and policy coherence; the notify–investigate model; cultural competency; variable practice; FGCs; section 78 (with- or without-notice uplift) practices; and monitoring and accountability (Wai 2915, 2021: 56).

The central issue for the Waitangi Tribunal to determine was whether 'policies and practices inconsistent with te Tiriti/the Treaty have caused significant and irreversible prejudice to tamariki Māori taken into State care, as well as their whānau, hapū, and iwi?' (Wai 2915, 2021: 1). The inquiry found that the policy and practice of the state child protection agency has resulted in significant harm to Māori:

The prejudice arising is profound. In confidential sessions we heard directly from those who had tamariki taken from them by Oranga

Tamariki. The impacts are felt over generations. We heard from those who had been in care about the effects of disconnection and we heard from a range of remarkable individuals and organisations working to help whānau in contact with the system. The case for substantial redress is obvious, but its form is less so. (Wai 2915, 2021: 25)

The Waitangi Tribunal report documents a violation of the partnership principle – 'a failure of both process (insufficient engagement with Māori in the design of the legislation and policy), and substance (significant intrusion into the sphere of Māori rangatiratanga without consent)' – and argues that 'the principle of active protection requires the Crown to not only return power and control to Māori – but to direct reliable and proportionate resources towards laying a durable foundation for whānau Māori to thrive as Māori' (Wai 2915, 2021: 99). It is concluded that the legislative policy and practice changes introduced since 2017 are not sufficient to secure outcomes consistent with Te Tiriti o Waitangi and its principles.

Transformational change

In addition to a range of operational shortfalls, the Waitangi Tribunal challenges the appropriateness of the notify–investigate child protection paradigm:

> Claimants support Associate Professor Keddell's arguments that the notify–investigate model reproduces social inequities and compounds societal racism and exposure bias at every decision point. Counsel for claimants submit that the Crown, in maintaining this model, despite evidence that it perpetuates and even worsens inequities, has breached its duty to actively protect Māori rangatiratanga over their kāinga. ... Counsel submit that a paradigm shift must be implemented to move from the notify–investigate model to a preventative model, with a genuine transfer of power and resources to a 'by Māori for Māori' approach being a prerequisite of any such model. (Wai 2915, 2021: 65)

Importantly, the 'report and detect' child protection juggernaut is now being questioned internationally. A 'notify and investigate' medico-legal focus locates causation in the abusive behaviour of individuals and families. It is increasingly driven by risk and surveillance (and associated racial and class-centred bias), and it effectively conceals the significance of the socio-economic inequality produced by contemporary neoliberal politics and market economics:

> These factors include poverty, alienation, transience, income and housing insecurity, health and education disparities, involvement

with the criminal justice system, and drug and alcohol dependency. Addressing these issues will require a bold and comprehensive all-of-government approach. Piecemeal reform of Oranga Tamariki, no matter how well designed, will ultimately fail another generation of children (Māori and non-Māori), if the same factors placing inhumane stress on families continue unabated. (Wai 2915, 2021: 179)

The analytical lens applied in the Wai 2915 Report focused on the specific needs and rights of whānau Māori, as it should and must do in this context. However, as suggested, this analysis of the social and economic determinants of contact with the child protection system – and many of the implications for policy reform – have universal application.

Although this report identifies and explores matters that need to be rectified for Te Tiriti o Waitangi compliance, the Waitangi Tribunal is cautious about prescription. It is very specific, however, about how the process of transformation should be initiated and led. A transition authority is recommended: 'with a clear mandate to design and reform the care and protection system for tamariki Māori, coupled with authority to work in genuine partnership with the Crown to ensure a modified system is properly implemented' (Wai 2915, 2021: xiv).

It is recommended that this authority should (initially) be comprised of the governance group associated with the recent Māori Inquiry (Ko Te Wā Whakawhiti), namely: Sir Toby Curtis, Sir Mason Durie, Dame Areta Koopu, Dame June Mariu, Lady Tureiti Moxon, Merepeka Raukawa-Tait, the Honourable Sir Pita Sharples, Sir Mark Solomon, Dame Iritana Tāwhiwhirangi and the Honourable Dame Tariana Turia. It is noted that two of the members of the governance group (Dame Naida Glavish and Sir Mark Solomon) were recently appointed to a panel to advise the minister on possible reforms to OT and that this process will need to be integrated with the new, larger and independent initiative that is proposed.

The Waitangi Tribunal urges the Crown to 'trust the judgement of this group and be guided by them on what is appropriate in terms of the next steps towards the establishment of a Transition Authority and the process by which its composition and functions can be settled' (Wai 2915, 2021: 188). This begs the question of the countless occasions where the Crown has asked for trust from Māori and subsequently failed to deliver.

It is unclear at the time of writing whether the current government will have the fortitude to accept and adopt the recommendation(s) set out. A political/historical account like the one contained within this book cannot, of course, keep pace with an evolving process of change, particularly during the volatile times within which this text has been constructed. Political controversy in the form of complex competing interests in relation to the future of statutory child protection in Aotearoa continues to unfold. The finer detail is not critical to the summary provided here.

Concluding messages

The conciliatory human rights arm of the wider liberal political system has become involved, through its watchdog bodies, to ensure that a quantum of restorative justice is administered – Bourdieu's left hand of the state. The current centre-left political establishment is looking to broker a constructive way forward through further processes of consultation with Māori. This is likely to continue to be an uneasy process. For, by and with Māori social services are vital, but it is also important to remember that cultural recognition within a framework of liberal capitalist economics cannot, by definition, be a complete remedy for endemic inequality.

The current child protection crisis has been brought about, in essence, because of the seemingly inbuilt predilection of the liberal capitalist state to afford a lesser set of rights to socially excluded sections of society. The issue of how a universal standard of respect can be extended to all individuals, as well as to groups who do not subscribe to the political and cultural tenets of liberal individualism, remains unclear. There is also a related question of where, if at all, the profession of social work might sit as part of the solution.

A series of broad lessons can be distilled from the narrative journey taken in this text. 'Notify, detect, assess and intervene' processes of statutory child protection social work impact differentially on the children of the working-class poor. In Aotearoa and comparable settler states, this intervention disproportionately targets Indigenous people. A profession that does not understand its history and its politics is flying blind. Discipline of the disadvantaged needs to be kicked back to the 19th century where it belongs. Complex problems beg complex solutions. Empowering social work is skilled and resource-intensive, and good thoughtful practice is better served by critical sociological and political theory than behavioural science. Social workers need to be poverty-aware, relationally engaged and well supported.

Understandings of how systemically generated inequality affects the lives of children, parents and whānau can be applied in practice (Hyslop and Keddell, 2018: 6). However, work with whānau where there is risk of harm will continue to be challenging. Social work approaches that build trust are more important than clinical risk assessment, but there is always a difficult balance. Compassion and respect need to be mixed with an equal dose of realism about risk and harm. Workers – be they whānau navigators or state social workers – need high-quality support systems and manageable workloads. Not much to ask, you would hope, but very elusive to date.

Progressive child protection policy and practice must listen to survivor voices, recognise the debilitating social effects of poverty, enable autonomous

Māori service provision and learn from its past. Social work is not essentially about efficient business practice or correcting faulty behaviour. As Garrett (2018) has argued, soft neoliberalism is not enough. In the wider economic context, an aggressive commitment to policies of redistribution is needed if the social suffering of children living at the edges of our fundamentally unequal liberal capitalist social system is to be effectively addressed (Gillies et al, 2017: 161). Middle-class love and kindness will not do that, and the state cannot be an effective substitute for whānau:

> The State is inherently a cold breast and dry nipple. The best it can do in loco parentis is to draw on the resources within the extended family or wider community to find people who might genuinely care for the child. Some of us fear this to be a diminishing resource. The State cannot enable the child to find the answers to the questions which are central to each of us: where do I come from; who do I belong to; who am I; and do I matter? (Scott, 2006: 4)

Although it is crucial to disassemble the generic 'detect and rescue' focus of the child protection system, and to devolve services for Māori to Māori, this is not a complete answer because social services do not remedy the structural injustices that inevitably flow from the social relations of liberal capitalism. It is, however, a good start. There are many pieces to this socially and politically constructed puzzle. Mechanisms for wider Māori self-determination will continue to develop as the pressure of history unfolds in the present. Part of the solution is for Pākehā New Zealanders to realise that we have nothing to lose and much to gain from realising the promise of Te Tiriti o Waitangi. Liberal capitalism constricts the life worlds of all people, and we can all come to live in better, more connected and more sustainable ways.

As part of the ongoing struggle for social and economic justice, there is an opportunity, as there was in 1989, to develop a world-leading, Te Tiriti o Waitangi-compliant and socially just child protection system. It will not be given to us on a plate, however; there is a great deal of work to be done. It is hoped that a deeper understanding of the often-circular historical and political journey set out in this book will help to inform a partial road map to this destination.

Notes

Chapter 1

1. Aotearoa is the Māori name for New Zealand. It is used throughout this text to signal the centrality of the Māori experience to the child protection narrative and to show appropriate respect for the first people of this land.
2. The Waitangi Tribunal is a standing commission of inquiry created by an Act of Parliament in 1975. It hears claims and makes recommendations relating to alleged breaches by the Crown of the promises made in the 1840 Treaty of Waitangi (Te Tiriti o Waitangi) between Māori and the Crown.
3. 'Whānau' refers to a family constellation that is normally larger than the European concept of family, encompassing a multigenerational group linked with common ancestry and ties of reciprocity. Related whānau make up a hapū (sub-tribe) and connected hapū comprise an iwi (tribal identity). It is important not to assume that these terms correspond directly to English-language translations.
4. 'Pasefika' is a generic term encompassing Indigenous peoples of Pacific Island nations.
5. This quotation is taken from a roundtable discussion between Foucault and colleagues in 1972. The translated text is reproduced in Chambon (1999).
6. Wakefield's New Zealand Company set out to promote systematic British settlement from a base of 'hard-working' wage earners attracted by the opportunity to take possession of small packages of land. It pivoted on the procurement of cheap land from Māori.
7. Although Smith's economic ideas are associated with his landmark 1776 *Wealth of Nations* text (1910), he was essentially a moral philosopher with a degree of paternalistic benevolence towards the morally vulnerable labouring classes.

Chapter 2

1. Reducing reliance on state benefits was an integral part of the 1990s' neoliberal turn, as exemplified by the international 'Beyond Dependency' conference held in Auckland in 1997.
2. In Aotearoa, applicants are currently required to satisfy 'fit and proper' criteria adjudicated by a state-appointed Social Workers Registration Board.
3. Compte's political philosophy is grounded in his concept of scientific positivism, which supports the search for objective 'facts' about social phenomena.
4. Foucault's concept of power-saturated human life owes a significant debt to the radical philosophy of Friedrich Nietzche.

Chapter 3

1. Te Tiriti o Waitangi is a foundational constitutional document that (in contemporary readings) is taken to guarantee Māori expectations of sovereignty over things Māori. It has been a politically contested vehicle for Māori rights since its signing in 1840.
2. Mermeri Penfold was a celebrated Māori linguist and educator.
3. MOOHR was an activist organisation that arose in Wellington, and Te Hikioi is associated with a leftist newsletter highlighting issues of social injustice.

Chapter 4

1. 'Pūao-te-Ata-Tū' translates as 'the new dawn (a new beginning)'.
2. Tāmaki Makaurau is the reo Māori ('Māori language') name for the city of Auckland.

Chapter 5

[1] 'Pounamu' is the Māori name for Jade or 'green stone' – a material treasured for many purposes.

[2] The 1987 case of 'baby C' who died at the hands of her caregiver while subject to multi-agency involvement was the first highly publicised death of a child under social work oversight. The subsequent review process had significant repercussions for practice development and for future review processes.

[3] The RES system was developed by researchers in Manitoba, though it was not adopted in the Canadian child protection context.

Chapter 6

[1] The concept of differential response combines the idea of demand management with the notion that families in need at a lower level of risk are more likely to engage cooperatively and productively with non-statutory social work services.

[2] A media storm followed the 2006 death (and investigative aftermath) of these infant twins in the care of family.

[3] The naming of the new organisation drew considerable controversy. The original title 'Ministry for Vulnerable Children' was withdrawn after concerted interest group disapproval – though not before significant corporate labelling material had been produced.

Chapter 7

[1] The concept of substantiation refers to the legislated requirement for a social worker to form a belief that a child is, or is likely to be, in need of care or protection as defined in the law.

[2] Dr Alan Detlaff is a US academic who has engaged in extensive study of risk bias in child welfare.

References

Ballantyne, N. (2019) 'The ethics and politics of human service technology: The case of predictive risk modelling in New Zealand's child protection system', *Hong Kong Journal of Social Work*, 53(1–2): 15–27.

Barretta-Herman, A. (1990) 'The restructuring of the Department of Social Welfare and implications for social work practice, 1986–1988: A dissertation presented in partial fulfilment for the requirements of a Doctorate in Philosophy at Massey University', Doctoral thesis, Massey University, New Zealand. Available at: https://mro.massey.ac.nz/handle/10179/3918

Barretta-Herman, A. (1994) 'Revisioning the community as provider: Restructuring New Zealand's social services', *International Social Work*, 37(1): 7–21.

Bauman, Z. (1999) *In Search of Politics*, Cambridge: Polity Press.

Bauman, Z. (2000) *Liquid Modernity*, Malden, MA: Polity Press.

Beddoe, L. (2014) 'Feral families, troubled families: The spectre of the underclass in New Zealand', *New Zealand Sociology*, 29(3): 51–68.

Beddoe, L. and Joy, E. (2017) 'Questioning the uncritical acceptance of neuroscience in child and family policy and practice: A review of challenges to the current doxa', *Aotearoa New Zealand Social Work*, 29(1): 65–76.

Belgrave, M. (2012) 'Forty years on, forty years back', Paper presented to the 'Affording our Future' Conference, 10–11 December, Wellington. Available at: www.wgtn.ac.nz/cpf/publications/pdfs/1.8-Belgrave-paper.pdf

Bell, A., Elizabeth, V., MacIntosh, T. and Wynyard, M. (eds) (2017) *A Land of Milk and Honey? Making Sense of New Zealand*, Auckland: Auckland University Press.

Bhattacharyya, J. (2004) 'Theorizing community development', *Journal of the Community Development Society*, 34(2): 5–29.

Bolger, S., Corrigan, P., Docking, J. and Frost, N. (1981) *Towards Socialist Welfare Work*, Basingstoke: Macmillan.

Booth, C. (1904) *In Darkest England and the Way Out*, London: International Headquarters of the Salvation Army. Available at: www.gutenberg.org/cache/epub/475/pg475.txt

Booth, W. (1904) *Life and Labour of the People in London, Vol. 1: East, Central and South London*, First Series: Poverty, London: Macmillan and Co.

Boshier, P. (2020) 'He Take Kōhukihuki: A matter of urgency – investigation report into policies, practices and procedures for the removal of newborn pēpi by Oranga Tamariki, Ministry for Children'. Available at: www.ombudsman.parliament.nz/resources/he-take-kohukihuki-matter-urgency

Boston, J. and Chapple, S. (2014) *Child Poverty in New Zealand*, Wellington: Bridget Williams Books.

Bourdieu, P. (2005) *The Social Structures of the Economy*, Cambridge: Polity Press.

Bourdieu, P. and Ferguson, P.P. (1999) *The Weight of the World: Social Suffering in Contemporary Society*, Oxford: Polity Press.

Bradley, J. (1997) 'Iwi and cultural social services policy: the state's best kept secret', *Te Kōmako: Social Work Review*, 8(1): 3–5.

Brodie, I., Nottingham, C. and Plunkett, S. (2008) 'A tale of two reports: Social work in Scotland from social work in the community (1966) to changing lives (2000)', *British Journal of Social Work*, 38(4): 697–715.

Brown, M. (2000) 'Care and protection is about adult behaviour: The ministerial review of the Department of Child, Youth and Family Services: Report to the Minister of Social Services and Employment Hon Steve Maharey'. Available at: www.msd.govt.nz/documents/about-msd-and-our-work/publications-resources/archive/2000-care-and-protection-is-about-adult-behaviour.pdf

Bywaters, P. and CWIP (Child Welfare Inequalities Project) Team (2020) *Child Welfare Inequalities: Final Report*, Huddersfield: University of Huddersfield. Available at: https://pure.hud.ac.uk/ws/files/21398145/CWIP_Final_Report.pdf

Bywaters, P., Brady, G., Bunting, L., Daniel, B., Featherstone, B., Jones, C., Morris, K., Scourfield, J., Sparks, P. and Webb, C. (2018) 'Inequalities in English child protection practice under austerity', *Child and Family Social Work*, 23: 53–61.

Cabinet Social Equity Committee (1985) 'Revision of child and young persons legislation', 16 September, Archives New Zealand, Corporate Records, Wellington, Ref. 19239307.

Callinicos, A. (2010) *Bonfire of Illusions: The Twin Crises of the Liberal World*, Cambridge: Polity Press.

Casassas, D. and Wagner, P. (2016) 'Modernity and capitalism: Conceptual retrieval and comparative-historical analyses', *European Journal of Social Theory*, 19(2): 159–71.

Caton, A. (1984) 'Minutes of South Auckland Sexual Abuse Committee', 12 January, Archives New Zealand, Corporate Records, Wellington, Ref. 19240874.

Chambon, A. (1999) 'Foucault's approach: Making the familiar visible', in A. Chambon, A. Irving and L. Epstein (eds) *Reading Foucault for Social Work*, New York, NY: Columbia University Press, pp 51–83.

Chatterjee, S. (1999) *The New Politics: A Third Way for New Zealand*, Palmerston North: Dunmore Press.

Choate, P.W. (2019) 'The call to decolonise: social work's challenge for working with indigenous people', *British Journal of Social Work*, 49(4): 1081–99.

Circular Memorandum (1983) 'Matua Whangai programme' (1983:125), Department of Social Welfare, Head Office, 12 September, Archives New Zealand, Corporate Records, Wellington, Ref. 19240714.

Circular Memorandum (1984) 'Child protection teams' (1984:121), 17 September, Archives New Zealand, Corporate Records, Wellington, Ref. 19240866.

Cnaan, R. and Dichter, M. (2008) 'Thoughts on the use of knowledge in social work practice', *Research on Social Work Practice*, 18(4): 278–84.

Connolly, M. and Doolan, M. (2007) 'Responding to the deaths of children known to child protection agencies', *Social Policy Journal of New Zealand*, 30: 1–1.

Connolly, M. and Harms, L. (2013) *Social Work: Contexts and Practice* (3rd edn), Melbourne: Oxford University Press.

Cook, L. (2020) 'A statistical window for the justice system: Putting a spotlight on the scale of state custody of generations of Māori', Brief of Evidence Wai 2915. Available at: https://forms.justice.govt.nz/ search/Documents/WT/wt_DOC_161895442/Wai%202915%2C%20 A040(a).pdf

Cox, L. and Irwin, K. (1999) 'Review of Iwi social services strategy', Children, Young Persons and Their Families Agency, Wellington, August.

Craig, M. (1982) New Zealand Foster Care Federation: Discussion paper on institutional and systems abuse of children', Archives New Zealand, Corporate Records, Wellington, Ref. 1924072.

Cram, F., Gulliver, P., Ota, R. and Wilson, M. (2015) 'Understanding overrepresentation of Indigenous children in child welfare data: An application of the Drake risk and bias models', *Child Maltreatment*, 20(3): 170–82.

Cree, V. (2013) 'New practices of empowerment', in M. Gray and S.A. Webb (eds) *The New Politics of Social Work*, Basingstoke: Palgrave Macmillan, pp 145–58.

Cummins, I. (2018) *Poverty, Inequality and Social Work: The Impact of Neoliberalism and Austerity Politics on Welfare Provision*, Bristol: Policy Press.

Dalley, B. (1998) 'Moving out of the realm of myth', *New Zealand Journal of History*, 32(2): 189–207.

Dalley, B. (2019) 'Family is culture review report', Independent Review of Aboriginal Children and Young People in OOHC, Sydney. Available at: www.familyisculture.nsw.gov.au/__data/assets/pdf_file/0011/726329/ Family-Is-Culture-Review-Report.pdf

Dean, G. and Pihema, J. (1981) 'Working Party for Recruitment of Maori Foster Parents', Maori Foster Recruitment Committee minutes, Department of Social Welfare, 20 August, Archives New Zealand, Corporate Records, Wellington, Ref. 19240711.

Dominelli, L. (2004) *Social Work: Theory and Practice for a Changing Profession*, Cambridge: Polity Press.

Dominion Sunday Times (1988) 'Trust is not enough', 11 September, Archives New Zealand, Corporate Records, Wellington, Ref. 19239876.

Doolan, M. (2005) 'Iwi social services: Why the lack of progress?', *Aotearoa Social Work Review*, 17(3): 26–33.

DSW (Department of Social Welfare) (1988) 'Guidelines on child abuse', September, Archives New Zealand, Corporate Records, Wellington, Ref. 19240963.

DSW (Department of Social Welfare) (1994) 'Te Punga: our bicultural strategy for the nineties', Wellington: The Dept.

Dugdale, R.L. (1970 [1910]) *The Jukes: A Study in Crime, Pauperism, Disease and Heredity, 4th ed,* New York, NY: GP Putnam's Sons.

Duncan, G. (2004) *Society and Politics: New Zealand Social Policy*, Auckland: Pearson Education.

Eketone, A. (2020) 'The "hidden depression" that never really went away', *Aotearoa New Zealand Social Work*, 32(3): 37–40.

Ely, R.T. (1981) 'Pauperism in the United States', *North American Review*, 152 (413): 395–409.

Engels, F., Marx, K. and Arthur, C.J. (1970) *The German Ideology.* United Kingdom: International Publishers.

EP (Modernising Child, Youth and Family Expert Panel) (2015) 'Final report', Wellington. Available at: www.msd.govt.nz/documents/about-msd-and-our-work/publications-resources/corporate/expert-panel-cyf/investing-in-children-report.pdf

Featherstone, B., White, S. and Morris, K. (2014) *Re-imagining Child Protection: Towards Humane Social Work with Families*, Bristol: Policy Press.

Featherstone, B., Gupta, A. and Morris, K. (2017) 'Bringing back the social: The way forward for children's social work?', *Journal of Children's Services*, 12(2–3): 190–6.

Featherstone, B., Morris, K., Daniel, B., Bywaters, P., Brady, G., Bunting, L., Mason, W. and Mirza, N. (2019) 'Poverty, inequality, child abuse and neglect: Changing the conversation in child protection?', *Children and Youth Services Review*, 97: 127–33.

Ferguson, H. (2004) *Protecting Children in Time: Child Abuse, Child Protection and the Consequences of Modernity*, Basingstoke: Palgrave Macmillan.

Ferguson, H. (2018a) 'How social workers reflect in action and when and why they don't: The possibilities and limits to reflective practice in social work', *Social Work Education*, 37(4): 415–27.

Ferguson, H. (2018b) 'Making home visits: creativity and the embodied practices of home visiting in social work and child protection', *Qualitative Social Work*, 17(1): 65–80.

Ferguson, I. (2008) *Reclaiming Social Work: Challenging Neoliberalism and Practicing Social Justice*, London: Sage Publications.

Ferguson, I., Ioakimidis, V. and Lavalette, M. (2018) *Global Social Work in a Political Context: Radical Perspectives*, Bristol: Policy Press.

Flanagan, K. (2018) ' "Problem families" in public housing: Discourse, commentary and (dis)order', *Housing Studies*, 33(5): 684–707.

Foucault, M. (1981) 'The order of discourse', in R. Young (ed) *Untying the Text: A Post-Structuralist Reader*, London: Routledge and Keegan Paul, pp 48–78.

Foucault, M. (2003) 'Security, territory, and population', in P. Rabinow and N. Rose (eds) *The Essential Foucault: Selections from Essential Works of Foucault 1954–1984*, New York, NY: The New Press, pp 259–62.

Foucault, M. (2013) 'Society must be defended', Lecture at the College de France, 17 March 1976, in T. Campbell and A. Sitze (eds) *Biopolitics: A Reader*, Durham, NC: Duke University Press, pp 61–81.

Fry, T. (2015) 'Valuation of the benefit system for working-age adults as at 30 June 2014', Sydney: Ministry of Social Development. Available at: www.msd.govt.nz/about-msd-and-our-work/newsroom/media-releases/2015/reforms-succeed.html

Garlick, T. (2012) *Social Developments: An Organisational History of the Ministry of Social Development and Its Predecessors, 1860–2011*, Wellington: Steele Roberts Aotearoa.

Garrett, P. (2013) *Social Work and Social Theory: Making Connections*, Bristol: Policy Press.

Garrett, P. (2018) 'What are we talking about when we talk about "neoliberalism?"', *European Journal of Social Work*, 22(1): 1–13.

Gilbert, N. (2012) 'A comparative study of child welfare systems: Abstract orientations and concrete results', *Children and Youth Services Review*, 34: 532–6.

Gillies, V., Edwards, R. and Horsley, N. (2017) *Challenging the Politics of Early Intervention: Who's 'Saving' Children and Why*, Bristol: Policy Press.

Ginsberg, N. (1979) *Class, Capital, and Social Policy (Critical Texts in Social Work and the Welfare State*, series ed P. Leonard), Basingstoke: Macmillan.

Gray, M. and McDonald, C. (2006) 'Pursuing good practice: The limits of evidence-based practice', *Journal of Social Work*, 6(1): 7–20.

Gray, M. and Webb, S. (eds) (2013a) *The New Politics of Social Work*, Basingstoke: Palgrave Macmillan.

Gray, M. and Webb, S. (2013b) 'The speculative left and new politics of social work', in M. Grey and S. Webb (eds) *The New Politics of Social Work*, Basingstoke: Palgrave Macmillan.

Gray, M., Coates, J., Yellow Bird, M. and Hetherington, T. (eds) (2013) *Decolonising Social Work*, Burlington: Ashgate.

Gupta, A. (2017) 'Poverty and child neglect: The elephant in the room?', *Families, Relationships and Societies*, 6: 21–36.

Hackell, M. (2016) 'Managing anxiety: Neoliberal modes of subjectivity, fantasy and child abuse in New Zealand', *Citizenship Studies*, 20(6–7): 867–82.

Hanna, S. (2008) 'Child protection practice in a call centre: An emerging area of social work', *Aotearoa New Zealand Social Work*, 3: 34–43.

Harris, A. (2007) 'Dancing with the state: Māori creative energy and policies of integration, 1945–1967', Doctoral thesis, University of Auckland, New Zealand. Available at: http://hdl.handle.net/2292/2605

Harris, J. (2008) 'State social work: Constructing the present form moments in the past', *British Journal of Social Work*, 38(4): 662–79.

Harvey, D. (2005) *A Short History of Neoliberalism*, Oxford: Oxford University Press.

Hauraki, D. (1987) 'Maori Perspective Advisory Committee, Recommendation 7: Maatua Whangai', DSW Cultural Development Unit, Department of Social Welfare, 4 November, Archives New Zealand, Corporate Records, Wellington, Ref. 1918949.

Heilbroner, R.L. (1985) *The Nature and Logic of Capitalism*, New York, NY: Norton.

Hetherington, R. (2006) 'Learning form difference: Comparing child welfare systems', in N. Freymond and N. Cameron (eds) *Towards Positive Systems of Child and Family Welfare*, Toronto: Toronto University Press.

Hewlett, N. (2007) *Badiou, Balibar, Ranciere: Re-thinking Emancipation*, London: Continuum Publishing.

Hibbs, S. (2005) 'The determination of "problem"', *Te Kōmako: Aotearoa New Zealand Social Work*, 17(2): 32–7.

Houston, S. (2014) 'Social work and the sociological imagination', in P.M. Garrett (ed) *Critical and Radical Debates in Social Work: Children and Families*, Bristol: Policy Press, pp 61–7.

Hunn, J.K. (1961) *Report on Department of Maori Affairs: With Statistical Supplement*, Wellington: Government Printer.

Hyslop, I. (1997) 'The promise and the practice: Child protection legislation in New Zealand', *Asia Pacific Journal of Social Work and Development*, 7(1): 59–67.

Hyslop, I. (2007) 'Twenty years in an open-necked shirt: A retrospective personal narrative', *Aotearoa New Zealand Social Work*, 19(1): 3–10.

Hyslop, I. (2009) 'Child protection policy and practice: A relationship lost in translation', *Social Policy Journal of New Zealand*, 34: 62–72.

Hyslop, I. (2012) 'Social work as a practice of freedom', *Journal of Social Work*, 12(4): 404–22.

Hyslop, I. (2013a) 'The "White Paper for Vulnerable Children" and the "Munro Review of Child Protection in England": A comparative critique', *Aotearoa New Zealand Social Work*, 25(4): 4–14.

Hyslop, I. (2013b) 'Social work practice knowledge: An enquiry into the nature of the knowledge generated and applied in the practice of social work', Doctoral thesis, Massey University, New Zealand. Available at: http://hdl.handle.net/10179/513

Hyslop, I. (2016a) 'Social work in the teeth of a gale: A resilient counter-discourse in neoliberal times', *Critical and Radical Social Work*, 4(1): 21–37.

Hyslop, I. (2016b) 'Where to social work in a brave new neoliberal Aotearoa', *Aotearoa New Zealand Social Work*, 28(1): 5–12.

Hyslop, I. (2017) 'Child protection in New Zealand: A history of the future', *British Journal of Social Work*, 47(6): 1800–17.

Hyslop, I. (2020) 'Child protection, capitalism and the settler state: Rethinking the social contract', *Policy Quarterly*, 16(1): 34–6.

Hyslop, I. and Keddell, E. (2018) 'Outing the elephants: Exploring a new paradigm for child protection social work', *Social Science*, 7(7): 105.

Hyslop, I. and Keddell, E. (2019) 'Child protection under National: Reorienting towards genuine social investment or continuing social neglect', *New Zealand Sociology*, 34(2): 93–122.

Ife, J. (2016) *Community Development in an Uncertain World* (2nd edn), Melbourne: Cambridge University Press.

Jackson, M. (1995) 'Comment Treaty of Waitangi: Special Issue', *Victoria University of Wellington Law Review 27*, 25: 245–8.

Jacobs, M. (2018) 'Seeing like a settler colonial state', *Modern American History*, 1(2): 257–70.

Jenson, T. and Tyler, I. (2015) ' "Benefit broods": The cultural and political crafting of anti-welfare commonsense', *Critical Social Policy*, 35(4): 470–91.

Jones, C. (1983) *State Social Work and the Working Class* (*Critical Texts in Social Work and the Welfare State*, series ed P. Leonard), Basingstoke: Macmillan.

Jordan, B. (2012) 'Individualisation, liberal freedom and social work in Europe', *Dialogue in Practice*, 1(14): 7–25.

Keddell, E. (2014) 'Current debates on variability in child welfare decision-making', *Social Science*, 3: 916–40.

Keddell, E. (2019) 'Harm, care and babies: An inequalities and policy discourse perspective on recent child protection trends in Aotearoa New Zealand', *Aotearoa New Zealand Social Work*, 31(4): 18–34.

Keddell, E. (2020) 'The case for an inequalities perspective in child protection', *Policy Quarterly*, 16(1): 36–8.

Keddell, E. and Cleaver, K. (2020) 'Joint brief of evidence of Emily Keddell and Kerri Cleaver', Waitangi Tribunal – Wai 2915, #A9, Urgent Oranga Tamariki Inquiry, 7 October. Available at: https://forms.justice.govt.nz/search/Documents/WT/wt_DOC_165023706/Wai%202915%2C%20A090.pdf

Keddell, E. and Hyslop, I. (2019) 'Ethnic inequalities in child welfare: The role of practitioner risk perceptions', *Child & Family Social Work*, 24(4): 409–20.

Keddell, E. and Hyslop, I. (2020) 'Networked decisions: Decision-making thresholds in child protection', *British Journal of Social Work*, 50(7): 1961–80.

Keddell, E., Davie, G. and Barson, D. (2019) 'Child protection inequalities in Aotearoa New Zealand: Social gradient and the "inverse intervention law" ', *Child and Youth Services Review*, 104: 104383.

Keenan, D. (1995) 'Pūao-te-Āta-tū: A brief history and reflection', *Te Kōmako: Aotearoa New Zealand Social Work*, 7(1): 11–29.

Kelsey, J. (1995) *The New Zealand Experiment: A World Model for Structural Adjustment?*, Wellington: Bridget Williams Books.

Kemp, A.P. (2020) 'Child protection practice: An unintended consequence of reform', PhD thesis, University of Tasmania, Australia. Available at: https://eprints.utas.edu.au/34789/

Kirby, G. (1994) 'Taku Whangai: My child that we nurtured', *Adoption: Past, Present and Future Conference*. Auckland: P. Morris, Uniprint, pp 19–30.

Krumer-Nevo, M. (2016) 'Poverty-aware social work: A paradigm for social work practice with people in poverty', *British Journal of Social Work*, 46(6): 1793–808.

Lorenz, W. (2017) 'Social work education in Europe: Towards 2025', *European Journal of Social Work*, 20(3): 311–21.

Lunt, N. (2010) 'Winning hearts and minds for the competition state', *Policy Studies*, 31(1): 23–37.

Marx, K. and Engels, F. (1964) *The German Ideology*, Moscow: Progress Publishers.

Mason, K.H. (1992) *Report of the Ministerial Review Team to the Minister of Social Welfare, the Hon. Jenny Shipley. Review of the Children, Young Persons and their Families Act*, Wellington: Government Printer.

McCartan, C., Morrison, A., Bunting, L., Davidson, G. and McIlroy, J. (2018) 'Stripping the wallpaper of practice: Empowering social workers to tackle poverty', *Social ScienUces*, 7(10): 193.

McClure, M. (1998) *A Civilised Community: A History of Social Security in New Zealand, 1898–1998*, Auckland: University of Auckland Press and Historical Branch of Internal Affairs.

McCulloch, O.C. (1888) *The Tribe of Ishmael: A Study in Social Degradation*, Indianapolis, IN: Charity Organization Society.

Mead, M. (1994) 'Tamaiti Whangai: The adopted child: Maori customary practices', *Adoption: Past, Present and Future Conference*, Auckland: P. Morris, Uniprint, pp 85–95.

Miller, P. and Rose, N. (1990) 'Governing economic life', *Economy and Society*, 19: 1–31.

Milner, V. (2004) 'He myth of best practice: Learning from the worst', *ANZSW Journal (Archives), Social Work Review*,16, Summer: 58–64.

Ministerial Advisory Committee (1988) 'Puao-te-Ata-Tu (day break): The report of the Ministerial Advisory Committee on a Maori Perspective for the Department of Social Welfare', Wellington. Available at: www.msd.govt.nz/documents/about-msd-and-our-work/publications-resources/archive/1988-puaoteatatu.pdf

Ministry of Social Development (2003) 'Report of the Department of Child, Youth and Family Services First Principles Baseline Review', Ministry of Social Development, Child Youth and Family and the Treasury, Wellington: New Zealand Government.

Ministry of Social Development (2011) *Every Child Thrives, Belongs, Achieves: The Green Paper on Vulnerable Children*, Wellington: New Zealand Government.

Ministry of Social Development (2012) *The White Paper for Vulnerable Children: Children's Action Plan: Identifying, Supporting and Protecting Vulnerable Children*, Wellington: New Zealand Government.

Moloney, P. (2002) 'State socialism and William Pember Reeves: A reassessment', in P. Moloney and K. Taylor (eds) *On the Left: Essays on Socialism in New Zealand*, Dunedin: University of Otago Press, pp 39–58.

Morris, K., Will Mason, W., Bywaters, P., Featherstone, B., Daniel, B., Brady, G., Hooper, J., Mirza, N., Scourfield, J. and Webb, C. (2018) 'Social work, poverty, and child welfare interventions', *Child and Family Social Work*, 23: 364–72.

Morrison, T. (1997) 'Emotionally competent child protection organizations: Fallacy, fiction or necessity?', in J. Bates, R. Pugh and N. Thompson (eds) *Protecting Children: Challenges and Change*, Aldershot: Arena.

Morrison, T. (2007) 'Emotional intelligence, emotion and social work: Context, characteristics, complications and contribution', *British Journal of Social Work*, 37(2): 245–63.

Munro, E. (2010) 'Review of child protection in England: Part one: A systems analysis'. Available at: www.basw.co.uk/resources/munro-review-child-protection

Munro, E. (2011a) 'Interim report: The child's journey'. Available at: www.basw.co.uk/resources/munro-review-child-protection-interim-report

Munro, E. (2011b) 'Final report: A child-centred system'. Available at: www.basw.co.uk/resources/munro-review-child-protection-final-report

Murdoch, I. (2006) *Imagined Orphans: Poor Families, Child Welfare, and Contested Citizenship in London* (Rutgers Series in Childhood Studies, ed M. Bluebond-Langner), New Brunswick, NJ: Rutgers University Press.

Murray, E., Lacey, R., Maughan, B. and Sacker, A. (2020) 'Association of childhood out-of-home care status with all-cause mortality up to 42-years later', Office of National Statistics Longitudinal Study. Available at: https://doi.org/10.1186/s12889-020-08867-3

Nash, M. (1998) ' "That terrible title, social worker": A time of transition in social work history 1949–73', *Aotearoa New Zealand Social Work*, 10(1): 12.

NZPC (New Zealand Productivity Commission) (2015) 'More effective social services'. Available at: www.productivity.govt.nz/inquiries/more-effective-social-services/

O'Brien, M. (2014) 'The world we're in: Social work now and then', *Aotearoa New Zealand Social Work*, 26(2/3): 6–16.

Office of the Chief Social Worker (2014) *Workload and Caseload Review: Qualitative Review of Social Worker Caseload and Management*, Wellington: Child, Youth and Family.

Office of the Commissioner for Children (2000) *Final Report on the Investigation into the Death of James Whakaruru*, Wellington: New Zealand Govt.

Office of the Commissioner for Children (2020a) 'Te Kuku O Te Manawa – Ka puta te riri, ka momori te ngākau, ka heke ngā roimata mo tōku pēpi' (Part 1). Available at: www.occ.org.nz/publications/reports/te-kuku-o-te-manawa/

Office of the Commissioner for Children (2020b) 'Te Kuku O Te Manawa – Moe ararā! Haumanutia ngā moemoeā a ngā tūpuna mō te oranga ngā tamariki' (Part 2). Available at: www.occ.org.nz/publications/reports/tktm-report-2/

O'Leary, P., Tsui, M. and Ruch, G. (2013) 'The boundaries of the social work relationship revisited: Towards a connected, inclusive and dynamic conceptualisation', *British Journal of Social Work*, 43: 135–53.

O'Malley, V. (1998) *Agents of Autonomy: Maori Committees in the Nineteenth Century*, Wellington: Huia Publishers.

Oranga Tamariki (2019) 'Professional practice group: Practice review into the Hastings Case', New Zealand Government. Available at: www.orangatamariki.govt.nz/assets/Uploads/About-us/News/2019/Practice-Review/Hawkes-Bay-Practice-Review.pdf

Oranga Tamariki (2020) 'Oranga Tamariki response to Ombudsman's He Take Kohukihuki: A matter of urgency', 7 August. Available at: www.orangatamariki.govt.nz/about-us/news/oranga-tamariki-response-to-ombudsmans-he-take-kohukihuki-a-matter-of-urgency/

Orford, S., Dorling, D., Mitchell, R., Shaw, M. and Smith, G.D. (2002) 'Life and death of the people of London: A historical GIS of Charles Booth's inquiry', *Health Place*, 8(1): 25–35.

Parton, N. (1985) *The Politics of Child Abuse*, Basingstoke: Macmillan.

Parton, N. (2014a) *The Politics of Child Protection: Contemporary Developments and Future Directions*, Basingstoke: Palgrave Macmillan.

Parton, N. (2014b) 'Child protection and politics: Some critical and constructive reflections', *British Journal of Social Work*, 44(7): 2042–56.

Parton, N. and Kirk, S. (2010) 'The nature and purpose of social work', in I. Shaw, K. Briar-Lawson, J. Orme and R. Ruckdeschel (eds) *The Sage Handbook of Social Research*, Los Angeles, CA: Sage Publications, pp 23–37.

Pease, B. (2009) 'From evidence-based practice to critical knowledge in post-positivist social work', in J. Allan, L. Briskman and B. Pease (eds) *Critical Social Work*, Crow's Nest, NSW: Allen and Unwin, pp 45–57.

Pease, B. (2010) 'Challenging the dominant paradigm: Social work research, social justice and social change', in I. Shaw, K. Briar-Lawson, J. Orme and R. Ruckdeschel (eds) *The Sage Handbook of Social Research*, Los Angeles, CA: Sage Publications, pp 98–113.

Pease, B. (2013) 'A history of critical and radical social work', in M. Gray and S.A. Webb (eds) *The New Politics of Social Work*, Basingstoke: Palgrave Macmillan, pp 21–43.

Pelton, L.H. (2015) 'The continuing role of material factors in child maltreatment and placement', *Child Abuse and Neglect*, 41: 30–9.

Poata-Smith, E.S. (2002) 'The political economy of Māori protest politics, 1968–1995: A Marxist analysis of the roots of Māori oppression and the politics of resistance' PhD thesis, University of Otago, New Zealand. Available at: http://hdl.handle.net/10523/151

Polanyi, K. (2001) *The Great Transformation: The Political and Economic Origins of Our Time*, Boston, MA: Beacon Press.

Potter, H. and Jackson, M. (2017) 'Constitutional transformation and the Matike Mai project: A korero with Moana Jackson', *Economic and Social Research Aotearoa*. Available at: https://esra.nz/constitutional-transformation-matike-mai/

Principal Social Worker Unit (1989) 'Te Ara Hou – The new path', Department of Social Welfare, Social Work Development Plan, Archives New Zealand, Corporate Records, Wellington, Ref. 19239457.

Procacci, G. (1991) 'Social economy and the government of poverty', in G. Burchell, C. Gordon and P. Miller (eds) *The Foucault Effect: Studies in Governmentality*, Chicago, IL: University of Chicago Press, pp 151–68.

Provan, S. (2012) 'The uncanny place of the bad mother and the innocent child at the heart of New Zealand's "cultural identity"', PhD thesis, University of Canterbury, New Zealand.

Rashbrooke, M. (2013) *Inequality: A New Zealand Crisis*, Wellington: Bridget Williams Books.

Rickard, T. (2014) 'He iwi moke, he whanokē: Iwi social services, policy and practice', Master's thesis, Massey University, New Zealand. Available at: http://hdl.handle.net/10179/5768

Roberts, D. (2002) *Shattered Bonds: The Color of Child Welfare*, New York, NY: Basic Cevatis Books.

Rogowski, S. (2010) *The Rise and Fall of a Profession?*, Bristol: Policy Press.

Roper, B.S. (2008) 'The welfare state: Origins, development, crisis, and redesign', in N. Lunt, M. O'Brien and R. Stephens (eds) *New Zealand, New Welfare*, South Melbourne: Cengage Learning, pp 10–18.

Rose, N. (2001) 'Governing "advanced" liberal democracies', in A. Barry, T. Osborne and N. Rose (eds) *Foucault and Political Reason: Liberalism, Neo-liberalism and Rationalities of Government*, London: Routledge, pp 37–65.

Rose, N. and Miller, P. (2010) 'Political power beyond the state: Problematics of government', *British Journal of Sociology*, 61(S1): 271–303.

Royal Commission of Inquiry into Historical Abuse in State Care and in the Care of Faith-Based Institutions (2020) 'Tāwharautia: Pūrongo o te Wā (Tāwharautia)', Interim report. Available at: www.abuseincare.org.nz/

Saar-Heiman, Y. (2020) 'The poverty-aware paradigm for child protection: A critical framework for policy and practice', *British Journal of Social Work*, 50(4): 1167–84.

Salomen, N. and Sturmfels, D. (2011) 'Making the most of child and family assessments', *Social Work Now*, 47: 3–9.

Schick, A. (1996) 'The spirit of reform: Managing the New Zealand state sector in a time of change', Public Service Commission – Te Kawa Mataaho. Available at: www.publicservice.govt.nz/resources/spirit-of-reform

Scott, D. (2006) 'Sowing the seeds of innovation in child protection', keynote paper presented to the 10th 'Australasian Child Abuse and Neglect' conference, Wellington. Available at: https://citeseerx.ist.psu.edu/viewdoc/download?doi=10.1.1.121.4966&rep=rep1&type=pdf

Smith, A. (1910) *An Inquiry into the Nature and Causes of the Wealth of Nations*, London: J.M. Dent.

Smith, C. (2001) 'Trust and confidence: Possibilities for social work in "high modernity"', *British Journal of Social Work*, 31(2): 287–305.

Smith, V., Moore, C., Cumming, J. and Boulton, A. (2019) 'Whānau Ora: An Indigenous policy success story', in J. Luetjens, M. Mintrom and P. 't Hart (eds) *Successful Public Policy: Lessons from Australia and New Zealand*, Acton, ACT: Australian National University Press.

Sorrenson, D. (1996) 'Kaupapa Maori responsiveness: New Zealand Children and Young Persons Service management responsiveness to Maori in the restructured state sector', Master's thesis, Massey University, New Zealand. Available at: mro.massey.ac.nz/handle/10179/5563

Spicker, P. (1990) 'Charles Booth: The examination of poverty', *Social Policy in Administration*, 24(1): 21–38.

Spolander, G., Engelbrecht, L. and Pullen Sansfaçon, A. (2015) 'Social work and macro-economic neoliberalism: Beyond the social justice rhetoric', *European Journal of Social Work*, 19(5): 1–15.

Stanley, L. and de Froideville, M.S. (2020) 'From vulnerability to risk: Consolidating state interventions towards Māori children and young people in New Zealand', *Critical Social Policy*, 40(4): 526–45.

Stanley, S. (2016) *The Road to Hell: State Violence against Children in Postwar New Zealand*, Auckland: Auckland University Press.

Stewart-Harawira, M. (2005) *The New Imperial Order: Indigenous Responses to Globalisation*, Wellington: Huia Publishers.

Sugarman, J. (2015) 'Neoliberalism and psychological ethics', *Journal of Theoretical and Philosophical Psychology*, 35(2): 103–16.

Sutherland, O. (2019) 'Witness statement of Dr Oliver Sutherland', Royal Commission of Inquiry into Historical Abuse in State Care and in the Care of Faith Based Institutions. Available at: www.abuseincare.org.nz/library/v/61/statement-of-dr-oliver-sutherland

Tawney, R.H. (1978) *History and Society: Essays by R.H. Tawney*, London: Routledge and Keegan Paul.

Tennant, M. (1989) *Paupers and Providers: Charitable Aid in New Zealand*, Wellington: Allen and Unwin and Historical Branch, Dept of Internal Affairs.

Tennant, M. (1993) 'McGregor, Duncan', in *Dictionary of New Zealand Biography, Vol 2, 1870–1900*, Wellington: Bridget Williams Books and Internal Affairs, pp 285–6.

Tennant, M. (2007) *The Fabric of Welfare: Voluntary Organisations, Government and Welfare in New Zealand, 1840–2005*, Wellington: Bridget Williams Books.

Todd, M. (1984) 'Report of the Child Protection Coordinating Committee', Archives New Zealand, Corporate Records, Wellington, Ref. 19240874.

Tudor, R. (2019) 'The biopolitics of community: An analysis of the recovery processes and school social work practices in the wake of the 2010 and 2011 Christchurch earthquakes', PhD thesis, Monash University, Australia. Available at: https://doi.org/10.4225/03/5aa74b608e9e9

Wai 2915 (2021) 'Report of the Waitangi Tribunal – He Pāharakeke, He Rito Whakakīkanga Whāruarua'. Available at: https://forms.justice.govt.nz/search/Documents/WT/wt_DOC_171027305/He%20Paharakeke%20W.pdf

Walker, R. (2004) *Ka whawhai tonu mātou – Struggle without End* (rev edn), Auckland: Penguin.

Walker, S. (2006) 'The Maatua Whangai Programme O Otepoti from a caregiver perspective', Master's thesis, University of Otago, New Zealand. Available at: http://hdl.handle.net/10523/8986

Wallace, J. and Pease, B. (2011) 'Neoliberalism and Australian social work: Accommodation or resistance?', *Journal of Social Work*, 11(2): 132–42.

Wanhalla, A.C. (2001) 'Gender, race and colonial identity: Women and eugenics in New Zealand, 1918–1939', Master's thesis, University of Canterbury, New Zealand. Available at: https://ir.canterbury.ac.nz/handle/10092/4237

Warner, A.G. (1889) 'Notes on the statistical determination of the causes of poverty', *Publications of the American Statistical Association*, 1(5): 183–205.

Warner, A.G. (1894) 'The causes of poverty further considered', *Publications of the American Statistical Association*, 4(27): 49–68.

Warner, J. (2015) *The Emotional Politics of Social Work and Child Protection*, Bristol: Policy Press.

Weir, R.E. (2002) 'Whose left/who's left? The knights of labour and "radical progressivism"', in P. Moloney and K. Taylor (eds) *On the Left: Essays on Socialism in New Zealand*, Dunedin: University of Otago Press, pp 21–38.

Welshman, J. (2013) *Underclass: A History of the Excluded since 1880*, London: Bloomsbury Academic.

Whānau Ora Commissioning Agency (2020) 'Ko Te Wā Whakawhiti, it's time for change: A Māori inquiry into Oranga Tamariki – Report'. Available at: https://apo.org.au/sites/default/files/resource-files/2020-02/apo-nid274231_1.pdf

Women Against Racism Action Group (1984) 'Institutional racism in the Department of Social Welfare – Tamaki Makaurau', Report. Available at: https://trc.org.nz/sites/trc.org.nz/files/Institutional%20Racism%20 WARAG.pdf

Workman, K. (2019) 'Witness statement of Sir Kim Workman', Royal Commission of Inquiry into Historical Abuse in State Care and in the Care of Faith Based Institutions. Available at: www.abuseincare.org.nz/ library/v/62/statement-of-sir-kim-workman

Young, V. (1983) 'Office of the Minister of Social Welfare', 21 December, Archives New Zealand, Corporate Records, Wellington, Ref. 19240711.

Žižek, S. (2014) *From the End of History to the End of Capitalism: Trouble in Paradise*, London: Penguin.

Index

www.ingramcontent.com/pod-product-compliance
Lightning Source LLC
Chambersburg PA
CBHW070926030426
42336CB00014BA/2560